Expert Advice From The Home Depot®

Landscape
Construction
1-2-3®

Meredith® BOOKS

Home Depot® Books
An imprint of Meredith® Books

Landscape Construction 1-2-3®
Senior Editor: John P. Holms
Art Director: Tom Wegner
Writer: Jeff Day
Graphic Designer: Tim Abramowitz
Copy Chief: Terri Fredrickson
Copy and Production Editor: Victoria Forlini
Editorial Operations Manager: Karen Schirm
Managers, Book Production: Pam Kvitne,
 Marjorie J. Schenkelberg, Rick von Holdt, Mark Weaver
Contributing Copy Editor: Kim Cantanzarite
Contributing Proofreaders: Genelle Deist, Heidi Johnson,
 David Krause, Janet Anderson
Illustrator: Jim Swanson
Indexer: Donald Glassman
Edit and Design Production Coordinator: Mary Lee Gavin
Editorial and Design Assistants: Renee E. McAtee,
 Karen McFadden

Meredith® Books
Editor in Chief: Linda Raglan Cunningham
Design Director: Matt Strelecki
Executive Editor, Gardening and Home Improvement:
 Benjamin W. Allen

Publisher: James D. Blume
Executive Director, Marketing: Jeffrey Myers
Executive Director, New Business Development: Todd M. Davis
Director, Sales-Home Depot: Robb Morris
Executive Director, Sales: Ken Zagor
Director, Operations: George A. Susral
Director, Production: Douglas M. Johnston
Business Director: Jim Leonard

Vice President and General Manager: Douglas J. Guendel

Meredith Publishing Group
President, Publishing Group: Stephen M. Lacy
Vice President-Publishing Director: Bob Mate

Meredith Corporation
Chairman and Chief Executive Officer: William T. Kerr

In Memoriam: E. T. Meredith III (1933–2003)

Photographers
Image Studios
Account Executive: Lisa Egan
Technical Consultant: Rick Nadke
Photographer: Bill Rein, Dave Classon
Contributing Photographer: John von Dorn
Assistant: Mike Clines

The Home Depot®
Licensing Specialist: Ilana Wilensky

Distributed by Meredith Corporation
Meredith Corporation is not affiliated with The Home Depot®

Note to the Reader: Due to differing conditions, tools, and individual skills, Meredith Corporation and The Home Depot® assume no responsibility for any damages, injuries suffered, or losses incurred as a result of following the information published in this book. Before beginning any project, review the instructions carefully, and if any doubts or questions remain, consult local experts or authorities. Because codes and regulations vary greatly, you always should check with authorities to ensure that your project complies with all applicable local codes and regulations. Always read and observe all of the safety precautions provided by any tool or equipment manufacturer, and follow all accepted safety procedures.

The editors of *Landscape Construction 1-2-3®* are dedicated to providing accurate and helpful do-it-yourself information. We welcome your comments about improving this book and ideas for other books we might offer to home improvement enthusiasts.

If you would like to purchase any of our home improvement, cooking, crafts, gardening, or home decorating and design books, check wherever quality books are sold. Or visit us at: meredithbooks.com

Contact us by any of these methods:
Leave a voice message at: 800/678-2093
Write to: Meredith Books, *Home Depot Books*
 1716 Locust St.
 Des Moines, IA 50309–3023
Send e-mail to: hi123@mdp.com

Landscape
Construction
1-2-3®

Meredith® BOOKS

LANDSCAPE CONSTRUCTION 1-2-3.

TABLE OF CONTENTS

HOW TO USE THIS BOOK Page 4

① OUTDOOR DESIGN Page 6

② FENCES AND GATES Page 12

Fences and Gates tool kit 14
Materials 15
Laying out fences and gates 17
Installing fence posts 19
Installing prefab fence panels 22
Installing wood fence rails 24
Hillside fencing 26
Hanging rails for stepped
   hillside fencing 27

Building your own fence sections . .28
Installing wood fencing 30
Putting up louver fencing 34
Making a basket-weave fence 35
Making and hanging a wood gate . .37
Building a post-and-rail fence 41
Installing mortised posts and rails 42
Building a wire fence 44
Installing a vinyl fence 46

Installing chain link fences 50
Assembling and hanging
   a chain link gate 53
Installing a pet fence 55
Repairing fences and gates 56

③ LANDSCAPING WALLS Page 62

Landscaping Walls tool kit 64
Materials 65
Mixing and working with mortar 66
Laying out a wall 68
Providing drainage for
   retaining walls 70
Building a wooden retaining wall . . . 72

Building a post-and-board
   retaining wall 75
Building a landscape block
   retaining wall 77
Building a dry stone wall 80
Building a footing for a stone
   or brick wall 82

Building a running-bond brick wall . 87
Laying a common-bond brick wall . . 90
Building a mortared stone wall 93
Building a concrete block wall 97
Stuccoing a block wall 101
Maintaining walls 104

④ SHEDS Page 108

Sheds tool kit 110
Materials 111
Laying out a shed 112
Installing a skid foundation 114
Installing concrete footings with
   fiber forms 115
Constructing a concrete
   slab foundation 117

Building a subfloor 121
Building a wood shed 123
Roofing a shed 131
Applying trim, hardware,
   and paint 133

Installing a shed window 135
Building a vinyl shed 137
Building a metal shed 144
Building a shed ramp 150

TRELLISES AND ARBORS Page 152

Trellises and Arbors tool kit 154
Materials 155
Building a trellis panel 156
Hanging trellises 159
Building an arbor 163
Building an arch-top arbor 172

 # ELECTRICAL Page 176

Electrical tool kit 178
Materials 179
Making wire connections 181
Extending a circuit 183
Adding a GFCI circuit 190
Running conduit and cable 192
Mounting electrical boxes 196
Installing a GFCI outlet 198
Installing switches 200
Installing automatic
    control devices 202
Installing outdoor light fixtures 204
Installing low-voltage lighting 208

PLUMBING AND DRAINAGE Page 210

Plumbing and Drainage
    tool kit 212
Materials 213
Making supply-pipe connections . . . 214
Tapping into supply pipes 218
Running supply pipes 220
Adding outdoor faucets 222
Gutters and downspouts 224
Installing outdoor
    drainage systems 226

CONCRETE Page 230

Concrete tool kit 232
Materials 233
Pouring a concrete pad 234
Mixing and pouring concrete 237
Anchoring posts for
    sports equipment 241
Special surface finishes 243
Repairing concrete 246

GLOSSARY Page 251

INDEX Page 253

How to use this book

A beautiful landscape starts with good bones—secure fences and gates, sturdy retaining walls, well-placed trellises and arbors, adequate drainage, and efficient storage. While these important elements provide functionality, they can also be attractive additions to the overall landscape design.

Creating the structure of a landscape involves basic construction techniques: working with materials such as stone, lumber, and concrete; and using many kinds of tools, from power augers to a hammer and tape measure. Successful installations mean:

- mastering some unfamiliar skills
- using the right tools and materials
- working safely
- doing the job right the first time

Landscape Construction 1-2-3 can help. It's accessible, easy-to-use, and full of the right information. Here's how to get the most value out of *Landscape Construction 1-2-3*:

TRUST THE WISDOM OF THE AISLES

A genuine desire to help people say, "I can do that!" is what the associates at The Home Depot® are all about. Landscaping experts from around North America have contributed their years of on-the-job experience and wisdom of the aisles to *Landscape Construction 1-2-3*. They've created a hardworking, accurate, and easy-to-follow guide to the basics of landscape construction.

THE ORGANIZING PRINCIPLE

Landscape Construction 1-2-3 consists of eight chapters that provide detailed coverage of the basics of landscape construction, plus a comprehensive landscaping glossary, an index, and a resource guide.

TAKE A LOOK INSIDE!

- **Chapter One:** Outdoor Design
  How structures fit into your overall landscape design
- **Chapter Two:** Fences and Gates
  Installing a variety of fencing options
- **Chapter Three:** Landscaping Walls
  Constructing walls from the most common building materials
- **Chapter Four:** Sheds
  Sheds from scratch or from kits
- **Chapter Five:** Trellises and Arbors
  Finishing touches that add beauty and functionality to outdoor spaces
- **Chapter Six:** Electrical
  Supplying power outdoors
- **Chapter Seven:** Plumbing and Drainage. Bringing water outside; installing gutters and drainage
- **Chapter Eight:** Concrete
  Concrete basics, from slabs to walkways

DOING THE JOB—STEP-BY-STEP

All the projects include **complete instructions** along with detailed, **step-by-step photography** to make successful completion simple and easy. You have everything you need to do the job right the first time, following standards set by manufacturers and the trades—just like the pros.

TIPS, TRICKS, AND TIMESAVERS

Each page contains more than just how to do the job. To help you plan your project and to schedule your time, you'll find expert advice: how hard a job is, how long it takes a pro, and how long it might take you.

Skill Scales fill you in on the skills you'll need, time involved, and variables that might complicate the job.

Stuff You'll Need at the beginning of each project provides a materials list along with commonly needed tools.

Additional features on the pages are filled with specific information—**Safety Alert, Buyer's Guide, Tool Tip, Time Saver, Homer's Hindsight,** and **Work Smarter** are all there to help you work efficiently and economically. Whenever a project involves something special—whether it's safety or getting the right tool—you'll be prepared for whatever comes up.

AND THERE'S MORE

Introductory information at the beginning of projects tells you what you need to know. **Real-World Situations** start each section and remind you that the world isn't perfect, so be prepared to deal with issues as they arise. **Tool Kits** at the beginning of each section show you the basic tools you'll need to do the projects.

GET THE MOST OUT OF YOUR LANDSCAPING EXPERIENCE

To make the best use of what's inside, read through each project carefully before you begin. Walk yourself mentally through the steps from beginning to end until you're comfortable with the process. Understanding the scope of the job will limit unnecessary mistakes and avoid the costs of doing things twice.

TAKE YOUR TIME

If you're not a landscaping contractor, don't expect to become one on your first project. What you learn on the job will make it easier as you go along. For every challenge you'll find a solution. Ask the experts and then listen to their advice. And don't forget to take a little pride in what you will accomplish with some good advice and a little old-fashioned elbow grease.

Support your local building inspector

Often confusing to the do-it-yourselfer, building codes exist to enforce consistent methods of installation and, more importantly, to ensure the safety of your family. Sometimes the reason for code is common sense, other times the code may seem silly. However you must follow codes, so find out what's required and do it from the start. This book is written to meet relevant national codes. Codes change, though, and local codes can sometimes be more stringent than their national cousins. Legally, it's up to you to make sure the job you're doing meets code because the consequences can be serious. Aside from potential danger, an inspector can make you start over (which can get expensive), and you may not be able to sell your house until you fix the violation. Find out what local standards you need to meet, and get some advice on how to best go about the job. Get a permit, do the job right, and sleep soundly at night.

Whether you're leveling a sled for a new storage shed or marking the curve for the top of a gate, success is measured by how carefully you've planned for each step of the project.

BUYER'S GUIDE

FINDING MATERIALS FOR LANDSCAPE CONSTRUCTION
The majority of products and materials used in landscape construction such as general building materials, and tools are available throughout the country and are similar size, shape, and quality even though they may be manufactured by different companies. However, some materials are regionally specific and may not be in stock or are simiply unavailable in your area. If that's the case, your local home improvement center will work with you to choose substitutes that will meet your needs or they can sometimes special order certain items if they are available and shipping is feasible.

Solid advice and tricks of the trade

Tips, insights, tricks, shortcuts, and even the benefit of 20/20 hindsight from the pros at The Home Depot are worth their weight in gold. Their years of experience translate into instant expertise for you. As you go through the book, look for these special icons, which signal detailed information on a specific topic.

Select the best materials.

Avoid common mistakes.

Prevent unsafe situations.

Design options to change your landscape.

Fix common mistakes.

Learn shortcuts that work.

Make smart work choices.

Use specialty tools to their best advantage.

SAFETY ALERT

Some aspects of home improvement can be dangerous, but it's hard to remember that when you're wrestling with a power auger to dig postholes. Being safe in potentially dangerous situations is a way of thinking—and the only way to work.

- Wear recommended safety gear including gloves, clothing, safety glasses, and ear protection when working with power tools. Flying debris can blind you or distract you long enough to create a disaster. Regular eyeglasses can shatter when hit.

- Wear a respirator or particle mask that's rated for the job you're doing. Breathing toxic fumes or inhaling particles can have serious consequences.

- Get in the habit of wearing safety goggles any time you're working.

- Always turn off the power at the circuit breaker when working with wiring.

- Choose the right tool for the job and know how to use it safely.

- Don't overreach. Move the ladder before you fall.

- Don't reach above your head to make a cut. Something is bound to fall on you. It may be the cutoff; it may be the saw.

- Ask questions. Store personnel can recommend the right tools and materials for the job; building inspectors can (and will) make sure you're doing the job right.

- Take your time. Read the directions carefully, consider the job at hand, and imagine what might go wrong. The surest way to avoid trouble is to be prepared.

Preparation and planning save both time and money. The Landscaper's Golden Rule? Don't start digging until you're sure where the hole is going to go.

1 OUTDOOR DESIGN

Landscape construction projects are primarily focused on creating solutions to poor drainage, issues of privacy, holding back the side of the hill, improving storage, adding outdoor lighting, or bringing water to the far reaches of your yard. But because the issues are more often about function than form doesn't mean their form can't be attractive and add to the overall appeal of your home as well.

A good fence can make a good neighbor or keep the dog out of the street, and it can be an architectural statement while doing so. A retaining wall will control the movement of dirt and help level a spot of ground; it can also become a location for planting flowers or shrubs or one or more sides of a raised patio. A well-sited shed can remove clutter from the landscape and still be attractive. Trellises and arbors are primarily decorative but they will add dimension and detail to a finished landscape. A beautifully executed stone wall defines the boundaries of your property while adding a touch of elegance to the surrounding environment.

The lesson here is that functionality isn't an end in itself. This book is about landscape construction but it's also about how to make practical solutions attractive ones as well.

On the following pages you will see examples of how solutions that work can add to the beauty of the landscape you're working so hard to improve.

CHAPTER 1

Defining the landscape 8

Be a legal eagle 10

Grading wood 11

REAL-WORLD SITUATIONS

CONSIDER THE BIG PICTURE

Putting up a fence or a retaining wall is a big job, not necessarily a hard one, but a big job nonetheless. There are a number of factors to consider as you make decisions about what you're going to do.

■ **What will the impact of your project be on the neighborhood in general?** Tour the streets and see how the neighbors have handled their projects. Your design objective should be to enhance the general ambience of your area. You goal is to solve your problem and make an individual statement without destroying the harmony of the whole.

■ **Do you want to do the whole project yourself?** Objectively evaluate your skills and experience against the complexity of the project and decide honestly whether you're up to all of it or part of it. Do you have the time, and enough friends to step in when you need help? There's nothing wrong with hiring a professional to do the more demanding or complex projects.

■ **Do you have the tools?** If you need tools such as a new circular saw or some other power tool, buy them. You'll use them again and again. A power auger or a cement mixer, on the other hand, are probably rentals, especially if you're only going to use them only once.

■ **Are you familiar with potential restrictions?** If not, you'll need to be. Building codes must be complied with, zoning ordinances respected, deed restrictions adhered to, and if you break a gas line while digging a foundation, not only is safety a concern, but it'll cost you time and will be expensive to repair.

Defining the landscape

Retaining walls, fences, driveways, sidewalks, and pathways are the bones of the landscape or what contractors call the hardscape. These elements define the basic structure of your property. Once they are in place you will begin to add landscaping details such as gardens, groupings of flowers and shrubbery, and structures that are primarily decorative such as arbors and trellises. But first you must decide where the bones will go and how they will function.

Some of these elements may already be in place—driveways, for instance, or sidewalks, patios, and flower gardens. If so, your goals may be more specific than devising a plan for the entire landscape. You may want a retaining wall to protect an existing garden from runoff or to keep the side of the hill from ending up in your house.

A fence may help define the boundaries of your property but it may also be needed to keep the deer from eating the vegetables.

If all you're looking for is security, a chain link fence may be the answer, especially if the area you are protecting is on a private section of the property. In either case as you make decisions about adding hardscape elements to your property, you should consider the differences between public and private spaces.

Retaining walls are good examples of how form and function combine in a landscape design. A retaining wall adds variety and visual interest while keeping a hillside in place.

PUBLIC SPACES

Public spaces are the areas of your property that are visible from the street—the front or sides of your home, the front yard, the driveway, and any paths or walkways that are in public view. Choices you make about public spaces will affect the entire neighborhood. Consider the impact on the neighborhood before you make a decision.

PRIVATE SPACES

Private spaces are out of public view, but that doesn't mean they should be solely utilitarian. Private spaces such as back yards or patios should ideally be considered as another room in the house—inviting and comfortable for you and your family.

MAKE A SITE MAP

Before you do anything you must have a plan. Maybe you already know where problem areas are, but maybe you're considered making major alterations in the landscape. In either case grab a long tape measure (100 feet), a pad, a pencil, and a helper and create a complete map of your property. Include the boundaries and all fixed structures, including the house, garage, and other buildings such

This graceful arbor defines the entrance to a patio and provides a secure base for climbing plants. Choose a style of arbor that compliments the architecture of your home.

as sheds. Chart the position of the driveway, sidewalks, patios, flower and vegetable gardens, groupings of shrubbery, trees, hedges, fences, and any other element or obstacle that may influence choices you will make.

Take your rough measurements and create a map in a scale that fits easily on a piece of paper. Make photocopies you can use to record ideas, and begin thinking about what you want to do. Spend some time walking your property, map in hand, so you can get a feeling for how your design will actually work when it's in place. This might be the time to consult a professional designer or, for a structural issue, a landscape contractor to review your ideas and make suggestions. They will usually do this for a fee, or if you hire them it will be part of the package.

SEEK INSPIRATION EVERYWHERE

Ideas come from many sources—books, magazines, friends, online, tours of finished landscapes that you like, garden shows on television, and in the garden departments of your local home center to name a few. Research materials that suit the architecture of your home and are compatible with the surrounding landscape.

A successful landscape is achieved with careful planning and attention to detail. Resolve basic questions and formalize your overall design on paper before you begin. Erasing a pencil line is easier than refilling a posthole and moving a fence.

THE ULTIMATE GOALS

The ultimate goals in any landscape construction project are to solve problems, add functionality and beauty to your outdoor spaces, and equally important, to do so in a manner that creates a harmonious, unified result.

The more time you spend thinking and planning before you start digging, the less likely you'll want to pull the whole thing out and start over. Remember, you're going to live with your wall, fence, or arbor for a long time—be sure you're getting what you want.

No matter how complex the design, landscape construction can be broken down into basic elements. Here the designer took advantage of a relatively steep hillside by combining stuccoed retaining walls and and a series of stone terraces to create an inviting entrance to the outdoor living space situated at the top of the hill.

Be a legal eagle

If you've broken a local code or ordinance when you installed your patio or walkway and the city finds out, you'll have to alter your design or even its siting to come into compliance. Saying, "Gee, I didn't know," won't get you very far with the inspector, and changes at the last minute can be costly indeed. Factoring in the extra time involved in doing your project twice and finding out what's acceptable before you begin is definitely worth the effort. Another issue to consider is whether there are deed restrictions in place in your neighborhood that define the limits on what can be installed and what can't. Do your research before you begin work to ensure that you can enjoy your patio or walkway in peace. Here are some important issues to consider as you create your design.

CHECK BUILDING CODES

Building codes exist to protect homeowners from potentially dangerous situations based on faulty construction methods and the use of unsafe materials. They're based on proven industry practices and approved for safety and uniformity. You have to abide by local and national codes, so it's best to know what they are and how they will affect your design as you prepare to install your patio or walkway. Contact your local building inspector's office for codes issues that can affect you.

RESEARCH ZONING ORDINANCES

Zoning ordinances define how a piece of property can be used and how structures can be placed on it. You usually won't be allowed to put up a gas station in the middle of a residential neighborhood even if it looks like the rest of the houses on the street. Residential zoning ordinances establish minimum setbacks from property lines, utility easements, and often even the size limits of a structure. Information will be available at the county clerk's office or at your local government center.

RESPECT DEED RESTRICTIONS

Some communities have adopted deed restrictions in order to maintain control over local property values or even architectural style. There may be restraints on the kind of installations that are allowed and even the style and the materials you can use. Other neighborhoods may have unspoken or informal restrictions on the kind of additions they allow. Their primary interest is in maintaining the integrity of the neighborhood. While you may not be legally bound to follow these guidelines, it's not fun to be feuding with the neighbors. Take a good look around the area and talk to the folks next door before you install a patio that looks like a carnival ride or build a retaining wall out of old rubber tires.

DON'T DIG UP THE GAS LINE

The placement of underground utility cables such as electric, communication and telephone, or television may affect the location of your patio even if they are buried deeper than you plan to excavate. Don't restrict access to them unless you're sure you'll never want to change. Sewer, water, and gas lines running to the house must also be considered. Utility and cable companies will be happy to visit your site and flag the position of underground lines. They don't like replacing or repairing broken pipes or cables any more than you do.

Even if you intend to do the job yourself it's a good idea to review your plans with an expert. Questions about construction techniques or compliance with zoning ordinances, deed restrictions, or local codes should be answered before you begin construction.

Grading wood

Lumber, like beef, is graded. Unlike beef, there's no single grading agency, so standards vary from species to species. With any wood, choosing the proper grade is always a matter of appearance vs. cost. The more you pay the fewer knots and the less sapwood you get. Spend your money on what people will see, and use a less expensive grade for posts, joists or beams. Grading standards for the three most common outdoor woods are shown here: Redwood, cedar, and softwood, which includes pressure-treated (PT) wood. Stores often carry a single grade of PT. Visit several and buy from whomever carries the best.

Stamp of approval

This representative grading stamp indicates standard grade dimension lumber of the species Douglas fir with a moisture content less than 20 percent. A mill's number, as shown here, or its name or symbol identifies the manufacturer. The certification symbol of the Western Wood Products Association means its grading guidelines were used.

Western red cedar grades

Architect Clear	Stable, defect free, uniform grain.
Custom Clear	Stable, a few small knots grain.
Architect Knotty	Stable, wider grain, knots allowed.
Custom Knotty	Not stable. Has not been dried.

Softwood lumber grades

DIMENSIONAL LUMBER (2 to 4 inches thick)

Select	Top grade, defect free
No. 1 (construction)	Few defects; no knots larger than 1½ inches, no checks, splits, or warps
No. 2 (standard)	More defects than No. 1; may have knots larger than 2 inches or checks, but no splits or warps
No. 2 and better	A commonly available mixed grade made of Select, No. 1, and No. 2
No. 3 (utility studs)	More defects than No. 2; may have checks, splits, or warps. Used where strength matters and where wood is unlikely to be seen.
Construction	Less strength and shorter span than No. 2 and better
Standard and better	A mix of all the grades above used in framing

BOARDS (less than 2 inches thick)

Select B and BTR	Highest quality, virtually free of defects or blemishes; expensive and not always available
Select C (choice)	High quality; few defects or blemishes
Select D (quality)	Quality; some defects and blemishes
No. 1 common	Small, minor defects and blemishes; limited size ranges and not always available

Redwood lumber grades

ARCHITECTURAL GRADES

Clear All Heart	Top grade; contains no sapwood, at least one face is defect free
Clear	Same as clear all heart, except contains some sapwood
Heart B	Heartwood with some knots
B Grade	Heart and sapwood with some knots

GARDEN GRADES

Deck Heart and Construction Heart	Similar grades of pure heartwood that contain knots and some imperfections
Deck Common and Construction Common	Same as deck and construction heart, but contain both heartwood and sapwood.
Merchantable Heart	Heartwood with knots, cracks at the end of the board (called checks), and some splits.
Merchantable	Same as above, but contains sapwood.

A fence can provide security and privacy. It can keep your dog in and your neighbor's dog out. But the fence that keeps the dog in may not be tall enough to keep out prying eyes. First consider why you want a fence, then find a few fences that meet your needs. Now look at the back of these fences. The front and back of a fence are almost always different. Any fence that is beautiful from your yard but unattractive from the neighbor's deck is probably a poor choice.

Once you've decided on a type of fence, decide on the material—chain link, vinyl, redwood, cedar, ornamental iron, or pressure-treated wood. While chain link wins no awards for beauty, it will keep the kids in the backyard, it doesn't block your view of the neighborhood, and it is maintenance-free. Vinyl comes almost exclusively in white, but it's a white that stays maintenance-free for years.

You can build almost any kind of fence with wood, then paint it, stain it, or simply admire the grain. Wood issues arise in regard to maintenance. Fortunately, pressure-treated wood pretty much solves the problem. Once you get above ground, the resistance to decay is considerably less important. Cedar, redwood, and pressure-treated wood will give you similar results. (If you're building the fence from scratch, pressure-treated timber rated "above ground" is made for everything except posts.)

Whether you're building from scratch or prefab panels, if you go with pressure-treated wood, stain it rather than paint it. Even the best paint will eventually chip. Cedar and redwood can both do with or without a finish. Both exterior-grade clear finish (other than varnish) and finishes made to match the wood apply easily. Both will also darken the wood somewhat, as will time and weather. Time and weather, however, won't lengthen the life of the fence. A good finish will.

CHAPTER 2

Fences and Gates tool kit 14

Materials 15

Laying out fences and gates 17

Installing fence posts 19

Installing prefab fence panels 22

Installing wood fence rails 24

Hillside fencing 26

Hanging rails for stepped hillside fencing . . 27

Building your own fence sections 28

Installing wood fencing 30

Putting up louver fencing 34

Making a basket-weave fence 35

Making and hanging a wood gate 37

Building and hanging a double gate 40

Building a post-and-rail fence 41

Installing mortised posts and rails 42

Building a wire fence 44

Installing a vinyl fence 46

Installing chain link fences 50

Assembling and hanging a chain link gate . . 53

Installing a pet fence 55

Repairing fences and gates 56

REAL-WORLD SITUATIONS

GOOD FENCES MAKE GOOD NEIGHBORS

Fences are simple to install, but they do require time and a certain amount of muscle.

In the lower half of the United States, a simple guideline keeps fence builders out of most trouble: Put your fence posts in holes that are at least half as deep as the fence is tall. A fence 4 feet high belongs in a hole that's 2 feet deep. A 6-foot fence belongs in a 3-foot hole, and an 8-foot fence belongs in a 4-foot hole. Looked at another way, this formula means that at least one-third of the total length of the fence pole is underground, more than enough to anchor the fence against high winds and backyard disasters.

As you go farther north, however, freezing and thawing soil causes the ground—and anything in it—to shift. To protect the posts, their holes must be dug at least 6 inches below the frost line, as well as at least half the height of the exposed fence. The map on page 82 will help you find the frost line in your area, but it's always a good idea to check with your municipality for local requirements.

To further anchor the posts, set the end and gateposts in concrete. If you expect the fence to face real abuse, you can set all the other posts in concrete too. Think twice about putting concrete around anything but end and gateposts, however. If you ever have to remove the fence, you'll also have to remove the concrete.

FENCES AND GATES TOOL KIT

3-POUND SLEDGEHAMMER	**DUST MASK**	**LEVEL**	**PLUMB BOB AND MASON'S LINE**	**RUBBER MALLET**	**SPADE**
CHALK LINE	**FENCE PULLER**	**LINE LEVEL**	**POST LEVEL**	**SAFETY GLASSES**	**SPEED SQUARE**
CIRCULAR SAW	**FENCING PLIERS**	**MASON'S TROWEL**	**POSTHOLE DIGGER**	**SCREWDRIVERS**	**TAPE MEASURE**
COLD CHISEL	**FRAMING SQUARE**	**MIXING TUB**	**POWDERED CHALK**	**SCRUB BRUSH**	**WHEELBARROW**
COMBINATION SQUARE	**HAMMER**	**PENCIL/MARKER**	**POWER AUGER**	**SHOVEL**	**WIRE CUTTERS**
DRILL AND BITS	**HANDSAW**	**PLIERS**	**POWER MITER SAW**	**SOCKET WRENCHES**	**WORK GLOVES**

FENCES AND GATES

Materials

Basic materials for constructing a wood fence include **Ⓐ pressure-treated 4×4s** for posts; a stamp indicates that they are suitable for ground burial. Protect the tops of posts from exposure to water with **Ⓑ post caps. Ⓒ Prefab fencing panels** go up quickly and come in a variety of styles. If you want to build a fence from scratch, nail **Ⓓ pressure-treated 2×4 rails** to the posts to build a frame for the fencing. Fence boards made from **Ⓔ 1×6s** apply to fencing styles such as the alternate board, louver, or basket weave. You can also make your own pickets by cutting shapes from **Ⓕ 1×4s. Ⓖ Cedar** and **Ⓗ redwood** fence boards resist rot naturally and are virtually maintenance-free. **Ⓘ Wire fencing** is yet another option. Build a rustic fence without the old-time work, using **Ⓙ precut mortised posts and rails,** or nail rails to a 6-inch post.

Vinyl fences come with ready-to-assemble **Ⓐ balustrades, Ⓑ posts, Ⓒ top rails, Ⓓ bottom rails, Ⓔ fence boards, and Ⓕ post caps.**

Local home improvement centers offer preassembled fence panels of both wood and vinyl, which speed installation time.

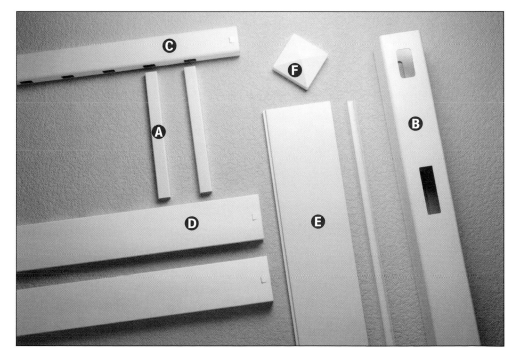

Materials (*continued*)

Mix **A** **concrete** and put it in end, corner, and gatepost holes to anchor the posts in the ground. Put **B** gravel underneath the other posts to help drain away water.

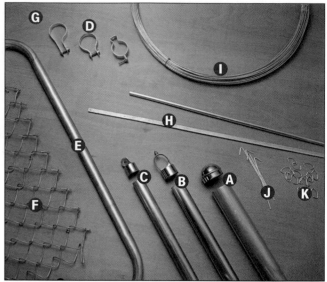

A chain link fence is easy to put up—don't be scared off by its large number of parts. For the basic frame you'll need **A** **2½-inch-diameter end posts and caps,** **B** **1⅝-inch-diameter line posts and caps,** and **C** **1⅜-inch-diameter rails and caps.** Attach rail caps to posts with **D** **brace bands.** Assemble a gate with **E** **top, bottom, and side rails** or buy all the parts together in a kit. Install **F** **chain link fencing** with **G** **tension bands,** **H** **tension bars,** **I** **tension wires,** **J** **tie wires,** and **K** **hog rings.**

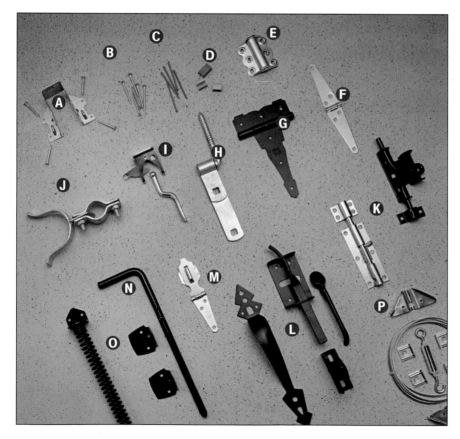

Choose fasteners and hardware suited to the type of fence and gate you're building. Fit rails edge up between posts with **A** **hangers and galvanized hanger nails.** Fasten fence boards with **B** **deck screws** or **C** **galvanized nails.** Attach wire fencing to wood posts and rails with **D** **staples.** Hang a gate with **E** **self-closing butt hinges,** **F** **strap hinges,** **G** **T hinges,** or **H** **lag-and-strap hinges.** **I** **Strike latches.** Other types of latches include **J** **a drop latch,** **K** **a slide-bolt latch,** **L** **a thumb latch,** and **M** **a hasp latch.** For a double gate, install **N** **a barrel bolt.** **O** **A spring closure** swings a gate shut automatically. Correct a sagging gate with a turnbuckle-style **P** **antisag kit.**

Laying out fences and gates

The best way to lay out a fence is with batterboards, which are a bit fancier than stakes and string but allow you to reposition the string without moving the stake. For string, use mason's line—it won't sag like regular string does.

If the fence has two or more sides, they need to be at right angles to each other. It's not the sort of thing you can easily check with a square, so you'll have to measure the diagonal between two points near the corner.

Once you've run the lines, you can put tape on them to mark where the posts will go. Depending on the fencing you're using, the posts will be either 6 or 8 feet apart.

SKILL SCALE

EASY	MEDIUM	HARD

REQUIRED SKILLS: Measuring, using a plumb bob, some basic carpentry.

HOW LONG WILL IT TAKE?

Laying out an 80-foot run of fence should take about:

Experienced . . . . 1 hr.
Handy . . . . 1.5 hrs.
Novice . . . . 2 hrs.

STUFF YOU'LL NEED

✔ MATERIALS:

2×2s, 2×4s, 12-inch landscape spike, 10d (3½-inch) nails, masking tape

✔ TOOLS:

Tape measure, mason's line, hammer, 3-pound sledgehammer, circular saw, line level, plumb bob, powdered chalk

1 BUILD BATTERBOARDS. Build a pair of batterboards for each run of fencing. Start by cutting points into the ends of two 2-foot 2×4s. Nail a 2×4 crosspiece to them about 2 inches from the top.

2 DRIVE THE BATTERBOARDS INTO THE GROUND about 18 inches beyond the planned end points of the fence. Tie mason's line to one of the crosspieces, stretch the line to the other crosspiece, and tie the line in place so it's taut.

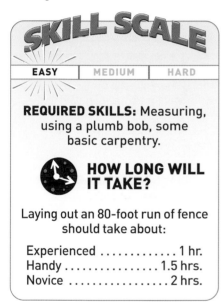

3 CHECK FOR LEVEL. Hang a line level on the middle of the line. Drive one of the batterboards farther into the ground to level the line, if necessary. Measure from a fixed object, such as the house or patio, and slide the line along the crosspiece until the line matches the exact path of the fence.

4 LAY OUT ADJOINING SIDES OF THE FENCE. Drive more batterboards and stretch line to lay out adjoining sides of the fence. Level the line as needed by driving one of the batterboards farther into the ground, then adjust so the line replicates the path of the fence.

Laying out fences and gates (continued)

5 **CHECK FOR SQUARE.** Start at the corner where the lines cross; measure 3 feet along one line and mark the spot with tape. Put a piece of tape 4 feet from the intersection on the other piece of line. The lines are square if the distance between the pieces of tape is 5 feet. If they're not square, slide one of the lines along the batterboard until they are.

6 **MARK THE CORNERS AND ENDS OF THE FENCE.** Drop a plumb bob from the corners that the mason's line forms. Mark the spot below the plumb bob with chalk. If the fence ends without forming a corner, measure along the line to lay out the end point. Mark it with tape, drop a plumb bob, then mark the ground with chalk.

7 **LAY OUT THE POSTS.** Measure along the mason's line, and put tape on the line to indicate the position of the fence posts. Drop a plumb bob from the tape and mark each spot with chalk or a piece of paper and a nail.

LAYING OUT A CURVED FENCE

1 **FIND A CENTER POINT THAT'S THE SAME DISTANCE FROM EACH END OF THE CURVE** and make a "compass" from string and a chalk bottle.

2 **TO LAY OUT THE POSTS ON A CURVE,** measure in a straight line between points on the curve.

Installing fence posts

If you want your fence to outlast its first summer, you need to set the posts deep enough in the ground to withstand wind, rain, and frost. With that in mind, there is only one hard-and-fast rule when you're digging a fence posthole: Dig a hole for the post that is half as deep as the fence is high. In areas with frost, dig the hole at least that deep or 6 inches below the frost line, whichever is deeper. Other than that, everything is variable:

■ You can set the post in concrete or fill the hole with the dirt that came out of it and tamp the dirt in place.

■ You can dig the hole a bit deeper than you otherwise would and put 4 inches of gravel on the bottom for drainage.

■ Generally speaking the hole should be 4 inches wider than the widest dimension of the post, but the size of the hole depends on the height of the fence and quality of the soil. (See "Sizing Footings" on page 20.)

On the following pages you'll see how to set posts two different ways—in concrete or in tamped soil. For the best job set end, corner, and gateposts in concrete. You can set the other posts, called line posts, in concrete, too, but it isn't strictly necessary. The tamped soil is usually enough.

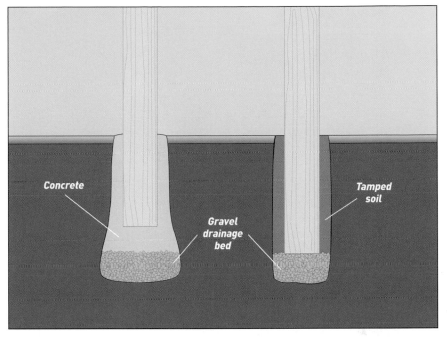

AS A RULE, A POSTHOLE SHOULD BE ABOUT 4 INCHES WIDER THAN THE POST. If no frost is present, dig a hole for the post that is as deep as half the height of the fence. In areas with frost, the holes should be the same depth and at least 6 inches below the frost line. Add 4 inches to the depths of the holes if you're putting in a gravel drainage bed. Ideally, set end and gateposts in concrete: Widen the bottom of the hole a few inches, pour in the concrete, and set the post so that it's 6 inches from the bottom of the hole.

SKILL SCALE

EASY	MEDIUM	HARD

REQUIRED SKILLS: Using a shovel, mixing concrete, using a level.

HOW LONG WILL IT TAKE?

Setting an 80-foot run of wood fence posts should take about:

Experienced .... 8 hrs.
Handy .... 10 hrs.
Novice .... 12 hrs.

VARIABLES: The type of soil will affect work time.

SAFETY ALERT

Locate underground utilities before you start to dig postholes.

STUFF YOU'LL NEED

✔ MATERIALS:
Gravel; pressure-treated 4×4s, 2×4s, and 2×2s rated for ground burial; duplex nails; bagged concrete

✔ TOOLS:
Power auger, tape measure, post level, wheelbarrow, shovel, hammer, clamps, level, mason's trowel, line level, drill and bits, chalk line, speed or combination square, circular saw, stepladder, clamps, safety glasses, dust mask, work gloves

Regional variation

Gas-powered augers are a good way to dig fence postholes in loose or sandy soil but can catch and turn into a merry-go-round in rocky ground. If you have rocky or hard ground, consider hiring a fencing contractor whose auger is mounted on a truck or tractor. You'll save yourself time—and possible injury. Lay out the holes in advance so you don't pay the contractor to wait while you get ready.

It's usually a good idea to dig postholes a few at a time rather than all at once so you can account for variations in panel widths and contours in the terrain as you go. This ensures that all the holes will be in the right place.

Installing fence posts (continued)

Sizing footings

FENCE HEIGHT	FOOTING DIAMETER × DEPTH (INCHES)		
	Loose Soil	Medium Soil	Hard Soil
4'	9×24	8×24	7×24
5'	9×24	8×24	7×24
6'	10×30	8×30	7×30
7'	11×36	9×36	7×36
8'	12×42	10×42	8×42
9'	13×48	11×48	9×48
10'	14×48	12×48	10×48
11'	15×48	14×48	12×48
12'	16×48	14×48	12×48

If you live in a frost-free area, the table above gives you the diameter and depth of footings for fence posts 4 inches in diameter. For fences with 10-foot sections, add 25 percent to either the diameter or depth. If you're putting in a 4-inch layer of gravel, dig postholes that much deeper.

1 DIG THE HOLES. Consider hiring a contractor to dig the holes in rocky soil. Rent a power auger for holes that aren't in rocky soil. Work with a helper and follow the manufacturer's instructions. Raise the auger after every few inches of digging to clear out soil. Dig to the depth required for the posts, plus 4 inches for a gravel base.

2 POUR FOOTINGS for end, corner, and gateposts. You'll set corner posts, end posts, and gateposts in concrete. The others are set in tamped soil. Start by lining the bottom of all the holes with 4 inches of gravel. Then mix concrete in a wheelbarrow and fill the end, corner, and gatepost holes with 6 inches of concrete. (If you're setting more than two posts in concrete, pour and set one hole at a time.)

3 PUT IN END, CORNER, AND GATEPOSTS. Restring the layout lines and use them as guides to set the end, corner, and gateposts. (You'll set the line posts later.) While the concrete is still wet, put the posts in their holes. Plumb each post with a level and hold it in place with braces and stakes.

4 PUT CONCRETE ON TOP OF THE FOOTINGS. Mix more concrete in the wheelbarrow. Shovel the concrete around the posts that will be set in concrete. Fill the hole about one-third of the way.

5 TAMP TO REMOVE TRAPPED AIR. Air trapped in the concrete will weaken it. Work a 2×4 up and down in the concrete to release the air.

6 **FILL THE HOLES.** Continue filling the holes with concrete up to about 2 inches above ground level. Smooth the surface of the concrete with a mason's trowel. As you smooth the surface, slope it away from the post so rain will drain away from it.

7 **SET THE LINE POSTS IN THEIR HOLES** using the mason's line as guides. Align and plumb each post, then backfill around it and tamp the soil. (Footings aren't needed for line posts.) Slope the soil at the top of the holes away from the posts for drainage.

WORK SMARTER

SETTING POSTS WITH DECORATIVE TOPS

Cutting posts to height after they've been set in the ground isn't something you'll want to do if the posts have a decorative top already in place. If this is the case, set the end posts at the desired height, then run a level mason's line between them. Double-check the height of each post against the mason's line. Working one post at a time, dig a hole until it holds the post at the right height. Plumb and brace the post and backfill around it before digging the next hole.

Let the concrete harden at least 48 hours before trimming the post and removing the braces.

TRIMMING POSTS

1 **MARK A LEVEL LINE ON ALL THE POSTS.** Start by marking one of the end posts at the desired height. Hold chalk line against the mark and stretch it to the other end post. Level the line with a line level and snap it against the line posts. If the fence is long, work no more than three or four posts at a time to avoid problems caused by sag in the line. Extend the chalk line across all four faces of each post with a combination square.

2 **CLAMP A SPEED SQUARE TO THE POST.** Position the square so when you rest the saw on it, it will make a cut along the line, marking the top of the post.

3 **CUT THE POST TO LENGTH.** Guide the saw along the top of the square to cut off the top of the post. If your saw won't cut deep enough to cut through a fence post (most saws won't), remove the jig and screw it to the opposite side of the post. Cut as before to cut through the post.

Installing prefab fence panels

Prefab fence panels are one of the fastest ways to build an attractive fence. Panels come in a variety of designs, from picket fences to board fences topped with lattice. It pays to shop around for the panels that best suit your house, your pocketbook, and your tastes.

Compared to other fencing styles, for which a lot of cutting and nailing is required, prefab fencing is both fast and easy. You dig holes for the fence posts and put the posts in place. But before you plumb the posts and fill the holes, you attach the fence section to each post so the fence fits perfectly between the poles. (Imagine how unlikely that would be if both posts were already anchored in the ground.) Doing so also makes it easier to plumb the posts: Plumb the panel, and the posts are automatically plumb too.

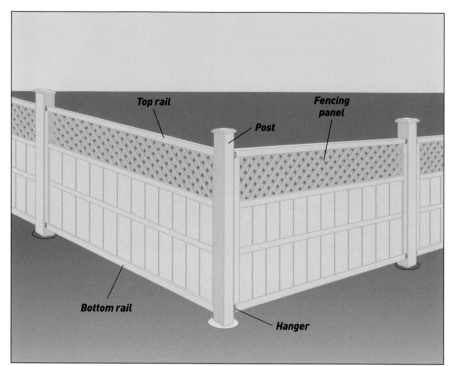

Top rail

Post

Fencing panel

Bottom rail

Hanger

SPACE THE POSTS TO MATCH THE PANELS. 6- and 8-foot lengths are standard. Add ¼ to ½ inch at each end. Attach the panels so they clear the ground by 3 or 4 inches. Because you may need to install the panels at different heights due to changes in the ground level, wait until you've installed the entire fence before trimming the posts to length.

SKILL SCALE

EASY	**MEDIUM**	HARD

REQUIRED SKILLS:
Basic carpentry.

HOW LONG WILL IT TAKE?

Installing an 80-foot run of prefab fencing should take about:

Experienced . . . . .5 hrs.
Handy . . . . .10 hrs.
Novice . . . . .12 hrs.

STUFF YOU'LL NEED

✔ **MATERIALS:**
Prefab wood panels, rail hangers, hanger nails, post caps, galvanized 8d (2½-inch) nails, construction adhesive

✔ **TOOLS:**
Tape measure, mason's line, line level, framing square, speed or combination square, level hammer, circular saw, safety glasses, work gloves

WORK SMARTER

WOODEN FENCE HANGERS

Instead of securing panels to the post with metal hangers, you can use grooved wooden U-channels. Nail the channel to the fence, then slide the panel into the groove. The channels provide support along the full height of the panel. Spacing is as critical as for hangers, so follow the same technique: Set both posts in the ground but don't fill the holes around them until you've attached the panel.

AN ALTERNATE APPROACH TO PREFAB PANELS

No rule stops you from installing prefabricated fence panels across the face of the posts instead of between them. You might even hang alternate panels on alternate sides of the posts. A benefit of this approach is that spacing between posts doesn't have to be as exact, and small differences go unnoticed. For a strong fence, fasten the panels to the posts with #8 2½-inch deck screws.

HANGING PANELS

1 **INSTALL AN END POST.** Plumb the end post, brace it, then fill in the hole with concrete. Measure and mark layout lines where the top and bottom of a panel will meet the post. Brace the next post temporarily in place, then transfer the layout lines with a mason's line and line level.

2 **INSTALL HANGERS.** Extend the layout marks to the inner faces of the posts using a square. Measure from the top of the fence to the rails and nail hangers this distance from the mark you made. Bend down the flange on the top bracket before nailing the bracket in place. Don't bend the flange on the bottom bracket.

3 **PUT THE PANEL IN PLACE.** Put the first panel between the end post and the next post, sliding it into place until the bottom rail sits on the hangers. Check the panel for level and adjust the braces, if necessary. Plumb the loose post and fill the holes with soil, tamping the soil as you go.

4 **NAIL THE FENCE IN PLACE.** Nail the sides of the brackets to the panels. Once the first panel is installed, work your way down the fence, installing one panel at a time. Set any gateposts, corner posts, or end posts in concrete.

If hangers are unavailable in your area, nails will secure the panels just as effectively.

5 **CUT OFF THE POSTS.** Draw a line where you want to cut the posts. Because most circular saws don't cut deep enough to cut through a fence post, use a combination or speed square to extend the line all the way around. Clamp a speed square to the post to guide the saw, cut through the post, then move the saw to the opposite side of the post and cut again.

6 **INSTALL CAPS ON THE POSTS TO PROTECT THEM FROM WATER.** Spread construction adhesive or exterior glue on the post, center the cap, and drive in two 8d (2½-inch) nails at an angle.

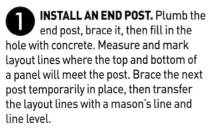

Installing wood fence rails

Even in the age of prefab panels, it's possible to build a fence from scratch. The job starts with posts. You dig the holes, align the posts, and fill in the holes. The rails come next, followed by the fencing (pickets, basket weave, or countless other possibilities). You can attach a rail several ways; none is necessarily better than the others. If your fence will be taller than 4 feet or particularly heavy, however, you'll need to install a third rail midway between the other two.

SKILL SCALE

EASY	MEDIUM	HARD

REQUIRED SKILLS:
Using a line level, measuring.

HOW LONG WILL IT TAKE?

Installing an 80-foot run of fence rails should take about:

Experienced . . . . 2 hrs.
Handy . . . . 3 hrs.
Novice . . . . 4 hrs.

STUFF YOU'LL NEED

✔ **MATERIALS:**
Pressure-treated or rot-resistant rails (2×4, 2×2, or 2×1 depending on the fence), rail hangers, #8 2½-inch deck screws, galvanized 10d (3-inch) nails

✔ **TOOLS:**
Tape measure, pencil, mason's line, line level, combination square, hammer, ⅜-inch drill and bits, safety glasses, work gloves

YOU CAN INSTALL RAILS BETWEEN POSTS OR ACROSS THEM, and you can fasten them with hangers, nails, or screws. Rails placed wide side up resist side-to-side pressure. Rails placed narrow side up sag the least and are recommended for heavy fences and those whose posts are 6 feet or more apart. When attaching rails to the sides of posts, use 16-foot rails and stagger them so there is only one joint per post. Don't cut notches in the posts to hold the rails. Not only is it a lot of work, it weakens the post.

LAYING OUT RAILS ON POSTS

1 **LAY OUT RAILS ON THE FIRST POST.** Start at an end post and measure up from the ground to draw layout lines marking the location of each rail.

2 **TRANSFER THE LINES TO OTHER POSTS.** Transfer the layout lines to the other posts using a line level and mason's line. (Don't use ordinary string because it stretches). If you're hanging the rails between posts, use a square to transfer the lines to the inside faces of the posts.

HANGING RAILS BETWEEN POSTS

NARROW EDGE UP. Nail rail hangers to the posts. Slide the ends of each rail into the hangers, then nail the side flanges of each hanger to the rail.

FACE UP ON CLEATS. Fasten 2× cleats to the fence with #8 2½-inch deck screws. Place the rails on the cleats and drive two screws at an angle through the ends of the rails into the cleats.

ATTACHING RAILS TO THE SIDE OF THE POSTS

NARROW EDGE UP. Cut the rails so joints fall at the center of posts and the ends butt together tightly. Fasten the rail to the posts with #8 2½-inch deck screws.

CAP RAILS. Cut rails so the joints fall at the center of the posts and the ends butt together tightly. Cut a 45-degree miter on rails that meet over corner posts. Fasten with 10d (3-inch) nails or #8 2½-inch deck screws.

HANGING RAILS FOR CURVED FENCING

CUT RAILS SO THE JOINTS FALL AT THE CENTER OF THE POSTS. Put the rails on the posts, butting the ends tightly. Fasten the rails to the posts with #8 2½-inch deck screws.

Hillside fencing

If you're installing a fence on a hill, you'll need to take the slope into account. You have two choices: You can follow the contour or you can build a stepped fence. This page covers contoured fencing; stepped fences are discussed on the next page.

To lay out a contoured fence, first drive 2×2 stakes at the top and the bottom of the slope. Run a level mason's line between the stakes, measure along it, and mark locations for line posts with tape. Transfer the taped marks to the ground with a plumb bob, and mark each spot with powdered chalk.

Dig holes for the posts and install them before trimming them to the uniform height.

THE RAILS ON A CONTOUR FENCE FOLLOW THE SLOPE OF THE GROUND. Lay out the posts as described below. Once they're in place, measure up from the ground to lay out the bottom rails. Measure up from the bottom rails to lay out the top rails. Cut the rails so the ends fall at the middle of the posts and fasten them with #8 2½-inch deck screws.

1 **RUN A MASON'S LINE BETWEEN THE END STAKES.** Drive a stake at the top and bottom of the slope. Tie a line to each stake and level it with a line level. Measure along the line to lay out the locations of the posts, and mark the locations with tape.

2 **TRANSFER THE MARKS TO THE GROUND.** Drop a plumb bob from the tape to transfer the marks to the ground. Mark the spot with powdered chalk, then with stakes. Dig holes and install the stakes so that each is a little more than finished height above the ground.

Hanging rails for stepped hillside fencing

Some fences, such as alternate-board fences, work best when they step down a hillside. To lay out a stepped hillside fence, drive a 2×2 stake into the ground at the top and bottom of the slope. Run a level mason's line from the base of the top stake to the bottom stake. The distance between the ground and the line at the bottom post is the drop in elevation between stakes. Divide the drop by the number of fencing sections (not posts) to find the drop per section. In the example below, the overall drop is 24 inches over three sections of fence. Divide 24 inches by the three sections to come up with the drop per section: 8 inches.

When installing the posts, set each one slightly higher than the desired height. Measure to find the top of the upper post, and transfer the drop per section to the other posts with the help of a line level. Once the posts are laid out, trim the posts to height.

AS ITS NAME IMPLIES, STEPPED HILLSIDE FENCING GOES DOWN THE HILL IN A SERIES OF STEPS. First lay out the top of the upper post. Measure down by the amount of drop, and transfer this height to the next post with the help of a line level. Continue measuring and transferring until you reach the bottom of the hill.

1 LAY OUT THE POSTS. Drive a stake at the top and bottom of the fence run. String a mason's line from the base of the top stake to the bottom stake, then level the line with a line level. Measure the distance between the line and the ground at the bottom stake to find out how much the fence drops along the run. Measure along the line and mark the location of the posts with masking tape. Count the sections of fence you'll need, then divide the overall drop of the fence by the number of sections to find the drop per section.

2 LAY OUT THE TOP OF THE POSTS. Dig holes and install the posts so each one is slightly taller than the finished height of the fence. Measure to find where the top of the upper post will be and draw a line to mark where you'll cut it. Measure down by the drop per section—which you figured out in Step 1—and tie a line at that point. Tie the other end to the next post, and level the line. The point at which it crosses the second post will be the top of that post. Mark the top, move the line down by the drop per section, then stretch it to the third post and level it. Mark as before. Continue down the hill, marking the top, measuring down, and stretching a level line until you reach the bottom of the hill. Cut off the tops of the posts at the layout lines.

Building your own fence sections

You can nail almost anything to a standard post-and-rail skeleton. The most popular fence types are picket, alternate board, solid board, louver, and basket weave.

Building any of these fences is a three-step process: install the posts, install the rails, and screw on the fencing. Intervals of 4, 6, and 8 feet between posts are typical. Choose one (such as picket) and adjust the spacing of the fence boards so they are spaced evenly. Factor in the type of fence style, too, when you put up rails. The rails of some styles, such as louvered fencing, must be installed with the wide face up. Others such as the basket weave require the addition of a cap rail. Fences 48 inches or taller require a middle rail.

Check local codes for restrictions on fence height. Install the fence at least 2 inches above the ground to prevent the boards from rotting.

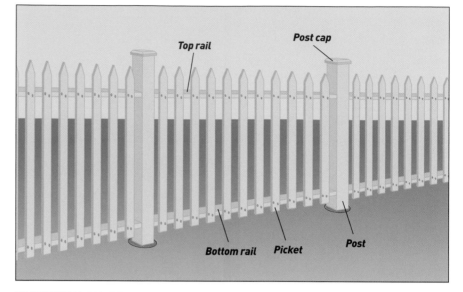

Top rail · Post cap · Bottom rail · Picket · Post

TRADITIONAL PICKETS ARE 4 FEET HIGH. They are typically 1×3s with the space between them equal to the width of each picket. Rails to hold the pickets are installed at the top and bottom; taller pickets need the support of a middle rail. No matter what size or shape you install, space pickets at intervals less than 4 inches or greater than 6 inches to minimize the risk of children or pets getting stuck between them.

SKILL SCALE

EASY · **MEDIUM** · HARD

REQUIRED SKILLS:
Basic carpentry.

HOW LONG WILL IT TAKE?

Building an 80-foot fence should take about:
Experienced . . . . 8 hrs.
Handy . . . . 12 hrs.
Novice . . . . 16 hrs.

STUFF YOU'LL NEED

✔ MATERIALS:
1× fence boards, pressure- treated
1×2s, 2×2s, 2×4s, #8 2-inch and 2½-inch deck screws

✔ TOOLS:
Tape measure, mason's line, line level, level, circular saw, saber saw, power miter saw, clamps, ⅜-inch drill and screwdriver bit, hammer, safety glasses

1 LAY OUT AND CUT THE PICKETS. Many pickets are flattop, but you can also lay out your own custom shapes. For customized pickets, make a pattern, trace the shape onto the boards, and cut outside curves with a saber saw. Cut inside curves with a drill bit, if possible. (See inset.) To speed up the job, clamp a couple of boards together and cut them at the same time.

2 MAKE A SPACER. Make a spacer that is as wide as the space between pickets. Screw a 2×2 block to the top of the spacer so when you hang it from the rail, the top of the spacer is level with the top of the pickets. Screw a small torpedo level to the spacer to tell if the pickets are plumb.

3 **ATTACH THE FIRST PICKET.** Butt the spacer against the post and butt a picket against the spacer. Use a level to make sure the picket is plumb, then screw the picket to the rails with #8 2-inch deck screws.

After installing the pickets, add caps to the tops of the posts to keep out water.

4 **ATTACH THE REMAINING PICKETS.** Butt the spacer against the first picket, position the next picket against it, and screw the picket to the rails. Continue installing pickets the same way, checking for plumb as you go and making any necessary adjustments.

CONTOUR PICKET FENCING
To lay out pickets that follow the contour of the ground, hold them upside down next to the spacer. Draw a line where the picket meets the top of the spacer; which if it's built correctly, aligns with the top of the pickets. Cut at the line and install the picket right side up.

BUILDING AND INSTALLING CURVED-TOP PANELS

1 **BUILD A FRAME FOR THE PICKETS.** You can dress up ordinary pickets by cutting a curve along the top of each section. First assemble a frame of 2×4s that fits snugly between the posts. Fasten the rails together with #8 2½-inch deck screws, then screw or nail the pickets to the frame.

2 **LAY OUT AND CUT THE CURVE WITH A SABER SAW.** Drive a nail into the pickets, marking each end of the curve. Drive a third nail into the center picket, marking the center point of the curve. Have a helper flex a thin piece of wood—roughly ¼ inch thick—between the end and center nail while you use it as a guide to trace along the panel. (Lattice or doorstop molding also works well.) Repeat, flexing the wood between the center nail and other end.

3 **INSTALL THE COMPLETED PANEL.** Put the completed panel between the posts, propping it on blocks at the desired height above the ground. Fasten the panel to the posts with #8 2½-inch deck screws.

Installing wood fencing

Astandard post-and-rail skeleton supports many styles of fencing. You'll find the most popular types on the following pages. Most styles have posts that are mounted at intervals of 4, 6, or 8 feet, and the space between boards (or "pickets") is usually uniform. Choose a fence style and picket, then cut rails to a multiple of the picket width.

Factor in the fencing style, too, when you put up rails. The rails for some styles, such as the louver, are installed face up. Others such as the basket weave require a cap rail after the fencing is installed. Fences more than 48 inches high need a third rail in the middle.

Check local codes for restrictions on height. Install fencing so the bottom of each board is at least 2 inches above the ground to prevent premature decay.

SKILL SCALE

EASY | **MEDIUM** | HARD

REQUIRED SKILLS: Layout, basic carpentry.

HOW LONG WILL IT TAKE?

Installing an 80-foot run of wood fencing should take about:

Experienced . . . . 8 hrs.
Handy . . . . 12 hrs.
Novice . . . . 16 hrs.

STUFF YOU'LL NEED

✔ MATERIALS:

1× fence boards, 1×2s, 2×2s, 2×4s, galvanized 6d (2-inch) nails, #8 2-inch and 2½-inch deck screws

✔ TOOLS:

Tape measure, mason's line, line level, level, circular saw, saber saw, power miter saw, clamps, ⅜-inch drill and screwdriver bit, hammer, safety glasses

ALTERNATE-BOARD FENCING

Post cap   *Top rail*

Bottom rail   *Fence board*   *Post*

AN ALTERNATE-BOARD FENCE IS MADE OF BOARDS—usually 1×6s—that alternate between opposite sides of the fence. The space between boards on either side of the fence is usually equal to the width of the boards, but you can increase privacy by making the space slightly narrower so that the boards overlap. Opt for 1×4s instead of 1×6s to create a taller, narrower look. Stay away from 1×8s; they tend to warp when installed vertically.

1 **SPACE THE POSTS TO MATCH THE WIDTH OF THE FENCE BOARDS.** Space the posts so that you can attach the fence boards without having to cut them to width. If necessary you can make small adjustments as you install the boards so that they'll fit on a standard 6- or 8-foot rail. Once the posts are in, attach the rails. (See "Installing wood fence rails," page 24.)

2 **MAKE A SPACER.** Make a spacer that is as wide as the space between boards. Screw a 2×2 block to the top of the spacer so that when you hang it from the rail, the top of the spacer is level with the top of the boards. Screw a small torpedo level to the spacer so you can tell if the boards are plumb.

HOMER'S HINDSIGHT

FOR THE WANT OF A NAIL...
More than one customer has told me that nailing fence boards in place requires enough force to knock the fence down before it's finished. They always ask if there are any tricks to nailing correctly, and I have to tell them that there aren't. That's why I always recommend deck screws for fence work. They drive easily with the help of a drill, and I've never seen anyone knock over a post with a screw. Get #8 deck screws. They're galvanized to prevent rust.

3 **LAY OUT THE BOTTOM OF THE FENCE BOARDS.** Run a mason's line between posts and level it at the desired height above the ground. The location of the line will affect the length of the vertical boards. Measure up from the mason's line to the top of the post to determine the proper length of the fence boards.

4 **CUT THE BOARDS TO LENGTH.** Clamp two or three boards together and cut them at the same time to speed up the job.

Designer Tip

KICKBOARDS

To close the gap under the fence, install kickboards before putting in the fence boards. Make the kickboard from rot-resistant lumber such as cedar, redwood, cypress, or .60 pressure-treated wood. You can either screw the kickboard to the face of the rail and the post (below left) or center it beneath the rail and secure it with a screw through the rail (below right). A kickboard attached to the face of the rail is stronger, but the centering option is a little more attractive. If you're attaching to the face, keep the top edge level so that you can rest the fence boards on it as you install them.

Keep burrowing animals out of the yard by extending the kickboard into a 4- to 6-inch trench dug between the posts.

5 **PUT IN THE FIRST BOARD.** Align a fence board with the mason's line and butt it against the first post. Check that it is plumb and screw it to the rails with #8 2-inch deck screws.

Installing wood fencing

ALTERNATE-BOARD FENCING (continued)

6 **INSTALL BOARDS ON ONE SIDE OF THE FENCE.** Hang the spacer on the top rail and butt it against the first fence board. Butt a fence board against the spacer. Put a board against it, check to make sure it's plumb, and screw the board to the rails with #8 2-inch deck screws. Work your way along the fence, positioning the spacer and screwing the boards in place.

7 **INSTALL BOARDS ON THE OTHER SIDE OF THE FENCE.** Go to the other side of the fence. Put the spacer against the first post, and install a board against the spacer. Install boards along the entire side, spacing them with the spacer.

WORK SMARTER

LEVELING THE PLAYING FIELD
Sometimes it's impossible to remove rocks and other obstructions on the ground. If you have an obstruction you can't get rid of, cut the fence board to follow the shape of the obstruction. To lay out the cut, clamp the full-length board plumb and in position. Scribe the shape of the ground onto the board with a scrap 2×4 and a pencil. Make the cut with a saber saw, then trim the board to length and install it.

Fences and trees

Incorporate a tree into the fence rather than build around it or cut it down. Set posts within 4 feet of the tree and install the rails as you normally would. Continue the fence rails from the post to within 4 inches of each side of the tree. Connect the rails with a rail that follows the slope of the tree, and create a frame that's rigid enough to hold fence boards. Don't nail anything directly to the tree, however. A tree gets wider as it grows and will eventually knock down anything attached to it.

1 **INSTALL TOP AND BOTTOM RAILS THAT COME WITHIN A FEW INCHES OF THE TREE.** Prop the bottom rail in position on a block. Nail a 2×4 brace to the top rail to temporarily support it. Hold a third rail in place at the end of these rails and trace along them to draw a line on the third rail. Cut along the line, then screw the third rail between the top and bottom rails using #8 2½-inch deck screws.

2 **INSTALL FULL-LENGTH FENCE BOARDS** until the tree prevents you from doing so, then remove the temporary brace. Lay out the rest of the fence boards, one at a time, tracing along the sloped rail to get the proper shape.

INSTALLING SOLID-BOARD FENCING

A SOLID-BOARD FENCE IS MADE OF POSTS AND RAILS like any other fence. A few changes, however, make it both more durable and more attractive. Most important is the cap rail that runs across the top. The cap rail protects the tops of the posts, which absorb water more readily and are more likely to rot than any other surface of the post. The fence is also designed to look the same from both sides—something your neighbor is likely to appreciate.

1 BUILD THE STRUCTURE. Install 4×4 posts and 2×4 top and bottom rails, then nail a 1×4 cap rail over the top rail. Cut two 1×1 supports to fit between each post. Screw the supports along the outside edge of the bottom rail on one side of the fence, fastening them every 6 to 8 inches with #8 2-inch deck screws. Repeat on the top rail.

2 INSTALL THE FENCE BOARDS. Put the first board in place next to a post, make sure it's plumb, and screw it to the supports with #8 1⅝-inch deck screws. Work your way down the fence, using a nail as a spacer between boards so they have room to expand in humid weather. When you're done screw a second set of 1×1 supports tightly against the fence boards.

INSTALLING BOARD-AND-BATTEN FENCING

BOARD-AND-BATTEN FENCING MIMICS THE SIDING ONCE APPLIED TO FARM SHEDS, barns, and similar outbuildings. An important part of this fence is the cap rail. Without it the end grain of every board would be exposed to the weather, shortening the life of the fence.

1 BUILD THE STRUCTURE. Install the posts, top and bottom rails, and a cap rail that overhangs the side of the rail on which you'll hang the fence boards. Cut the fence boards to length and tuck them under the cap rail, spacing them with the narrow edges of a batten. Plumb the boards with a level and fasten them with 1⅝-inch deck screws.

2 INSTALL THE BATTENS. Cut the battens to length with a circular saw or power miter saw. Center each batten over the space between boards and screw it to the top rail. Plumb with a level, then screw to the lower rail.

Installing wood fencing

PUTTING UP LOUVER FENCING

Louver fencing is a fancy version of standard board fencing. The boards are mounted at an angle to the face of the fence, and because of the angle, they provide nearly as much privacy as a board fence, along with ventilation. The trick to getting a uniform angle from board to board is to put angled spacers between the boards. Ideally use a power miter saw to cut spacers.

THIS LOUVERED FENCE IS MADE OF 1×6s MOUNTED AT AN ANGLE ON THE RAILS. The boards are sandwiched between 1×4 spacers that are cut at an angle to hold the boards in place.

BUILD THE STRUCTURE. Install posts and rails. The top rails overlap the posts and are nailed to them. The bottom rails butt into the posts and are supported by small blocks nailed to the posts. Once the rails are installed, measure the exact distance between them and cut fence boards to this length.

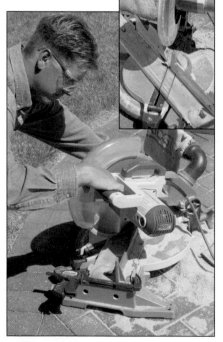

2 MAKE SPACERS. Set the blade of a power miter saw to 45 degrees. Cut a 45-degree angle on a piece of scrap and clamp it to the saw so it's 2 inches from the blade. (See inset.) Using the board as a stop, butt a 1×4 gently against it and cut the 1×4 to length. Continue cutting: Each section of fence has a triangular spacer at each end and parallelogram-shape spacers between all other boards.

3 FASTEN THE SPACERS. Drill pilot holes into the spacers to reduce the potential for splitting. Fasten an end spacer to the top and bottom rails with #8 2-inch deck screws. Don't drive the screws all the way in until you have plumbed the first fence board.

4 **PUT IN THE FIRST BOARD.** Butt a board against the end spacers so one edge is flush with the post. Plumb the board with a level and move a spacer, if necessary, to support the board firmly. Fasten the board to the spacer with #8 2-inch deck screws.

5 **PUT IN THE REMAINING BOARDS.** Put a parallelogram-shape spacer against the top and bottom of the first picket. Screw the spacers to the rails, then screw the next fence board to the spacers. Continue installing spacers and boards until you reach the next post.

6 **PUT IN THE FINAL SPACER.** Screw the last picket of the section in place. Put two triangular spacers between the post and board (top and bottom), then screw the spacers to the rails.

MAKING A BASKET-WEAVE FENCE

A simple trick to achieve a fancier fence is to weave spacers between fence boards. Start by installing the bottom rail, then nail supports to the posts. Screw one end of the fence boards to a support, and insert a spacer. Put in a second spacer a bit farther down the section, then screw the free end of the boards to their support. Add a cap rail to protect the tops of the posts from weather.

OOPS!

ANOTHER BOARD BITES THE DUST
Because of the spacers, each fence board needs to be longer than the distance between posts. Be sure to cut the boards to fit each section individually, or you're sure to need more wood.

Cap rail

Bottom rail   Fence board   Spacer   Support   Post

TO MAKE A BASKET-WEAVE FENCE, WEAVE 2×2 SPACERS BETWEEN 1×6 FENCE BOARDS. Hold the ends of the boards in place by sandwiching them between two 1×2 supports nailed to each post. Fasten a 2×4 cap rail to the tops of the rails and posts to protect them from rain, snow, and hot sun.

Installing wood fencing

MAKING A BASKET-WEAVE FENCE (continued)

1 **BUILD THE STRUCTURE.** Install posts and rails. Cut two 1×2 supports that fit between the rails and fasten them to the back edge of the rails with #8 2½-inch deck screws. Cut two 2×2 spacers to weave between the fence boards and mark their locations on the bottom rail.

2 **CUT THE FENCE BOARDS TO FIT.** Cut three fence boards 2 inches or so longer than the distance between two posts. Tack one end of each board to one of the supports and weave the spacers between them. Draw a line on the board showing where the free end meets the other support. Cut the boards at the line, then fasten one end of each to the supports.

3 **WEAVE THE SPACERS.** If the first three boards fit properly, cut the remaining boards to length. Screw one end of each to a support and weave the 2×2 spacers into place. Use a level to plumb the spacers.

4 **FASTEN THE LOOSE ENDS OF THE BOARDS.** Working up from the bottom, fasten the loose ends of the fence boards. Level each board as you screw it in place.

5 **INSTALL A SECOND SET OF SUPPORTS.** Cut a second set of 1×2 supports and screw them to the posts on the side opposite the first set of supports.

6 **WORK YOUR WAY DOWN THE FENCE.** Install supports, fence boards, and spacers one section at a time. Once all the pieces are in place, nail a cap rail across the top of the fence with 10d (3-inch) nails.

Making and hanging a wood gate

SKILL SCALE

EASY	MEDIUM	HARD

REQUIRED SKILLS: Cutting, measuring, assembly.

HOW LONG WILL IT TAKE?

Building and hanging a wooden gate should take about:

Experienced . . . . 3 hrs.
Handy . . . . 5 hrs.
Novice . . . . 6 hrs.

STUFF YOU'LL NEED

✔ MATERIALS:

2×4s, fence boards, #8 2-inch and 2½-inch deck screws, hinges, latch assembly, barrel bolt assembly

✔ TOOLS:

Tape measure, pencil, framing square, circular saw, saber saw, ⅜-inch drill and bits, screwdriver, level, safety glasses

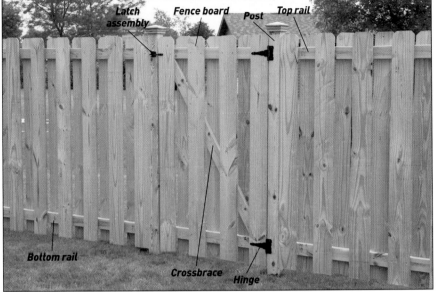

WHEN YOU BUILD A GATE, MAKE SURE THE POSTS THAT SUPPORT IT ARE PLUMB (straight up and down). If not, the gate won't swing properly, and depending on how far the posts are out of plumb, the gap at one edge could vary by as much as an inch from top to bottom. To help ensure plumb gateposts, lay out and install the gateposts first, then build the rest of the fence around them. When it comes time to build the gate, build the frame first. Then run a crossbrace from the bottom hinge to the top of the latch to keep the gate square. Last apply the boards that make the surface of the gate.

G ood fences make good neighbors, and good gates make good fences. Unfortunately a gate that isn't wide enough is no good at all. It must be 3 feet wide to handle equipment such as lawn mowers, wheelbarrows, and even larger machinery. Measure your garden equipment, add 6 to 12 inches for clearance to the widest piece, and make the opening at least that wide. A single gate handles an opening up to 4 feet wide. Make it wider, and you'll need a double gate.

Make sure the gate swings in the right direction, which is usually into your yard. Across a slope, however, hang the gate so it opens downhill. If there are steps on either side of the gate, it's best for the gate to swing away from them. (You don't want to knock anyone down the steps.)

BUILDING THE GATE

① CUT PARTS FOR THE FRAME. Measure between posts to double-check the width of the opening. Subtract the space required by the hardware and cut 2×4 top and bottom rails to this length. For this gate, measure from the *bottom* of the lower fence rail to the *bottom* of the upper rail and cut two gate side rails to this length. If you redesign the gate, cut the pieces to allow for joinery.

② CUT JOINTS AND ASSEMBLE THE FRAME. The top and bottom rails are notched to house the side rails. Cut the notches with a saber saw—each notch is as wide as a side rail and half as deep as the top rail. Clamp the pieces together and drill pilot and countersink holes for #8 2-inch deck screws with a combination bit. Screw the frame together.

Making and hanging a wood gate

BUILDING THE GATE (continued)

3 **CUT THE CROSSBRACE.** Check the gate for square by measuring its diagonals. The measurements will be the same if the gate is square. If not, push gently on the corners of the long diagonal until they are. Lay a 2×4 crossbrace against the frame and trace along the frame to lay out the ends of the brace. Cut along the lines with a saber saw or circular saw.

4 **ATTACH THE CROSSBRACE.** Put the crossbrace into place between the rails, trimming it to fit, if necessary. Drill pilot holes at an angle and drive #8 2-inch deck screws through the crossbrace into the rails.

5 **ATTACH THE FIRST FENCE BOARD.** Cut fence boards to length and make a spacer as long as the fence boards and as wide as the space you want between them. To help position the fence boards, screw a cleat to the top of the spacer so when the spacer sits on the top rail, you can position the fence boards by aligning them with the spacer. Fasten the first board to the top and bottom rails with #8 2-inch deck screws.

6 **ATTACH THE REST OF THE BOARDS.** Align subsequent fence boards one at a time with the spacer and screw them to the rails. If the fence has boards on both sides, turn the gate over and attach boards that match.

Framing a heavy gate

Tall, wide gates not only need strong hinges, they need extra reinforcement. Build them with side rails and top, bottom, and center rails. Run two diagonal crossbraces: one from the bottom rail on the hinge side to the latch side of the center rail and the other from the hinge side of the center rail to the latch side of the top rail. Hang the latch on the center rail.

HANGING THE GATE

1 **SCREW THE HINGES TO THE GATE.** Put the hinges on the gate so the hinge barrels edge the gate, as shown. Center the hinges on the rails, mark the screw holes, then bore pilot holes slightly narrower than the screw shank. Screw the hinges to the gate.

2 **PUT THE GATE TEMPORARILY IN PLACE BETWEEN THE POSTS.** Prop it on a block of wood so it's at the desired height. Position the gate so the latch side is slightly higher than the hinge side. Once you hang the gate, its natural sag will bring the latch side into alignment with the rest of the fence.

3 **SCREW THE HINGES IN PLACE.** Mark the screw holes on the post. Drill pilot holes slightly smaller than the screw's diameter, then screw the hinges to the post.

For a stronger gate, install the hinges with screws a bit longer than the ones with which they're packed.

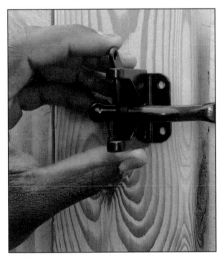
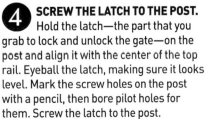

4 **SCREW THE LATCH TO THE POST.** Hold the latch—the part that you grab to lock and unlock the gate—on the post and align it with the center of the top rail. Eyeball the latch, making sure it looks level. Mark the screw holes on the post with a pencil, then bore pilot holes for them. Screw the latch to the post.

5 **SCREW THE STRIKE BAR TO THE GATE.** Put the strike in the latch and hold it against the gate, aligning it so it looks level. Mark screw holes on the gate with a pencil, and bore pilot holes. Screw the strike bar to the gate. Test the latch and make any necessary adjustments.

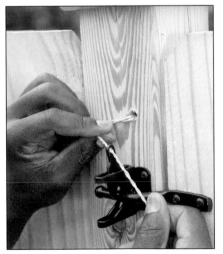

6 **ATTACH A LATCH STRING, IF NECESSARY.** On tall fences, it's difficult to reach over the gate to unfasten the latch. If you'd like to make the latch more accessible, bore a ⅜-inch-diameter hole through the center of the post a few inches above the latch. Tie one end of a string to the latch, thread it through the hole, and tie the other end to a pull ring. Pull on the ring to open the latch.

Making and hanging a wood gate

INSTALLING LAG-AND-STRAP HANGERS

1 **SCREW HOLES FOR THE LAGS.** To make a drill guide, drill a hole into a 2×4, then make two 45-degree cuts, centered on the hole, to create a 90-degree notch. Make marks on the post to show where you want the center of the lags to be. Put the drill guide over one mark and drill a ½-inch-deep hole for the lag into the post. Repeat at the other mark, then screw the lags in place so the pins are plumb.

2 **SCREW ON THE STRAP.** Prop the gate in place at the proper height. Put the straps on the lag pins, then put the straps against the gate. Mark the screw holes, drill pilot holes, then screw the straps to the gate.

WORK SMARTER

...AND CLOSE THE GATE BEHIND YOU

Install a spring closer so the gate closes on its own. Screw one end of the closer to the hinge side of the gate and the other end to the post. Tighten or loosen the adjustment nut to control the speed at which the gate closes.

BUILDING AND HANGING A DOUBLE GATE

If your gate crosses a driveway, you'll need an opening that's at least 8 feet wide. The only way to achieve such an opening is with a double gate. Each side should be the same size and hang the same way on the posts.

HOMER'S HINDSIGHT

BOTTOMS UP

Hanging two gates isn't that much harder than hanging one, and the same rules apply. The gates need crossbraces that run diagonally from the lower hinge to the latch. I've had more than one customer wonder why their gates sag, and it's usually because the braces run in the wrong direction. When you install the gate, make sure you do it right side up.

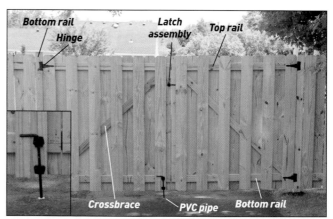

Bottom rail *Hinge* *Latch assembly* *Top rail* *Crossbrace* *PVC pipe* *Bottom rail*

WHEN COVERING A LARGE OPENING, BUILD TWO SINGLE GATES, each one half the distance between the posts minus 1½ to 2 inches clearance for hardware. Install crossbraces on the gates at diagonals so each one fits between the bottom rail on the hinge side and the top rail on the latch side. Install the latch on the top rail and a barrel bolt along the bottom rail to keep the gates in position when latched. Drill a hole in the driveway and insert a piece of PVC pipe so you can slide the barrel bolt into the driveway. A 2×4 block above the bolt will keep it in place when it's in the raised position. (See inset.)

Building a post-and-rail fence

The simplest wood fences are post-and-rail fences, three of which are shown on the following pages. The fence and the way you install it depends on whether the posts are square, round, or premortised. Set square posts in the ground, trim them to height, and install rails. Before setting round posts into the ground, cut notches for the rails. Set and plumb mortised posts as you install the rails.

SKILL SCALE

EASY	MEDIUM	HARD

REQUIRED SKILLS:
Measuring, cutting, layout, basic carpentry skills.

HOW LONG WILL IT TAKE?

Installing an 80-foot run of post-and-rail fence should take about:

Experienced . . . . 8 hrs.
Handy . . . . 12 hrs.
Novice . . . . 16 hrs.

STUFF YOU'LL NEED

✔ MATERIALS:
4×4 posts; pre-mixed concrete in bags; 1×6, 2×6, or precut tapered rails; 10d (3-inch) deck screws, roofing cement, wire, masking tape

✔ TOOLS:
Tape measure, pencil/marker, mason's line, hammer, line level, 3-pound sledgehammer, posthole digger, shovel, drill and screwdriver bit, circular saw, wood chisel, rubber mallet, level, framing square, wheelbarrow, safety glasses, work gloves

Cross rail

Post

Bottom rail

Cross rail

BEGIN BUILDING A BASIC POST-AND-RAIL FENCE BY SETTING THE POSTS IN THE GROUND AT REGULAR 6- TO 8-FOOT INTERVALS. Trim the posts to height and screw on the rails. Fasten the bottom rail 3 to 4 inches above ground level and the top rail so it's flush with the top of the posts. Cut cross rails and fasten them so the joints fall in the center of each post.

1 INSTALL THE RAILS. Lay out the fence and set the posts into the ground. Mark the posts for bottom rails that are 3 to 4 inches above the ground and top rails flush with the top of the posts. Install top and bottom 1×6 rails long enough to span three posts. The joints should fall at the center of the posts so two joints never fall on the same post. Level each rail and nail in place with galvanized 10d (3-inch) nails or screw it in place with 3-inch deck screws.

2 INSTALL THE CROSS RAILS. Tack cross rails to the posts and mark them for cutting with a framing square. Remove the cross rails, make the cuts with a circular saw, then fasten the cross rails to the posts with galvanized 10d (3-inch) nails or screw them in place with 3-inch deck screws.

Installing mortised posts and rails

Amortised post-and-rail fence is laid out much like the post-and-rail fences discussed on earlier pages. The parts are prefabricated, and because of the rail lengths, the posts are usually spaced 6 feet apart and no taller than 5 feet. Both round and square posts are available; round posts tend to give the fence a more rustic feel.

The rails have tapered ends that fit into mortises in the posts. The mortise runs completely through the post: One rail comes in from one side, the other from the other side. Corner posts are mortised on adjacent sides. Mortises for corners aren't as deep as they are for line posts, so you may have to shorten a rail in order to fit it snugly in the post.

Start a post-and-rail fence by digging holes for all the posts. Put a corner or end post in its hole, plumb it, brace it, and fill the hole with soil. Put the neighboring post in its hole and run the rails from mortise to mortise. Plumb and brace the post, and backfill the hole. Work your way along the fence, installing rails and posts one section at a time.

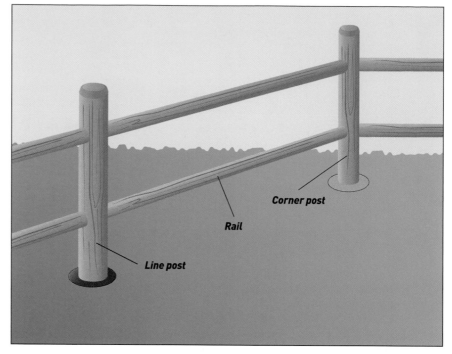

THE MORTISED POST-AND-RAIL FENCE HAS FEWER COMPONENTS THAN MOST FENCES, which makes it easier to install. Line posts usually have mortises at 10 and 24 inches from the top. Corner posts have mortises at the same height but are mortised so the rails meet at 90 degrees. The rails are identical and tapered to fit in the mortises.

1 **LAY OUT THE POSTS.** Lay out the fence with batterboards or stakes and string. Assemble the posts and fence rails on the ground along the string. Put a piece of tape on the string to mark the center of each post.

2 **DIG THE POSTHOLES.** Dig postholes below each piece of tape using a posthole digger. Make sure you dig deep enough so the post is at least 6 inches below the frost line or so one-third of the overall length of the post is buried (whichever is deeper).

3 **PUT IN A CORNER OR END POST.** Coat the bottom of a corner or end post with roofing cement and plumb and brace it in its hole with scrap 1×4s or 2×4s. Verify that the post is plumb and screw the braces into place.

4 **FILL THE HOLE WITH CONCRETE.** Mix fast-setting concrete in a wheelbarrow and pour it in the hole. Work a board up and down in the concrete to remove trapped air bubbles. Slope the top of the concrete with a trowel to direct water away from the post.

5 **PUT IN A LINE POST.** Coat the bottom of a line post with roofing cement and place it in its hole. Put one end of a rail in the end or corner post, then put the other end in the line post, wiggling as needed to get it to fit. Repeat with the second rail. Plumb the line post and check the rails for level. Fill the hole with concrete as before. If the concrete won't hold the post in place, brace it as before.

6 **PUT IN MORE LINE POSTS.** Once you've set the first line post, continue working down the run one section at a time. Plumb and brace each line post and level the rails before filling the hole with concrete and moving on to the next. Finish each run of fence with either an end post or corner post.

HOMER'S HINDSIGHT

CLOSING THE DOOR AFTER THE HORSE IS GONE

Many of our stores have a big demand for horse fencing. Post-and-rail fences are a popular choice, but many a customer has had to chase a horse that escaped the fence. If you're fencing in horses, build a fence that has a top rail that is at least 5 feet above the ground. Make sure you buy posts with mortises for a third rail to keep curious colts from squeezing through.

Building a wire fence

A wire fence may not be a thing of beauty, but it isn't meant to be. It's meant to be a good, strong utilitarian fence that goes up quickly. The quickest are made with metal posts simply driven into the ground. A sturdier version features regular wood posts set in holes. To build the wood version, set the posts every 8 feet on center, then nail a 2×4 top rail across two sections. Install bottom rails between every set of posts, then staple the wire in place. Finish the fence off with a 1×6 cap rail.

Whether you opt for metal posts or wood posts, the height of the fence depends on the mesh you buy. It usually comes in rolls that are 4 or 5 feet wide.

A WIRE FENCE IS BUILT ON A WOOD FRAME OR ON METAL POSTS. A wood-framed fence has 4×4 posts with 2×4 top and bottom rails to which the mesh is stapled. A 1×6 cap rail dresses up the fence and further strengthens it.

SKILL SCALE

EASY	MEDIUM	HARD

REQUIRED SKILLS:
Basic carpentry.

HOW LONG WILL IT TAKE?

An 80-foot run of wire fence should take about:

Experienced . . . . 8 hrs.
Handy . . . . 12 hrs.
Novice . . . . 16 hrs.

STUFF YOU'LL NEED

✔ **MATERIALS:**
Wire mesh, fence staples, galvanized 10d (3-inch) nails, 2×4s, 4×4s, 1×6s

✔ **TOOLS:**
Hammer, level, fencing pliers, safety glasses, work gloves

1 **BUILD THE FENCE FRAME.** Install the posts and cut the top rails long enough to span three posts. Nail the rails in place on top of the posts so their ends are on the center of the posts. Then cut the bottom rails to fit and toenail them into place between the posts.

2 **STAPLE MESH TO THE POST AND TO THE TOP RAIL.** With a helper, unroll enough mesh to reach from end post to end post. Align the end of the mesh with the edge of the post and attach it to the post with fence staples. To prevent sagging, staple the mesh to the top rail every 3 inches, temporarily leaving the bottom unattached. Work your way to the next post.

③ STAPLE MESH TO THE POST AND BOTTOM RAIL. When you reach the post, pull the mesh taut. Starting at the top, staple the mesh to the post every 6 inches with ½-inch or larger staples. When you reach the bottom of the post, work your way back along the bottom rail, stapling the mesh to it as you go.

④ TRIM EXCESS MESH. Work your way along the fence, attaching mesh in the same order as before: along the top rail, down the post, then back along the bottom rail. When you reach the end of the roll, use fencing pliers to trim any mesh that extends beyond the post.

⑤ SPLICE IN A NEW ROLL, IF NECESSARY. If you need more than one roll of fencing, cut the first roll even with the edge of the post, as described in the previous step. Begin the new roll on the same post, positioning it so at least one row of rectangles overlaps those already on the post.

⑥ ADD A CAP RAIL. Once you have attached the mesh to the posts and rails, center a 1×6 cap rail on the 2×4 top rail, positioning the 1×6 so the seams between boards never fall above those in the 2×4s. Nail the cap rail in place with 10d (3-inch) nails.

Faster fencing

Metal posts are a quick alternative to wooden posts. Space metal posts—also known as T stakes—8 feet apart and drive them into firm ground. You can use a 3-pound sledgehammer, but you're better off using a post driver

made specially for the job. A post driver is a hollow 2½-foot-long metal tube with handles and a cap at the top. Fit it over the post, lift the tube, and ram the top down on the posts. Once all the posts are set, hook the mesh over the hooks on one end post. Pull the mesh taut, then attach it to the next post, working your way from post to post until the fence is complete.

Installing a vinyl fence

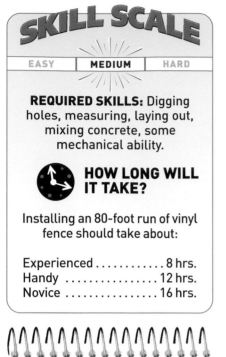

SKILL SCALE

EASY	MEDIUM	HARD

REQUIRED SKILLS: Digging holes, measuring, laying out, mixing concrete, some mechanical ability.

HOW LONG WILL IT TAKE?

Installing an 80-foot run of vinyl fence should take about:

Experienced . . . . 8 hrs.
Handy . . . . 12 hrs.
Novice . . . . 16 hrs.

STUFF YOU'LL NEED

✔ MATERIALS:

Vinyl posts, rails, fence sections, and gate; hinges; latch assembly; pre-mixed bags of concrete; duct tape; CPVC or PVC primer and cement

✔ TOOLS:

Tape measure, mason's line, level, plumb bob, powdered chalk, posthole digger, post level, screwdriver, shovel, garden trowel, adjustable wrench, drill and bits, power miter saw, safety glasses, work gloves

Assume nothing when putting in a new fence. Study the manufacturer's recommendations for installation before you begin assembly. Test-fit pieces and double-check measurements before you begin digging holes and making cuts. It's easier to make adjustments before the concrete is poured and posts are set.

Installing a vinyl fence is much like installing a prefab wood fence (see "Installing Prefab Fence Panels," page 22). You put a post in a posthole, attach a fence section, and attach the section to a second post. Don't fill in the holes until you've attached all the sections to all the posts so that you can space the posts to match the fence sections exactly.

Some manufacturers diverge from the general rule that says one-third of the overall length of a post should be in the ground. Almost all of them, however, recommend that you set the post in concrete. Follow the directions that come with the fence.

Vinyl fences look much like wood fences but require virtually no maintenance. They come in a variety of colors, sizes, and styles and, if necessary, can be cut just like wood to fit any size yard. Sections come 6 and 8 feet long and are generally available in 3-, 4-, 5-, 6-, and 7-foot heights.

BECAUSE VINYL FENCES ARE MANUFACTURED, THE EXACT INSTALLATION TECHNIQUE DEPENDS ON THE MAKER. Most manufacturers call for an 8- to 12-inch-diameter posthole lined with gravel for drainage and filled with concrete for strength. The fence sections won't fit if the posts are too close together or too far apart, so attach the fencing to the posts as you go. Don't fill in the holes until you've attached all the fencing and verified that it's level and plumb.

LAYING OUT THE FENCE

1 **LAY OUT THE FENCE** with mason's line and batterboards. Mark all the post positions on the lines with pieces of masking tape. Drop a plumb bob from the tape, and mark the ground with powdered chalk.

2 **DIG THE POSTHOLES.** With a posthole digger, dig holes 12 inches in diameter and 6 inches below the frost line or as directed by the manufacturer. Add another 6 inches of depth for a gravel bed to provide drainage. Pour in the gravel and tamp it with the end of a 2×4.

INSTALLING THE GATE

1 **ATTACH THE GATE HINGES.**
Installation begins with the gate.
Work on a flat surface and place a spacer between each gatepost and the gate (sizes vary depending on the manufacturer). Insert a metal support, if provided, into the post for the hinges, and screw the hinges to the post and gate. If necessary, drill your own holes.

2 **ATTACH THE LATCH.** Screw the
latch assembly to the gate, then put the strike bar in the latch and screw it to the posts.

HOMER'S HINDSIGHT

DON'T STOP YET

What turns out to be a mistake often starts as a good idea. While one of our fencing customers preassembled the gate, posts, and hinges, he decided to screw the gate stop in place too. But once everything was set in concrete, the world wasn't quite as perfect as it was when he attached the stop. The posts had settled a bit, and the stop was no longer in the right place. It was easy enough to fix: The customer simply remounted the stop. As timesavers go, however, this one was a loser.

3 **TEMPORARILY TAPE THE GATE
ASSEMBLY TOGETHER.** Tape the two posts and gate together with strips of duct tape. Leave the tape in place until all of the posts have been set and the concrete around them has hardened.

4 **SET THE GATE ON BLOCKS.** Place
4×4 blocks, bricks, or other spacers between the postholes. Pick up the gate with a helper, place the posts in the holes, and rest the gate on the blocks or bricks.

5 **PLUMB THE GATE AND SET IT IN
CONCRETE.** The posts must be straight up and down in two directions: left to right and front to back. Put a post level on the post so you can check both directions at the same time. Have a helper put tapered shims (sold at hardware stores and home centers) between the gate and blocks until the gate is plumb in both directions. Fill the posthole with concrete and let it dry.

Dig postholes a few at a time and set panels and posts as you go to ensure that the holes are in the right place.

Installing a vinyl fence

INSTALLING FENCING PANELS

1 **REINFORCE THE BOTTOM RAIL.**
Many fences have a metal bar that slides inside the bottom rail to strengthen it. If yours does, slide the bar into each of the bottom rails. Rails longer than 8 feet will have metal inserts while rails shorter than 8 feet usually do not.

2 **ASSEMBLE THE FENCE PANELS.**
Fence panels come either assembled or disassembled. To assemble, slide the fence boards or pickets into the bottom rails, then slide the pickets or boards into the top rail. Assemble all the panels you'll be using.

3 **PUT THE PANELS IN THE FIRST POST.** This section has been cut to fit the yard, but you can install a full section in the same way. Fit the rails of the assembled panels into the holes of the first post, put the next post in place, and slip the rails into it too. Plumb the post and support the rails on blocks.

4 **PUT THE RAILS IN THE NEXT POST.**
Move to the next posthole. Put the next post in its hole and insert the fence rails into the post. Prop the rails on blocks and leave them until you fill the postholes with concrete.

5 **WORK YOUR WAY DOWN THE FENCE ONE SECTION AT A TIME.**
Put a fence section into the last post you installed and put a post in the neighboring hole. Slide the rails into the holes in the posts as you go.

6 **PLUMB, LEVEL, AND BRACE THE POSTS.** Plumb all the posts in both directions. If the post is out of alignment, correct the problem with wooden shims: Use the same technique you used for the gate.

Many fences come with hardware to attach the panels to the posts, making installation easier. Check with your local home improvement center.

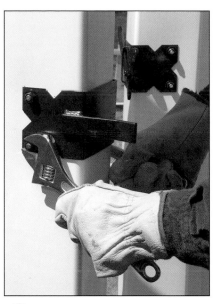

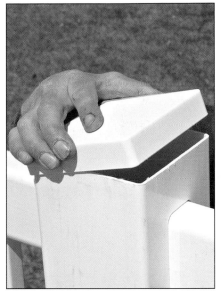

7 **SHOVEL CONCRETE IN THE HOLES.** Mix enough concrete to fill a posthole, leaving the mixture somewhat stiff so it will hold the posts in place as it dries. Verify that the post is plumb, pour the concrete into the hole, and let the concrete harden. Work your way along the fence, filling the postholes with concrete.

8 **INSTALL THE GATE STOP.** Once the concrete has hardened, return to the gate. Close it and mark where the stop goes. Open the gate, put the stop in place, and mark where the holes for it go. Drill them and then screw the stop to the post with the screws provided.

9 **INSTALL POST CAPS.** Put a post cap on the top of each post with the primer and cement recommended by the manufacturer. Once the concrete dries, remove the blocks that support the fence.

Cutting vinyl fencing

Not all yards evenly divide into 6- and 8-foot sections. If your yard is one of them, you can cut fence sections to size with a handsaw, circular saw, jigsaw, or power miter box. A power miter box makes the cleanest, truest, and squarest cut. Measure and make the cut on the rail so that you remove **full** pickets or boards. (They're hollow and look pretty silly if you try to cut one to width.) Cut the rails before you put in the pickets or fence boards. If your fence has lattice across the top, it's probably at least partially preassembled, and the lattice may have a piece of trim on each end. If so, cut enough off each side to remove the trim.

You can cut vinyl with standard woodworking tools. A power miter box (sometimes called a chop saw) will give you the best results.

Installing chain link fences

Chain link fences have a language all their own: brace band, rail cap, tension band, and tension bars. A chain link fence has a skeleton made of posts and rails. The pieces holding the framework together are called caps. The chain link itself is stretched tightly across the skeleton after the skeleton is installed. A metal bar called a tension bar is woven into the end of the mesh and attached to the end posts with tension bands.

Mesh is usually sold in rolls 4, 5, or 6 feet tall. Steel is the strongest mesh. Aluminum is lighter. As for the posts, they come in two diameters. The wider diameter, 2 3/8 inches, is for corner and end posts. The smaller diameter is 1 5/8 inches and is for the other posts in the fence, or line posts. When laying out the gateposts, leave an extra 3 3/4 inches (or as directed by the manufacturer) between them to make room for the hinges and latch.

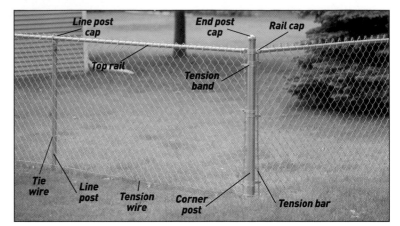

POSTS AND RAILS PROVIDE THE BASIC STRUCTURE FOR A CHAIN LINK FENCE. The rails fit through looped caps on the line posts and are attached to corner and end posts by rail caps. The chain link mesh is stretched across the posts, and tension bands slip around the end post to hold what's called a tension bar. Fasten the top of the mesh to the rails and the line posts, and run a wire through the bottom of the mesh to hold it in place.

EASY	MEDIUM	HARD

REQUIRED SKILLS: Digging, using a level, mechanical skills.

HOW LONG WILL IT TAKE?

Installing an 80-foot run of chain link fence should take about:

Experienced . . . . 8 hrs.
Handy . . . . 12 hrs.
Novice . . . . 16 hrs.

STUFF YOU'LL NEED

✔ MATERIALS:

Chain link mesh, rails, posts, caps,
hinges, latch, tension bars and bands,
brace bands, tie wires, tension wires or
hog rings, gravel, pre-mixed concrete

✔ TOOLS:

Posthole digger, pipe cutter or hacksaw,
shovel, trowel, mason's line, line level,
plumb bob, level, rubber mallet, socket
wrenches, fence puller, pull bar, pliers,
safety glasses, work gloves

ASSEMBLING POSTS AND RAILS

1 DIG THE POSTHOLES. Dig postholes three times wider than the post diameter: 6 to 8 inches for end and corner posts, 4 to 6 inches for line posts and 1/3 of the length of the pole plus 4 inches for gravel. Fill all the holes with 4 inches of gravel and tamp. Add 6 inches of concrete to the corner, gate, and end postholes only. Put posts in the wet concrete and plumb them with a level.

2 FILL END, GATE, AND CORNER POSTHOLES WITH CONCRETE. Finish filling in the corner, gate, and end postholes with concrete. Check the posts for plumb after every few shovelfuls and adjust as needed. Slope the top of the concrete so water drains away from the posts. Let the concrete cure for two to three days. Do not fill the holes for the line posts with concrete, and don't put the line posts in place.

3 **ATTACH TENSION BANDS AND GATE HARDWARE.** Slide tension bands onto each corner, gate, and end post. (The bands will help hold the mesh in place once it's installed. You will use 3 for a 4-foot fence, 4 for a 5-foot fence, and 5 for a 6-foot fence.) Put hinges and latch hardware onto the gateposts at roughly their final positions—they're hard to install later. Use a rubber mallet to drive end post caps onto the gate, corner, and end posts and slip a brace band over each installed post.

4 **INSTALL LOOPED CAPS, END POST CAPS, AND RAIL CAPS.** Drive looped caps onto the line posts with the mallet and put the posts in their holes, but don't fill the holes. Bolt a rail cap to each brace band, tightening just enough to hold the cap in place. Feed the rails through the looped caps. Cut rails with a pipe cutter or hacksaw, if needed. If you need longer rails, join them together using rails with a slightly smaller wedged end that fits into a full-size rail.

5 **ATTACH THE RAILS.** Fit the rails into the rail caps and raise or lower each cap to the final height of the mesh, including 2 inches clearance at the bottom. Tighten the brace bands, fill the holes around the line posts with dirt, and tamp until firm.

INSTALLING THE CHAIN LINK

Fence puller

Tension bar

Yoke

1 **UNROLL THE MESH AND INSTALL A TENSION BAR.** Lay the chain link mesh on the ground outside the fence. Run a tension bar through the links at the end of the mesh. The bar makes the end of the fence rigid and provides something to attach to the posts.

2 **ATTACH THE TENSION BAR TO THE POSTS.** With a helper, stand the mesh up and use a socket wrench to bolt the tension bar into the tension bands on one of the end posts. Align the mesh so it overlaps the rail by 1 to 2 inches and sits about 2 inches above the ground.

3 **STRETCH THE MESH.** Chain link mesh must be pulled taut or it will sag. Stretching is done with a tool called a fence puller. Insert a pull bar through the unattached mesh a few feet from the final post. Attach the yoke to the pull bar.

Installing chain link fences

INSTALLING THE CHAIN LINK (continued)

4 **ATTACH THE OTHER END OF THE FENCE PULLER TO THE FINAL POST.** Crank the fence puller until the loops of mesh move no more than ¼ inch when you squeeze them together. If the mesh changed height or became distorted during tightening, pull on it to reshape it.

Tension bar

5 **INSERT A TENSION BAR.** Without releasing the fence puller, insert a tension bar in the mesh, close enough so it can be fastened to the tension bands on the end post nearest the fence puller. To remove the excess mesh between the tension bar and end post, open a loop at the top and bottom, then twist and pull the strand free.

6 **ATTACH THE TENSION BAR.** Pull the tension bar into the tension bands on the end post by hand, then tighten the bolts on the bands with a socket wrench. Release the fence puller and remove the pull bar to which it was attached. Repeat the entire hanging and stretching process along the remaining sides of the fence.

7 **TIE THE FENCE TO THE RAILS.** Bend one end of an aluminum tie wire into a hook and grab the bottom strand of the opening above the rail. Loop the tie wire around the top rail, pull it firmly, and tie it back onto the mesh. Space the tie wires every 12 to 16 inches along the rail, then attach them to the line posts.

8 **RUN WIRE THROUGH THE BOTTOM LOOPS OF MESH.** Thread a tension wire through the bottom loops of the mesh and tighten it around the end posts. Wrap the wire around itself several times to fasten it. An alternative to threading the wire is to attach it to the mesh every 2 feet or so with hog rings. (See inset.)

Designer Tip

PRIVACY SLATS
A chain link fence serves well to keep the dog in the yard, but it won't give you much privacy. Privacy slats, available at most home centers, let you keep the dog in (or out) and give you some privacy. Privacy slats are available in a variety of colors. The easiest to work with are thin and flexible, much like the slats of venetian blinds. Weave the slats on a diagonal through the mesh.

Assembling and hanging a chain link gate

Most of the time, the best way to buy a chain link gate is to buy one that's preassembled. Sometimes, however, you may want a custom gate—one large enough to accommodate a big landscaping tractor, for example. Building a gate is a lot like building a short section of fence except you won't need a fence puller. When building your own gate, first fit the frame together, then attach the mesh by slipping tension bars into the tension bands. You also can buy special corner brackets that let you customize the width of your gate.

SKILL SCALE

EASY	MEDIUM	HARD

REQUIRED SKILLS:
Mechanical skills.

HOW LONG WILL IT TAKE?

Experienced .... 1 hr.
Handy .... 1.5 hrs.
Novice .... 2 hrs.

STUFF YOU'LL NEED

✔ **MATERIALS:**
Top, bottom, and side rails; chain link mesh; tension bars; tension bands; tie wires; hinges; latch assembly

✔ **TOOLS:**
Socket wrenches, pliers, wire cutters

You'll find preassembled gates in most home improvement centers. If they'll fit your opening, use them. You'll save yourself time and effort.

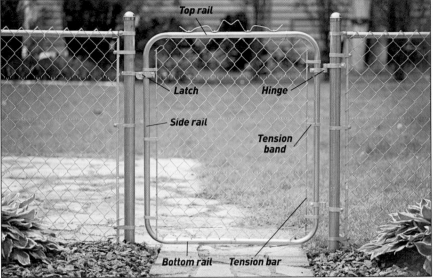

Top rail
Latch
Hinge
Side rail
Tension band
Bottom rail
Tension bar

A CHAIN LINK GATE IS AMAZINGLY STRONG. UNLIKE ITS WOODEN COUNTERPARTS, a chain link gate isn't likely to sag over time. The mesh is stretched across a frame of metal tubing and held by tension bars, which are anchored to tension bands. Standard tie wires hold the mesh at the top and bottom. Metal hinge pins hold the gate in place, while an adjustable metal latch keeps the gate securely closed.

ASSEMBLING THE GATE

1 **ASSEMBLE THE FRAME.** Slip tension bands onto the pieces of tubing that make up the frame. You'll need at least three tension bands for each tension bar—four if the gate is more than 4 feet high. Assemble the frame by sliding the pieces of tubing together.

2 **PUT A TENSION BAR IN THE MESH.** Insert a tension bar into the chain link mesh by sliding it through the end loops of the mesh.

Assembling and hanging a chain link gate

ASSEMBLING THE GATE *(continued)*

3 **ATTACH THE TENSION BAR TO THE FRAME.** Attach the tension bar to the tension bands on one side rail. Thread a second tension bar into the mesh close enough to the other side rail to hold the mesh taut once it's attached to the tension bands. Unhook the strand of mesh near the outside of the second tension bar and pull it out to remove the excess mesh.

4 **ATTACH THE SECOND TENSION BAR TO THE FRAME.** Pull the mesh and the second tension bar tightly and slip the tension bar into the tension bands. If the mesh isn't tight enough, unhook the tension bar and slip it into the next set of loops, then unravel the excess mesh and hook the bar back into the tension bands.

5 **TIE THE MESH IN PLACE.** Once the chain link mesh is firmly in place, attach tie wires to the top and bottom rails. Hook the tie wires around the mesh intersections, pull the mesh so it is slightly above the gate frame, and wrap the free end of the tie wire around the mesh.

HANGING THE GATE

1 **HANG THE HINGE STRAPS.** Install the hinge straps on the gate, spacing them evenly from the top and bottom. Position the gate and support it on wood blocks. Mark the gatepost to show where the hinge straps will meet it.

2 **HANG THE HINGES.** Set the gate aside, then slide the hinge pins into place at the marks and tighten them with the top pin pointing down and the bottom pin pointing up. Install the gate on the post, lifting the upper hinge strap onto the top hinge pin and lowering the bottom strap onto the lower pin.

3 **HANG THE GATE.** Position the latch catch on the gatepost opposite the hinges and tighten it. Slide the latch pin onto the side rail of the gate, line it up with the catch, then tighten it with a socket wrench.

Installing a pet fence

SKILL SCALE

EASY	**MEDIUM**	HARD

REQUIRED SKILLS: Digging, basic mechanical skills.

HOW LONG WILL IT TAKE?

Installing 100 feet of underground pet fence should take about:

Experienced . . . . 2 hrs.
Handy . . . . 4 hrs.
Novice . . . . 5 hrs.

STUFF YOU'LL NEED

✔ **MATERIALS:**
Transmitter, wire, marking flags, collar receiver

✔ **TOOLS:**
Wire cutter, spade, screwdriver

An underground pet fence isn't a fence in the traditional sense: It's more like a remote control system for your dog. You bury a wire antenna around the part of the yard in which you want to keep the dog, and whenever the dog approaches the wire, a transmitter sends a signal to a receiver in the dog's collar, and the dog gets a shock. (The shock is only about one-sixth the power of the shock you get from dragging your feet across the rug and touching a doorknob.) Plant small flags above the wire, and as Pavlov discovered, the dog soon learns its boundaries and avoids future shocks.

A word of warning: The fence will keep your dog in, but it won't keep other dogs out. If other dogs are likely to bother your dog, this fence probably isn't for you. If you do decide to install a pet fence, buy one of the kits that has all the materials you'll need in it.

① POSITION THE TRANSMITTER AS DIRECTED BY THE MANUFACTURER. Dig a narrow trench 2 to 3 inches deep, beginning at the transmitter and running around the area you want to fence. Connect the wire to the transmitter and run it through the trench.

② REFILL THE TRENCH AND MARK IT WITH FLAGS. Plug in the transmitter and put the collar/receiver on the dog. Take the dog on a few daily walks near the flags so it learns its boundaries. Once it does, you can remove the flags.

Repairing fences and gates

All good fences need help staying good. When faced with damage, the first decision is whether to repair or replace. Armed with the tricks shown here, you can make a fence as good as new (or nearly so) with minimal need to replace sections. Begin by removing any parts that get in the way of the repair. You can either remove the fencing with a pry bar or cut out the damaged section with a handsaw. When repairing a post, remove the fencing and rails connected to it. Once the repair is complete, use new nails to replace fencing and rails.

SKILL SCALE

EASY	MEDIUM	HARD

REQUIRED SKILLS: Basic carpentry and mechanical skills.

HOW LONG WILL IT TAKE?

Experienced .... Variable
Handy .... Variable
Novice .... Variable

VARIABLES: Repair time depends on the type of fence and extent of damage.

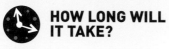

STUFF YOU'LL NEED

✔ **MATERIALS:**

Cleaners, 1×4s, 2×4s, 4×4s, nails, deck screws, lag screws, carriage bolts, mesh, pre-mixed concrete, antisag kit

✔ **TOOLS:**

Fiber scrub brush, cloth, wire brush, hammer, screw gun, ratchet and socket wrenches, handsaw, circular saw, drill and bits, spade, shovel, cold chisel, 3-pound sledgehammer, wood chisel, post level, pliers, wire cutters, mason's trowel, clamps, pliers, fence puller, pull bar, safety glasses, work gloves

CLEANING FENCES

SCRUB WOOD FENCES with a fiber scrub brush and a mild detergent solution to remove most stains. For tougher stains, add 1 to 2 cups of bleach to a bucket of warm water. Wear gloves and safety glasses when working with strong cleansers.

CLEAN VINYL FENCES with a sodium-bicarbonate-based cleaner. Bleach may stain the fence. Use a cloth instead of a brush so you don't scratch the surface of the fence. Wear safety glasses.

CLEAN METAL FENCES with a wire brush, scrubbing away old paint, dirt, and rust from metal posts, hardware, and other areas. You can take care of most stains with 1 cup of strong household detergent mixed with a gallon of warm water.

Pressure washing

Rent a pressure washer for hard-to-reach crevices in basket-weave and other fences or for stubborn stains on vinyl fences. Spray about 6 to 10 inches away from the fence. Don't use more than 1,000 psi of water pressure or the force may damage the wood. Many companies make commercial deck cleaners that are also good for cleaning fences. Consult the manufacturer's instructions before starting.

BRACING WOOD RAILS

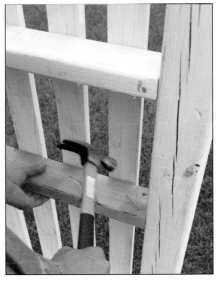

1 **REINFORCE RAIL ENDS WITH 2×4 CLEATS FASTENED TO THE POSTS.**
Screw the cleats in place with #8 deck screws or nail with galvanized 10d (3-inch) nails. Taller fences often have third rails in the center, which can be reinforced using this method as well.

2 **ADD A SISTER RAIL TO BOLSTER A DAMAGED RAIL.** It can span the entire rail or just part of it, depending on the damage. Clamp the sister rail under or on top of the original, then drill holes through both rails, bolt them in place with ⅜×4-inch carriage bolts, and remove the clamps.

3 **ADD A THIRD RAIL BETWEEN THE TOP AND BOTTOM ONES** if the fencing seems loose. Screw the rail to the posts with #8 deck screws or toenail with galvanized 10d (3-inch) nails. Fasten the fence boards to the new rails with #8 deck screws.

REPLACING A RAIL

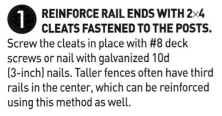

1 **REMOVE THE FENCE BOARDS.**
Remove all of the fence boards from the damaged rail. Unscrew the boards, as shown here, or pry off the boards and pull out the nails. Try not to damage the fence boards so you can reinstall them later.

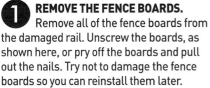

2 **REMOVE THE RAIL.** Pry out the nails or remove the hardware holding the old rail in place. Cut a new rail to fit between the posts. Nail or screw the rail in place, then reinstall the fence boards.

Splicing a rail

SAVE YOURSELF SOME WORK when you need to replace a short section of rail on a fence that has an exposed rail by splicing a new piece of rail in place. Remove the boards from the damaged section of rail, then cut off the damaged section at an angle. Put the new piece in place alongside the cut and trace along the cut in the old piece to transfer the angles to the new piece. Cut along each line, drill holes, and bolt the new piece in place with ⅜×4-inch carriage bolts.

Repairing fences and gates

FIXING POSTS THAT LEAN

1 **DIG OUT THE POST.** Dig around the post until you reach the bottom. As you dig, pile the soil on a newspaper or tarp so you can easily refill the hole later.

2 **BREAK UP THE FOOTING.** If the post is set in concrete, break up the concrete with a 3-pound sledgehammer and cold chisel. Wear gloves and protect your hands from the hammer with a shielded chisel, as shown here.

3 **PLUMB AND BRACE THE FENCE.** Screw braces to the post, plumb it with a level, then screw the braces to stakes driven in the ground. Check again for plumb and reset the braces, if necessary.

4 **POUR A CONCRETE FOOTING.** Mix bagged concrete, following the directions on the bag. You want it to be about as thick as oatmeal. Fill the posthole with the mix, sloping the concrete away from the posts for drainage.

Adding a sister post

You can reinforce a damaged post with a small post called a sister post. (If the post wobbles in the ground, either brace it or pour a new footing.) A sister post is half the thickness of the original post and the same width, but no higher than the fence's top rail. Cut the base of the sister post at a steep angle so you'll be able to drive it in like a stake. Put it in place against the original post. Place a block on top of the sister post to avoid splitting it and hit the block with a 3-pound sledgehammer to drive it 2 to 3 feet into the ground. Bolt it to the original post with $3/8 \times 4$-inch lag screws. Using a handsaw, cut a 45-degree angle on the top of the sister post so it will shed rain.

REPAIRING UNDERGROUND ROT

1 **REMOVE THE SOIL AROUND THE DAMAGE.** If a post has rotted in the ground, you can put a second, shorter post next to it and tie the two together. Begin by digging around the footing. Dig deep enough to reach the bottom of the post or concrete.

2 **BREAK UP ANY FOOTINGS.** Wearing safety glasses, break up any concrete with a 3-pound sledgehammer and cold chisel. Break the concrete into small, manageable pieces.

3 **BRACE THE POST.** Temporarily screw or nail 2×4 supports to the post. Plumb the post and hold it while a helper screws the braces to stakes driven in the ground.

4 **REMOVE THE DAMAGE.** Cut off the old post just above the damaged part and pull the bottom section out of the ground. Cut a new post section 1 foot or so longer than the section you removed, and bevel the top. Place the new section in the hole next to the undamaged part of the original post.

5 **BOLT THE OLD AND NEW PARTS TOGETHER.** Clamp the two post sections together. Counterbore 1-inch-wide holes for the heads of carriage bolts, drill ½-inch through holes, and insert ½-inch carriage bolts with washers. Put washers and nuts at the other end of the bolts and tighten with a socket wrench.

6 **POUR A FOOTING.** File the posthole with concrete. Slope the top to help drain water away. Let the concrete harden for two to three days before removing the braces and supports.

Repairing fences and gates

REPAIRING A CHAIN LINK FENCE

1 **LOOSEN THE MESH.** Remove the tie wires from the mesh with pliers. Connect a fence puller to both the post and fence and draw the fence tight enough to take tension off the tension bar. Remove the tension bar by loosening the bolts in the tension band. Loosen and remove the fence puller.

2 **REMOVE THE DAMAGED SECTION OF FENCE.** Open the loop at the top and bottom of a strand just outside the damaged area. Twist and pull the strand free. Take out a strand on the other side of the damage and remove the damaged section.

3 **WEAVE IN A PATCH.** Cut a section of mesh the same size as the one you removed. Weave it into the remaining fence using the strands you removed in Step 2. Loop the wire at the top and bottom of the strand back around the fence with pliers.

4 **ATTACH A FENCE PULLER.** Slide a pull bar through the mesh about 4 feet from the end post. Reattach the fence puller. Crank the bar until the strands in the mesh press together no more than ¼ inch when you squeeze them.

5 **REATTACH THE TENSION BAR.** Reattach the tension bar to the tension band and release the fence puller.

6 **TIE THE FENCE TO THE POSTS.** Attach new tie wires to hold the mesh firmly against the top rail and line posts. Thread a new tension wire through the bottom openings in the mesh.

FIXING GATES

IF A GATE DROOPS AND YOU DON'T HAVE DIAGONAL CROSSBRACES, INSTALL AN ANTISAG KIT, which includes a turnbuckle, some cable, and some eye hooks. Screw an eye hook into the corner on the hinge side and a second eye hook in the lower corner on the opposite side. Attach the turnbuckle and tighten to remove the sag.

IF A CHAIN LINK GATE GETS OUT OF ALIGNMENT, you can usually fix it by adjusting the hinge pins. Loosen the pins with a socket wrench and reposition them with a wood block and hammer. Check the gate's swing and reposition, if necessary, before tightening.

Gate stop

A gate that swings too far will gradually loosen its own hinges. The low-tech solution is to screw a 1×2 or 2×4 stop to the gatepost so the gate stops when it's flush with the fence. The high-tech solution is a hydraulic gate closer (available at home centers), which gently pulls the gate shut and stops it at the right point.

STRAIGHTENING METAL FENCING

1 **BREAK UP THE FOOTING.** Dig around the post footing, then break up the concrete with a 3-pound sledgehammer and cold chisel. If other posts are also leaning, break the footing around them too.

2 **PLUMB AND BRACE THE FENCE.** You can't nail into a metal fence, so drive a stake into the ground first, then screw it to the brace with a single screw. Plumb the fence, then clamp it to the brace.

3 **POUR NEW FOOTINGS.** Once the fence is plumb and in position, mix bagged concrete and pour new footings. Slope the concrete away from the posts so water will drain away from them. Remove the braces after the concrete has hardened for 48 hours.

LANDSCAPING WALLS

Make no mistake about it: Building a landscape wall is a lot of work, but it is extremely rewarding. Sometimes it's necessary; sometimes it's just attractive. Walls are usually necessary in yards that slope. Anything that's supposed to be flat, such as a garden, patio, or driveway, will cut through the contour of the land. You can plant gentle rises to hold back the soil, but anything higher than about a foot will keep sliding downhill.

As you'll see, these walls need a certain amount of strength. They also need to drain well—water that builds up behind them only adds pressure to the face of the wall. Landscaping block walls are designed to drain on their own; they're also built to automatically slope back into the hillside for strength.

Walls that are built for their aesthetic appeal don't have to be quite as strong as retaining walls. Stone and brick are good choices, built either with or without mortar. Cement block looks a bit utilitarian, but a coat of stucco changes its appearance entirely, and you can trowel or brush on a finish that gives it a handmade texture.

CHAPTER 3

Landscaping Walls tool kit 64

Materials 65

Mixing and working with mortar 66

Laying out a wall 68

Providing drainage for retaining walls 70

Building a wooden retaining wall 72

Building a post-and-board retaining wall . . 75

Building a landscape block retaining wall . . 77

Building a dry stone wall 80

Building a footing for a stone or brick wall . . 82

Building a running-bond brick wall 87

Laying a common-bond brick wall 90

Building a mortared stone wall 93

Building a concrete-block wall 97

Stuccoing a block wall 101

Maintaining walls 104

PAY ATTENTION TO THE HEIGHT OF YOUR WALL

Any stone or brick wall over 48 inches tall requires steel reinforcement for strength and stability. If you are planning a wall over 48 inches tall, you should have the installation done by a professional mason or bricklayer to ensure that the wall will stand and that you comply with local codes.

REAL-WORLD SITUATIONS

ALL WALLS ARE NOT CREATED EQUAL

Here's the big question: Should you build a mortared wall or dry-set? Dry-set stone walls may have been the first built by humans, and if the stones are stacked carefully, the wall is pretty stable. These walls require very little foundation—a course of stones set underground does the trick.

Mortared walls, of course, are stronger and more rigid. Before you start building, you have to realize that the ground is constantly moving under your feet. Though it's not moving enough for you to notice, it is enough to cause a rigid wall to crack over the course of the year. Dry-set walls can flex with changes in the ground, so for them, movement isn't a problem.

Once you put mortar in a wall, however, it can no longer flex, and if you look at an old house, you can often see cracks above spots where the ground has shifted.

Consequently, a mortared wall requires a foundation that is thick enough and strong enough to support it if the ground underneath shifts. Concrete and rebar do the trick, but they will need to extend below the frost line. Therefore, if you count the footing, you'll often find as much wall underground as above.

Whichever type of wall you settle on, have the materials delivered. They're far too heavy for even a large pickup, much less the family car, to transport.

LANDSCAPING WALLS TOOL KIT

3-POUND SLEDGEHAMMER

COLD CHISEL

GARDEN HOSE

MASON'S LINE

POWDERED CHALK

STONEMASON'S HAMMER

BRICK CHISEL

CONCAVE JOINTER

HAMMER

MASON'S TROWEL

SAFETY GLASSES

TAMPER

BROOM

CROWBAR

HANDSAW

METAL TROWEL

SCREWDRIVERS

TAPE MEASURE

CAULK GUN

DRILL AND BITS

LEVELS

MIXING TUB

SCRUB BRUSH

WHEELBARROW

CHALK LINE

DUST MASK

MASON'S BLOCKS

PLUGGING CHISEL

SHOVEL

WORK GLOVES

CIRCULAR SAW

FRAMING SQUARE

MASON'S HOE

PLUMB BOB

SPADE

Materials

Once you have your tools in order, you need to choose your materials. **A Pressure-treated lumber** is chemically treated for rot resistance. (For more on pressure-treated wood, see "Grading Wood," page 11.) Timbers are anchored into the ground with lengths of reinforcing steel better known as **B rebar.** Join courses of timbers with **C spikes.** Make retaining walls with **D lipped landscape blocks. E Bricks** are popular for building freestanding walls. **F Concrete blocks** are less expensive, making them a good choice for heavy-duty walls where appearance doesn't count. Dry walls (those without mortar) are best built with **G rubble stone,** which is uncut like stones you might find in a field. Once concrete has been poured, cover it with **H burlap** to help keep in moisture while it cures. **I Perforated plastic drainpipe** drains water away from the bottom of a wall. **J Landscape fabric** stops soil from getting into a gravel drainage field and blocking the flow of water.

Cement is the glue that makes sand and gravel stick together as concrete.

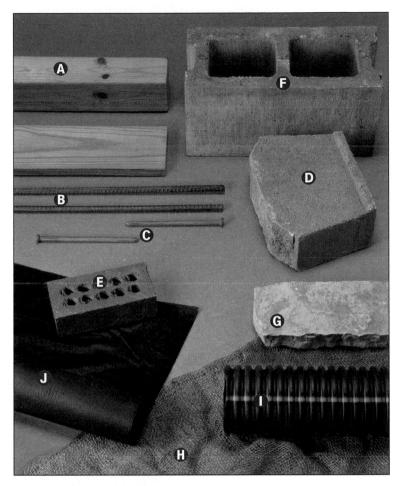

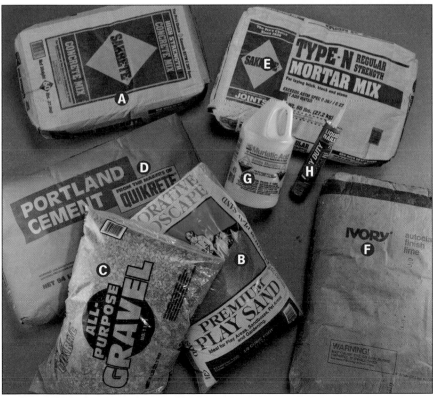

You can buy bags of **A pre-mixed concrete** or make your own mix out of **B building sand, C gravel,** and **D portland cement.** You can buy **E pre-mixed mortar** or make your own mortar by mixing sand, portland cement, and **F hydrated lime. G Muriatic acid** is actually a solution of hydrochloric acid and is used to clean masonry. Some walls require an application of **H construction adhesive** to help hold the top course in place.

TIME SAVER

THINK AHEAD
Make a list of all the materials you need and buy them all at the same time. Have the materials delivered so you don't end up overloading your own vehicle.

Mixing and working with mortar

TO TEST MORTAR, put ridges in it with a trowel or hoe. If the ridges collapse, the mortar is strong but too wet to support the weight of the masonry above it.

IF THE RIDGES CRUMBLE, the mortar will support weight, but it won't stick to and isn't strong enough to handle the masonry.

IF THE RIDGES REMAIN and the mortar sticks to the side of your trowel, the mix is strong enough to stick to and to support the weight of the masonry above it.

MIXING MORTAR

A good mortar is what masons call workable. It sticks to the brick or block you're working with, and it's strong enough to support the masonry above it but not so thick that it won't squeeze out when you push a brick down on it.

The trick to making mortar workable is water. Too much water and the mortar becomes runny; too little, and the mortar is crumbly and hard to manage.

But how much is the right amount?

The amount of water you'll need depends on many variables— temperature, humidity, the moisture of the mix in the bag, the quality of the ingredients—that it's pointless to think in terms of cups, pints, or gallons.

Instead think in terms of consistency. Work with a bagged mortar and mix it according to the directions on the bag, putting in about half or three-quarters of the water recommended. Mix it thoroughly with a mixer if you have one or a mortar hoe if you don't. Once the mortar and water are thoroughly mixed, make ridges in it with the hoe. If the ridges fall, the mixture is too wet; add more dry ingredients. If the ridges remain sharp and distinct, the mixture is right. If they crumble, add water.

Once you think you have it right, double-check with your trowel: Scoop up some mortar and turn the trowel on edge. If the water-to-mortar ratio is right, the mortar will stick to the trowel.

Making your own mortar

Most books, including this one, include recipes for mixing cement, sand, and lime to make your own mortar. And you'll find piles of sand and bags of lime and cement that masons use to mix their own mortar at most construction sites. So why would you buy mortar in a bag?

Mortar made from scratch isn't any better than mortar from a bag: It's less expensive, but it's not better. In fact, unless you've had some experience mixing mortar, you won't know how to adjust for the moisture in the materials or how the quality of the materials affects the mixture. Unless you have a mixer, you won't be able to get a homogeneous mix before you add the water.

In short, the recipes on the next page appear so you can understand what mortar is. When it comes to mixing the dry ingredients, however, bagged mortar is worth the price and may even be better than the stuff they mix on-site. Factories can balance the mix of ingredients more accurately because they can control the moisture of the contents. They also sell it in manageable sizes that are easier for you to transport and small enough so you don't end up mixing more than you can use.

MIXING MORTAR FROM SCRATCH IS LESS EXPENSIVE than buying it pre-mixed in bags, but it's not better.

RETEMPERING

About 30 minutes after you mix mortar, it will start to thicken. That's because some of the water will have evaporated. You can "retemper" and continue to use the mortar at this point by adding more water.

Around 2 hours after mixing, mortar will start thickening for a different reason: It's beginning to harden. The mortar is spent at this point. Don't use it, and don't retemper it. Mix a new batch.

In between these two points, the mortar is likely to thicken at least once or twice more. Unfortunately, you can't tell if it's drying out or hardening. The closer you get to the 2-hour mark, the more likely the mortar is hardening and the less likely retempering is to succeed. Retempering is generally successful during the first 1½ hours, though hot weather can shorten the time. Always replace mortar that's over 2 hours old.

SAFETY ALERT

Mortar is caustic. Wear work gloves, long sleeves, a respirator, and safety glasses when mixing or spreading it.

BUYER'S GUIDE

STONE MORTAR
Because the lime in most mortars stains stones, the mortars for laying stone are lime-free but rich in cement. Whether you're working in brick, concrete block, or stone, make sure you have the right mortar. If you're building a mortared stone wall, mix the mortar a bit on the dry side so it can support the weight of the stones while you work.

Estimating the mortar you'll need for walls

BRICK WALLS WITH 8×2×4-INCH BRICKS AND ⅜-INCH JOINTS
In simplest terms, you'll need a 60-pound bag of mortar for every 28 bricks you lay, or 4.1 square feet. An 80-pound bag is enough for 36 bricks, or 5.25 square feet. If you are using ½-inch joints, you'll need approximately one-third more mortar.

Since most walls are actually two bricks thick, figure out how much mortar you'll need for one face, and then double it.

CONCRETE BLOCK WALLS WITH 8×16×8-INCH BLOCKS AND ⅜-INCH JOINTS
A 60-pound bag is enough for 11 concrete blocks. When combined with the mortar around it, a concrete block covers an area of about 1 square foot.

An 80-pound bag is enough for 15 blocks, or 15 square feet.

Estimating for brick patios

Unlike a wall, a patio is laid with the wide faces exposed, so you'll only need 4⅓ bricks to cover a square foot. A 60-pound bag is enough to mortar between about 68 square feet of bricks.

An 80-pound bag is enough for about 90 square feet.

You'll need one-third more mortar if you're using ½-inch joints.

You'll need an additional 60-pound bag for every 10 square feet of ½-inch mortar bed underneath the brick. If you're buying 80-pound bags, each one will cover 13 square feet.

WORK SMARTER

USE THE RIGHT MORTAR MIX FOR THE JOB
Different types of premixed mortar cater to different applications and it's important that you use the proper mix for the job you're doing. There are three basic applications—masonary in contact with the ground, masonary that is above ground, and masonary that is exposed to strong winds. Tell an associate at your local home improvement center what you're doing with the concrete and they will lead you to the right material.

Consistency is the key when mixing multiple batches of concrete. Unevenly mixed batches won't bond and cure as effectively so take the time to be consistent.

Laying out a wall

Even the most complicated wall starts out as a few lengths of mason's line stretched between sets of stakes and crosspieces—what builders call batterboards. (You could a use single stake with no crosspiece, but batterboards let you reposition the line without having to move one of the stakes.) The ability to make adjustments is especially important when you're squaring up the layout using the 3-4-5 triangle, shown at *right*.

The wall you lay out can be as long as you like, but you're limited when it comes to height. If the wall stands more than 4 feet high, building codes require a professional engineer's design. If you're taking on a 6-foot hillside, however, you can avoid the cost of engineering work by terracing the hill with a pair of 3-foot-high retaining walls.

Mark 4 feet from corner

Mark 3 feet from corner

Corner is square if distance measures 5 feet

EVEN IF YOU DIDN'T PAY ATTENTION IN GEOMETRY, the easiest way to lay out a right angle is the 3-4-5 triangle. Lay out the corner by eye using batterboards and mason's line. Mark one line with a piece of tape 3 feet from the corner. Mark the other line 4 feet from the corner. Slide the lines until the distance between the two pieces of tape is 5 feet, at which point the corner is square.

SKILL SCALE

EASY	MEDIUM	HARD

REQUIRED SKILLS: Measuring, digging, leveling.

HOW LONG WILL IT TAKE?

Experienced . . . . 40 min.
Handy . . . . 55 min.
Novice . . . . 1.5 hrs.

STUFF YOU'LL NEED

✔ **MATERIALS:**
2×4s, 10d (3-inch) common nails, 2×2s, masking tape

✔ **TOOLS:**
Tape measure, circular saw, hammer, mason's line, line level, 3-pound sledgehammer, plumb bob, powdered chalk, safety glasses

LAYING OUT A STRAIGHT WALL

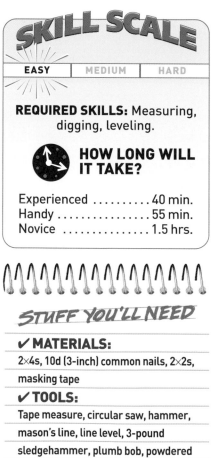

1 **BUILD BATTERBOARDS.** Start by cutting points on the bottoms of two 2×4s, creating stakes. Nail a crosspiece to the stakes about 2 inches from the top.

2 **SET THE BATTERBOARDS.** Drive a batterboard into the ground 12 to 18 inches beyond each end of the planned wall. Drive the stakes so they sit firmly in the ground, then level the crosspiece by hammering the top of the higher stake.

3 RUN LINE BETWEEN THE BATTERBOARDS. Tie a mason's line to the crosspieces. Attach a line level to the line and, if necessary, tap the batterboard that is at the high end to level the line.

4 POSITION THE LINE. Slide the line along the crosspieces until it marks an edge of the wall. Tape the line to mark the point you've decided on for each end of the wall. Drop a plumb bob from the taped points and use powdered chalk to mark where it meets the ground.

5 DRIVE STAKES TO MARK THE ENDS OF THE WALLS. Drive in 2×2 stakes at the chalked marks. Sprinkle chalk, sand, limestone, or flour along the mason's line to mark the edge of the wall. Before digging, mark where the line meets the batterboards and untie it. You'll put the line back in place later.

LAYING OUT A SQUARE CORNER

1 LAY OUT ONE WALL; DRIVE BATTERBOARDS FOR THE SECOND. Lay out the wall on one side of the corner with batterboards and mason's line, following the steps above. To lay out the second wall, drive in a second set of batterboards 12 to 18 inches beyond the corner and beyond the end of the second wall. Stretch a mason's line between the batterboards and position it by eye. Attach a line level and level the line.

2 SQUARE UP THE CORNER. Square up the corner using the 3-4-5 triangle. Mark one line 3 feet from the corner with a piece of tape. Mark the other line 4 feet from the corner. Measure between the two pieces of tape. Have the helper slide the line until the distance between the two pieces of tape is 5 feet. When it is, the corner is square.

3 MARK THE GROUND. Drop a plumb bob where the lines cross and mark the ground with powdered chalk. Measure to find the end of the wall, drop a plumb bob, and mark that point on the ground with chalk as well. Drive 2×2 stakes into the ground to mark the corner and ends of the wall.

Providing drainage for retaining walls

The life span of a retaining wall depends largely on its drainage. Dry soil places very little stress on a wall, but wet, heavy soil causes the wall to buckle or lean, and means extensive repairs can't be far behind.

No drainage system can handle a flood, but a good drainage system will prevent most water damage. The biggest trick—short of the excavation—is finding a place for the water to go. Bring the drainage pipe around the wall and continue running it until it comes to the surface.

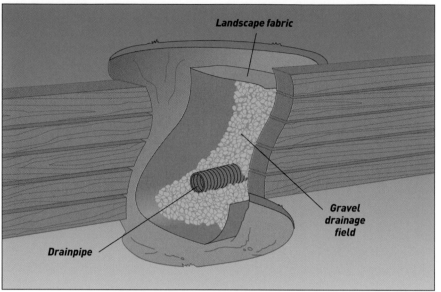

Landscape fabric

Gravel drainage field

Drainpipe

THE PARTS OF A DRAINAGE SYSTEM WORK TOGETHER. Gravel, which won't absorb water, replaces soil, which does. A layer of landscape fabric keeps the soil from clogging the gravel. A perforated drainpipe collects the water as it gathers at the base of the wall then guides the water along the wall into another part of the yard.

When you're digging, use your legs to help lift the dirt, otherwise there will be a break in the action while your back recovers from the inevitable strain.

SKILL SCALE

EASY	MEDIUM	HARD

REQUIRED SKILLS: Laying drainpipe requires basic excavating skills.

HOW LONG WILL IT TAKE?

Digging a trench for and laying 16 feet of drainpipe should take:

Experienced . . . . 4 hrs.
Handy . . . . 5 hrs.
Novice . . . . 6 hrs.

STUFF YOU'LL NEED

✔ **MATERIALS:**
Landscape fabric, gravel, perforated plastic drainpipe

✔ **TOOLS:**
Shovel, tape measure, level, garden rake, tamper, utility knife or scissors

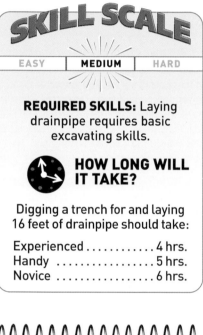

1 DIG A TRENCH. Lay out the wall with batterboards and level lines, and dig into the hill to create a level trench as deep as is required by the wall you're building. Place some of the excavated soil on the slope's low side to help flatten the area.

2 DIG A FOUNDATION. Make sure the trench is a uniform depth (and level) by taking measurements at various points along a level mason's line. If the measurements vary, add dirt (and tamp it) or remove dirt where necessary.

3 **COVER WITH LANDSCAPE FABRIC.** Landscape fabric prevents the soil from clogging your drainage system. Unroll enough fabric to run along the length of the trench twice, plus an amount a little more than the depth of the excavation. Pull the fabric across the back and bottom of the trench.

4 **LAY THE FIRST COURSES OF THE WALL AND THEN ADD A GRAVEL BED.** (See page 77.) Leave space at one end for the drainpipe to exit through the wall. Behind the wall, lay a gravel bed that slopes 1 inch every 4 feet as it travels across the hill. Check the slope with a 4-foot level sitting on a straight 2×4 with a 1-inch spacer under one end. Add or remove gravel to get a level reading.

5 **LAY DRAINPIPE.** Lay drainpipe along the back of the wall. It, too, should slope 1 inch every 4 feet. Continue the pipe around a sidewall, if any, without kinking the pipe. Continue to run the pipe downhill until it reaches the surface.

BACKFILLING THE EXCAVATION

1 **LAY GRAVEL IN THE TRENCH.** Cover the drainpipe with gravel as you build the wall. Lay the first few courses and fill in behind them with gravel. Tamp the gravel firmly. Continue to build the wall, filling in with 4-inch layers of gravel and tamping as you go.

2 **CONTINUE BUILDING THE WALL.** Lay gravel behind the wall until it is about 6 inches from the top. Pack down the gravel with a tamper, then fold the landscape fabric over the gravel.

3 **LAY TOPSOIL.** Fill the remaining space with soil and tamp it in place. Fill any low spots that result, then rake the area level. Sod, seed, or plant with the groundcover of your choice.

Building a wooden retaining wall

If you want to move the earth, build a retaining wall—by the time you're done, you'll feel as though you've moved half the planet.

Because a retaining wall is going to be in contact with the ground, make sure you use lumber that's rated for ground contact. Your best choice is a pressure-treated wood that has a rating of .40 or higher. (Regular pressure-treated wood, which is commonly used on decks, has a .25 rating; it holds less preservative and won't hold up well.) Avoid railroad ties—they're heavy and soaked with creosote, which is messy and can harm plants.

SKILL SCALE

EASY	MEDIUM	HARD

REQUIRED SKILLS:
Basic carpentry skills.

HOW LONG WILL IT TAKE?

Building a retaining wall 3 feet high and 16 feet long should take about:

Experienced .... 10 hrs.
Handy .... 14 hrs.
Novice .... 18 hrs.

STUFF YOU'LL NEED

✔ MATERIALS:
Landscape fabric, gravel, drainpipe, pressure-treated 6×6s or 2×12s, No. 4 (½-inch) rebar, 10-inch landscape spikes, ½×4 inch lag screws, concrete

✔ TOOLS:
Tape measure, shovel, ⅜-inch drill and ½-inch spade bit with extension, chainsaw, level, framing square, paintbrush, 3- and 6-pound sledgehammers, shovel, tamper, posthole digger, socket wrenches, safety glasses, work gloves

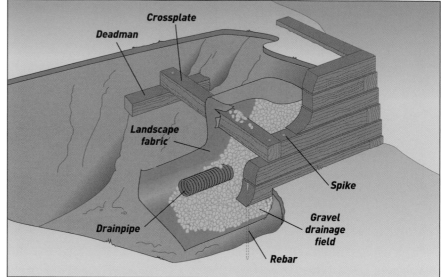

THIS RETAINING WALL'S HEFTY 6×6 TIMBERS HOLD BACK THE SOIL. A drainpipe at the base of the wall carries water away. Set the first course of timbers below grade as a foundation and anchor them with rebar. To counteract the pressure caused by the soil pushing against the wall, offset the courses so the back of each timber overhangs the back of the timber below by ½ inch. Anchor the wall with deadmen and tiebacks spaced at least 4 feet long installed every 4 feet along the wall.

1 REMOVE SOIL AND DIG A TRENCH. Lay out the wall, excavate the soil behind it, and dig a trench 8 inches deep for the first course of timbers. Line the trench and excavation with landscape fabric, then add 2 or 3 inches of gravel and tamp it in place. (See "Providing Drainage for Retaining Walls," pages 70–71.) Make sure the trench is level and flat.

2 PREPARE THE TIMBERS. Drill a ½-inch hole 6 to 12 inches from the end of each timber to hold the rebar stakes (see Step 4). If necessary, cut the last timber to fit with a chain saw. Treat cut ends with a preservative to keep them from rotting, and set the timbers in the trench.

3 **LEVEL THE FIRST COURSE.** Any irregularity in the first course will show up in all the other courses. Use a level to make sure the timbers are level from end to end and from side to side. At corners, check for square with either a 3-4-5 triangle or with a framing square. Add or remove gravel and move the timbers as necessary.

4 **DRIVE REBAR STAKES.** Drive 42-inch lengths of #4 (½-inch) rebar through the holes in the ends of the timbers with a 6-pound sledgehammer. Mark the location of the rebar on the face of the timber so you'll know where they are when you fasten the next course.

5 **LAY THE SECOND COURSE OF TIMBERS.** Offset the ends of the second course by at least 4 inches from the ends of the course below. Place the timbers so the front of the upper timber steps back ½ inch from the face of the lower timber.

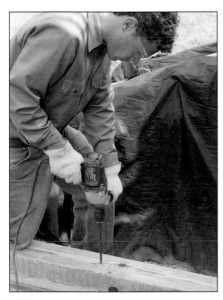

6 **DRILL HOLES FOR SPIKES.** Each row of timbers is fastened to the one below with 10-inch landscape spikes. Lay out holes for the spikes 6 to 12 inches from each end of the timbers and every 4 feet in between. Make sure the holes won't hit the rebar that holds the first row in place. Drill the holes with a ⅜-inch bit in an electric drill.

7 **DRIVE THE SPIKES.** Drive the spikes into the holes with a 3-pound sledgehammer. Mark the location of the spikes on the face of the timbers with chalk so you won't hit them when you drive the spikes for the next course.

8 **LAY THE DRAINPIPE.** Once you have nailed the second course in place, lay a thin bed of gravel on the ground behind it, sloping it 1 inch every 4 feet. (See "Providing Drainage for Retaining Walls," pages 70–71.) Lay drainpipe on the gravel and against the wall. (If a sidewall turns uphill, lay the drainpipe before you put in the sidewall's second course.)

Building a wooden retaining wall (continued)

Deadman trench

Tieback trench

9 DIG TRENCHES FOR THE DEADMEN AND TIEBACKS. Deadmen and tiebacks are installed on every other course to anchor the wall. They should be offset from the ones on lower courses. Fold the landscape fabric out of the way, cover the drainpipe with gravel, and dig trenches for the deadmen and tiebacks at 4-foot intervals. Make each trench large enough for a 4-foot tieback and a 3-foot deadman. Dig so the bottom of the trench is level with the top of the first course. Cut a hole in the landscape fabric for each deadman.

10 PUT THE DEADMEN AND TIEBACKS IN PLACE. Cut the deadmen and tiebacks. Set one end of each tieback on the second course of timbers, the other end on the crosspiece. Make adjustments as needed to level and square the deadmen and tiebacks.

11 NAIL THE DEADMEN AND TIEBACKS TOGETHER. Bore two ⅜-inch pilot holes through each tieback and deadman for a 10-inch landscape spike. Drive spikes into the holes, attaching the tiebacks to the deadmen and the wall.

To help prevent spikes from splitting timbers, let the end of the tieback overhang the deadman by about 2 inches.

12 LAY THE NEXT COURSE. Lay the next course, offsetting the timber ends by at least 4 inches from the ones below. Position the timbers so the front edge of the upper course steps back from the lower course by ½ inch. Drill and spike as before.

13 FILL THE TRENCH WITH GRAVEL AS YOU BUILD. Fill the trench with gravel to the top of each course as you lay it, and firmly pack down the gravel with a tamper.

14 LAY THE REMAINING COURSES. As you lay the timbers, the front of each course should step back from the front of the one below. Install deadmen and tiebacks every other course. Spike the courses to each other. For the top course, drive a spike through the corner.

15 **FILL WITH TOPSOIL.** After installing the top course, fold the landscape fabric over the gravel and fill the remaining space with topsoil. Tamp it, fill any resulting low spots, and rake it smooth.

IF YOU LIVE IN A WET AREA, bore a 1-inch drainage hole every 4 feet at a slightly upward angle through the second course. If you'd rather not drill holes, leave 1-inch gaps between the timbers and cover the back of the openings with galvanized screening.

BUILDING A POST-AND-BOARD RETAINING WALL

WORK SMARTER

A+

NO MORE THAN FOUR (FEET)
Building codes usually require that a licensed engineer design the system for a retaining wall that is more than 4 feet tall. This is to ensure that the wall can support the weight of all the dirt behind it.

If you need a tall wall and don't want to hire a professional, consider terracing the hill with a series of lower walls. But don't attempt to build a single wall; it isn't worth the risk.

If digging trenches for deadmen takes you into a neighbor's yard or presents other problems, a post-and-board wall gives you the look of wood with a fraction of the digging.

Begin by digging for a drainage pipe as explained in "Providing Drainage for Retaining Walls," pages 70–71. Then dig holes for 6×6 posts—the holes need to be half as deep as the wall is high. Align, plumb, and brace the posts, then pour the concrete footings.

The wall itself is made of 2×12 or 2×6 boards, which you screw onto the posts once the concrete has dried for at least three days. Use a level to make sure the first row is level, then screw the boards to the posts with deck screws before putting in the drainpipe and gravel. Put in the remaining rows, filling in behind them with gravel as you go.

1 **DIG POSTHOLES.** Lay out the wall, then level the ground at the base of the hillside. Dig postholes about 10 inches in diameter at 2-foot intervals along the length of the wall. Dig until the hole is at least half as deep as the wall is high. In cold climates, dig 6 inches below the frost line.

Building a wooden retaining wall

BUILDING A POST-AND-BOARD RETAINING WALL (continued)

2 **PLUMB AND BRACE THE END POSTS.** Enlarge the bottom of all the holes to a diameter of about 14 inches. Begin by setting the end posts so their tops are 1 inch shorter than the finished wall height. (See Designer Tip, below right.) Trim the posts, if necessary, with a chain saw. Screw boards to the posts, plumb the posts, and nail the boards to stakes to brace them.

3 **PLACE THE LINE POSTS.** Run a level mason's line between the tops of the end posts and align the tops of the other posts with it. Set, plumb, and brace all the posts, then fill the holes with concrete. Slope the concrete away from each post so water drains away from it.

Designer Tip

4 **PUT THE 2×12s IN PLACE.** Put the 2×12s for the first course on the uphill side of the posts. Level the boards and cut them, if necessary, so they'll meet at the center of the posts. Butt the ends together and hold them against the post. Bore two $^{7}/_{16}$-inch-diameter holes slightly smaller than the diameter of a $^{1}/_{2}$×4-inch lag screw through the boards into each post.

5 **BOLT THE BOARDS IN PLACE.** Put washers on the lag screws and drive them into the holes. Line the area behind the wall with landscape fabric, add gravel, and lay drainpipe. Cover with gravel and tamp. Fill in behind the wall and tamp the gravel as you build. About 6 inches from the top of the wall, fold the fabric over the gravel and fill the remaining space with topsoil.

CHAMFERED POSTS
When you chamfer the tops of the posts, you give a wall a more finished look that helps drain water from the top of each post. Cut the chamfer after you've braced the posts and cut them to length but before you attach the boards. The chamfer can be any width you like. Experiment by cutting a sample 2-inch bevel on a piece of scrap. If it's not quite what you like, keep cutting samples until you find one you do like. Note that the finished wall is one inch higher than the post.

Building a landscape block retaining wall

Landscape blocks are some of the best things to happen to walls in a long time. Made of precast concrete, they have textured faces that make them look a lot more like stone than concrete. They require neither footing nor mortar, and stacking them automatically creates a wall that leans into the hillside for strength. Two major types exist: lipped and pinned. The ones with lips work best for this project. The ones with fiberglass pins are used for large structural walls that require engineers and earthmoving equipment. Solid landscape blocks are durable and can easily be cut into smaller pieces to offset courses as you build your wall.

SKILL SCALE

EASY	**MEDIUM**	HARD

REQUIRED SKILLS: Using a level and a shovel.

HOW LONG WILL IT TAKE?

Building a landscape block wall 3 feet high and 16 feet long should take about:

Experienced .... 10 hrs.
Handy .... 14 hrs.
Novice .... 18 hrs.

STUFF YOU'LL NEED

✔ **MATERIALS:**
Landscape fabric, gravel, drainpipe, landscape blocks, construction adhesive

✔ **TOOLS:**
Tape measure, shovel, tamper, level, circular saw, 3-pound sledgehammer, rubber mallet, torpedo level, brick chisel, caulk gun, safety glasses, work gloves

Laying curves

The keystone shape of most blocks makes it easy to create a curved wall—the shape and size of the block determines how tight the radius can be. Lay out free-form curves with a garden hose. To lay out a precise arc, drive in a pipe at the desired center point. Tie one end of a mason's line to the pipe and the other end to a bottle of powdered chalk. Pull the line tight and walk around the pipe in a circle, marking the ground as you go.

Take your time leveling the surface that will hold the blocks. High and low spots will make it difficult to lay the stones evenly and will affect the overall strength and look of the wall.

1 DIG AND LEVEL A TRENCH. Lay out the wall with batterboards and mason's line. Dig a trench as wide and deep as the manufacturer recommends. Line the bottom with an inch or so of sand, rake it level, and compact it with a tamper. Place some of the soil you remove on the downhill side of the trench to level the slope.

2 LAY LANDSCAPE FABRIC. Line the back and bottom of the trench with landscape fabric. Unroll enough fabric to cross back over the trench later, plus about a foot more than the height of the wall. If you have to piece together lengths of landscape fabric, overlap any adjoining edges by 3 to 4 inches.

Building a landscape block retaining wall (continued)

3 **LAY THE FIRST BLOCK.** Some manufacturers instruct you to set the first block lip up; others instruct lip down. Follow the directions. Lay the first block and check for level from side to side and front to back. Tap with a rubber mallet to make small adjustments. Put sand under the block to solve bigger problems.

4 **LAY THE REST OF THE FIRST COURSE.** Lay the remaining blocks one at a time. Make sure each block is level, checking both side to side and front to back. Put the level across the new block and at least one of its neighbors to make sure the tops of the blocks are level with each other. The spaces at the ends of the course may not require a full block. Buy smaller blocks or trim larger ones to fit.

CUTTING BLOCKS
If you're working with solid blocks, you can trim them to fit smaller openings. Score along the line you want to cut with a circular saw and masonry blade. Split the block at the scored line by striking it with a brick chisel and 3-pound sledgehammer. If you're working with hollow-core blocks, don't plan on cutting them to size because they'll break. Instead buy half blocks and smaller blocks to fit openings that are less than a full block long.

5 **LAY THE SECOND COURSE.** If the first course ended with a full block, begin the second course with a half block. If you started the first course with a partial block, trim a full block so it overlaps the seam below by at least 3 inches. (Check the manufacturer's instructions.) Lay a second course of blocks with their lips pointing down, over the back of the wall. Position each block so it spans a joint in the course below. As you work, verify that the blocks are level; if not, shim the low end with asphalt shingle or some landscape fabric.

6 **TRIM BLOCKS FOR THE END OF THE WALL.** As you come to the end of the wall, trim a block to fit in the opening. When you begin building the rest of the wall, alternate so one row begins with a full block and the next with a half block.

Building corners

If your wall turns a corner, lay full blocks for the first course. On the second course, cut a block in half. Place the block as shown. On the remaining courses, lay the half block at a right angle to the one below. Chisel the lip off a block if it interferes with construction, then secure the block in place with a bead of construction adhesive.

7 **LAY A THIRD COURSE AND SOME DRAINPIPE.** Not all block walls require a drainpipe, though it's never a bad idea. Lay the third course the same way you laid the second course, leaving an exit point for the drainpipe at one end of the wall. Add a bit more gravel behind the wall to create a flat surface that slopes 1 inch in 4 feet, and tamp the gravel. Tuck a drainpipe behind the wall. Fill in completely behind the wall to the top of the course and tamp.

8 **LAY THE REMAINING COURSES.** Continue building the wall, adding gravel and tamping after every course. When you're a course or two below the top of the wall, fold the landscape fabric over the gravel and trim off any excess.

9 **LAY CAPSTONES.** The keystone shape of the blocks leaves triangular gaps between the stones, which are covered up with special blocks called capstones. Apply a bead of construction adhesive along the top of the wall and set the capstones in place.

10 **FILL IN AROUND THE WALL.** Put topsoil in the space between the landscape fabric and the top of the wall and fill what remains of the trench in front of the wall. Rake to make a flat surface and tamp.

HOMER'S HINDSIGHT

ONE BLOCK SHORT OF A FULL LOAD

More than one customer has come in to buy the exact number of blocks they need. A slight miscalculation, however, or a couple of blocks that break during trimming leaves them short. An extra trip to the store is bad enough, but when they get home they often discover that the color of the new blocks differs from the blocks they have at home. Dying concrete is not an exact science, and the color can vary from batch to batch. When you buy the blocks, make sure they come from the same batch. Verify that the store will let you return any extras, and add 10 percent to the number of blocks you think you'll need.

Building a dry stone wall

Dry stone walls are built without mortar, which has many advantages and saves a lot of work. Unlike mortared stone walls, a dry stone wall will flex as the ground beneath it shifts, eliminating the need for a foundation. Because no mortar is drying as you work, you can work at your own pace, and no mistake is permanent. (A dry stone wall is a bad choice in areas prone to earthquakes, however, and codes in such areas may prohibit building one.) If you choose to build a dry stone wall, remember that you'll be working with large, heavy stones. After a few days, working on a stone wall feels like a sentence to hard labor.

Sort stones into groups according to their functions before you start. Look for bondstones—those with a solid base, flat top, and one or more straight sides. Corners require stones with two sides that meet at 90 degrees. Save the flattest stones for the wall cap.

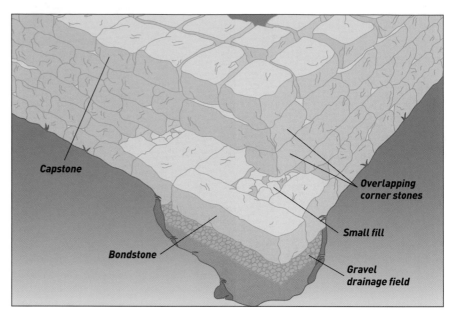

Capstone

Overlapping corner stones

Small fill

Bondstone

Gravel drainage field

A TYPICAL DRY STONE WALL HAS TWO PARALLEL FACES, CALLED WYTHES. A wythe is any continuous vertical section of a wall one masonry unit thick. The face of the wall is made of large stones; smaller stones fill the center. Bondstones—long stones that run the width of the wall—are positioned every 4 to 6 feet to tie the two sides of the wall together. Bondstones are also placed at the corners, with their long faces at 90 degrees to each other from course to course. For stability, the wall has a broad base that supports a narrower top. The resulting inward slope, or batter, should be 1½ to 2 inches for every vertical foot.

SKILL SCALE

EASY	MEDIUM	HARD

REQUIRED SKILLS: Basic masonry skills.

HOW LONG WILL IT TAKE?

Building a dry stone wall 3 feet high and 16 feet long should take about:

Experienced .... 16 hrs.
Handy .... 20 hrs.
Novice .... 24 hrs.

STUFF YOU'LL NEED

✔ **MATERIALS:**
Gravel, stones, 1×2s, 4d (1½-inch) common nails

✔ **TOOLS:**
Shovel, mason's line, tamper, circular saw, hammer, stonemason's hammer, level, safety glasses, work gloves

1 **LAY OUT AND DIG A TRENCH FOR THE WALL.** Stretch a mason's line between stakes to mark each edge of the wall. Sprinkle powdered chalk or sand over the lines to mark the wall's path on the ground. Dig a trench about 8 inches deep within the marked outlines.

2 **LINE THE TRENCH WITH GRAVEL.** Place a 4-inch layer of gravel in the trench. The gravel will drain water away from the finished wall. Tamp the gravel and use a level to make sure the bed is flat and even.

3 **LAY THE FRONT FACE OF THE FIRST COURSE.** Begin the first course by placing a long stone, called a bondstone, across each end of the trench. Then lay the front face of the first course, placing bondstones every 4 to 6 feet. Because the top and bottom of a stone are seldom parallel, arrange the stones so any resulting slope declines toward the middle of the wall.

4 **LAY THE REAR FACE OF THE WALL.** Lay the rear face along the back edge of the trench. Fill the spaces between the two faces of the wall with small stones or rubble.

5 **LAY THE SECOND COURSE.** Start the next course by laying a long stone at a right angle to the bondstone below it. Work your way down the wall one face at a time. Lay the stones so the space between two stones is always spanned by another stone. Lay bondstones every 4 to 6 feet, varying the positions from course to course.

TOOL TIP

BUILD A BATTER GAUGE

For strength, a wall needs to be narrower at the top than at the bottom. Because of this, the face of the wall slopes slightly. Build a batter gauge to check the slope, or batter. Cut two 1×2s equal to the wall's final height. Screw two ends to a spacer that is 1½ to 2 inches long for every foot of wall height. Screw the other two ends together and tape a level to either outer face of the 1×2s. Hold one leg of the gauge against the wall. The batter is correct when the level's bubble is centered in the vial.

6 **CHECK THE BATTER.** Constantly check the batter with your batter gauge and a level. Reposition stones as needed to get a plumb reading. Continue to build the wall, checking the batter after every few courses. Pick the flattest, broadest stones for the top course. Slope the top stones slightly outward by propping them up on small stones. The slope helps drain water away from the top of the wall.

Building a footing for a stone or brick wall

Whether you're building a brick wall, a stone wall, or any other wall that requires mortar, the job starts underground with a footing. A mortared wall is rigid and won't flex as the ground moves with seasonal changes. Without the footing, the wall would crack, and weather would compound the damage. With a footing, the wall sits on a strong, rigid platform. If the ground shifts enough to move the platform, the platform and wall move as one piece, minimizing cracks.

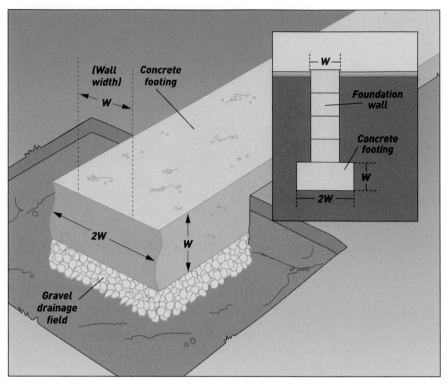

(Wall width) W

Concrete footing

W

Foundation wall

Concrete footing

W

2W

2W

W

Gravel drainage field

SKILL SCALE

EASY	**MEDIUM**	HARD

REQUIRED SKILLS:
Masonry skills.

🕐 HOW LONG WILL IT TAKE?

Constructing a wall footing 16×2×1 should take about:

Experienced . . . . 8 hrs.
Handy . . . . 12 hrs.
Novice . . . . 16 hrs.

STUFF YOU'LL NEED

✔ MATERIALS:
Gravel, 2×4s, 2×8s, 1×2s, 10d (3-inch) nails, concrete, burlap

✔ TOOLS:
Spade, tamper, mason's line, plumb bob, level, crowbar, 3-pound sledgehammer, circular saw, wheelbarrow, mason's hoe, garden hose, dust mask, safety glasses

⏰ TIME SAVER

HOME DELIVERY
Concrete and gravel are heavy. Have them delivered—it's not worth the wear and tear on your car or truck.

TYPICALLY A FOOTING IS AS THICK AS THE WALL IT SUPPORTS and twice as wide. If the wall is one foot wide, the footing should be at least one foot thick. Those in frost-free areas can pour their footings in a trench. Those in colder climates must pour their footings below the frost line—anywhere from 6 to 48 inches below the surface. If your footing needs to be deep underground, pour it at the bottom of a deep trench, then build a foundation wall on top, as shown *above*.

Regional variation

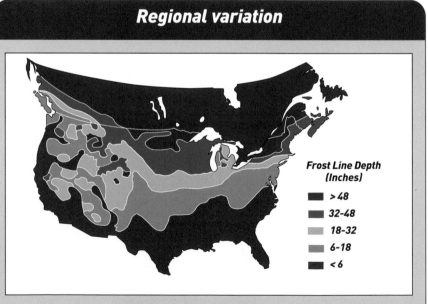

Frost Line Depth (Inches)

■	> 48
■	32-48
■	18-32
■	6-18
■	< 6

In a climate where the ground freezes, pour a footing so the bottom is at least 6 inches below the frost line. Check local building codes to find out exactly how deep that is in your area. In deep-frost areas, pour the footing and build a foundation wall on top of it once it's dry.

PREPARING THE SITE

1 **LAY OUT THE EDGES OF THE FOOTING WITH BATTERBOARDS AND MASON'S LINE.** The footing should be as thick as the wall it supports and twice as wide. Stretch mason's line to lay out the width, then use sand or flour to lay out lines on the ground that are 4 to 6 inches outside the lines. Measure the distance between the ground and the mason's line and write it on the batterboard for reference later. Mark the positions of the lines on the batterboards, then untie the lines.

2 **DIG A TRENCH FOR THE FOOTING.** Start the trench at the lines you made on the ground, then dig it about 3 inches deeper than the wall is wide. If the ground freezes where you live, dig down at least 6 inches below the frost line. In either case, line the trench with an inch of gravel, and tamp it down.

ASSEMBLING THE FORM

1 **LAY OUT THE OUTSIDE OF THE FORMS.** The lines you originally tied to the batterboards marked the inside edge of the forms. Move them 1½ inches closer to the outside edge of the trench in order to mark the outside edge of the form. Drop a plumb bob from the line and mark the end of the foundation with a nail put through a piece of paper.

2 **DRIVE STAKES TO SUPPORT THE FORM.** Drive stakes into the ground just outside the nails and run mason's line between them. Drive the stakes no more than 8 feet apart to ensure that the forms won't bow from the weight of the concrete.

3 **ATTACH THE FORMS TO THE STAKES.** Place a 2×8 against the stakes on each side of the trench. (Use 2×8s even if the footing will be deeper than 8 inches because excess concrete can flow underneath the form and make the footing stronger.) Measure down from the mason's line to make sure the board is both level and a couple inches below ground level (the distance you wrote on the batterboard in Step 1). Clamp the boards to the stakes and attach them. If you need to join two boards, drive a stake so it straddles the ends and nail it to both of the boards.

Building a footing for a stone or brick wall

ASSEMBLING THE FORM (continued)

4 **ATTACH ENDS TO THE FORMS.** For the ends of the form, cut 2×8s that are long enough to span the existing forms and the stakes. Attach each end to the forms and stakes. Trim all the stakes flush with the top of the form, using a handsaw. Apply form release agent to the inside surfaces of all the forms.

5 **DRIVE STAKES EVERY 2 FEET.** Lay a level across the form to make sure the sides are level. Hammer on the stakes as needed to adjust the boards. Drive in additional stakes flush with the top of the side boards every 2 feet along them. If two boards meet end to end, drive in a stake that spans the seams. Nail the stakes to the boards and trim them flush at the top.

6 **ATTACH SPREADERS.** Concrete weighs enough to bend the boards outward when it's poured. Reinforce the forms with 1×2 spreaders nailed every 2 to 3 feet.

WHEN THE GROUND IS TOO SOFT TO HOLD THE STAKES SECURELY, brace the sides of the form with kickers, pieces of 1×2 that extend out to firmer soil. Nail an end of the kicker to the form, drive a stake into firm ground at the other end of the kicker, and nail them together.

Regional variation

In areas prone to earthquakes or hurricanes, footings may need special reinforcement. (Walls more than 3 feet high also need reinforcement, but leave that job to professionals.) Check your local building codes for special requirements in your area. Often a footing must be reinforced with rebar; #4 (½-inch) rebar is a common standard. You may need to lay two parallel runs of rebar the entire length of the form. Wire the rebar to wire supports (sold separately) that hold the rebar in the middle of the slab. Overlap any lengths of rebar by at least 12 inches and tie them together with wire. If vertical reinforcement is required, drive rebar into the ground, spacing it as local codes require.

SAFETY ALERT

Concrete is caustic. Wear a long-sleeved shirt, work gloves, a respirator, and safety glasses.

POURING CONCRETE

1 MIX THE CONCRETE. Mix pre-mixed concrete following the directions on the bag. Empty out the dry ingredients, then make a crater in the middle and pour in about half the required water. Fold the ingredients together and slowly add the rest of the water.

2 TEST THE CONSISTENCY. Properly mixed concrete has the consistency of oatmeal. A more accurate way to test the mix is to smooth out the concrete and make grooves in it with a hoe. If the edges hold, the concrete is ready. If they fall in (like these did), add dry ingredients. If they crumble, add water.

TRUCK IT

If you're doing a job that involves less than 1 cubic yard of concrete, bags of pre-mixed concrete are probably easiest to handle. Anything bigger is going to take quite a few bags: One 90-pound bag of concrete yields only ⅔ cubic foot. You'll need 41 bags to get a cubic yard.

For large jobs have ready-mixed concrete delivered. Tell the suppliers what you're building so you get the right mix. Have plenty of help on hand when the truck arrives.

Concrete is a mix of sand, lime, cement, and water. Many books tell you how to mix your own, but there's no advantage to it. You're still going to have to buy sacks of sand, lime, and cement, and you'll need a cement mixer on top of that. Let the professionals do the mixing, whether they're at the factory that bags the mix or driving the concrete truck that pours it for you.

3 DUMP CONCRETE IN THE FORMS. Set up a wheelbarrow ramp that leads to the edge of the form. Prop up the high end on a 2×4 or bricks. Resting it on the forms could knock them out of alignment. Pour the concrete into the form from the wheelbarrow, dumping one load up against another until the form is filled to the top.

4 REMOVE TRAPPED AIR. Work a shovel or spade in and out of the concrete to remove air pockets. Pay particular attention to corners and edges, where air often gets trapped.

LANDSCAPING WALLS

Building a footing for a stone or brick wall

POURING CONCRETE *(continued)*

5 **SCREED THE FORM.** Lay a 2×4 across the form and pull it along the length of the footing, shimmying from side to side and removing the spreaders as you go. This process, called screeding, levels and smoothes the concrete.

6 **COVER WITH BURLAP.** Cover the footing with burlap and keep it damp, but not soaked, with water for two or three days while the concrete cures. The moisture keeps the concrete from drying too quickly and cracking.

7 **REMOVE THE FORM.** Once the concrete has cured, pull the nails out of the form. Work stakes loose with a crowbar and remove them, then gently pry the boards off the footing.

8 **REPLACE THE DIRT.** Fill in around the footing with soil and tamp it firmly. Wait until you've finished the wall to replant.

TOOL TIP

SHAKE THAT THING

Instead of working concrete by hand to eliminate pockets of air, you can rent a concrete vibrator. Follow the manufacturer's instructions to operate the vibrator, immersing it in the concrete for 10 to 15 seconds every foot or so along the edges of the form. Don't overdo it: Too much vibrating is just as bad as none at all.

HOMER'S HINDSIGHT

SMOOTH OPERATOR

I once had a customer who was very proud of the job he had done pouring his footing. He'd read every book he could on concrete work and bought the best tools he could find. He smoothed the surface carefully with a float, then troweled it even smoother. When it was done, he was pretty darn proud.

But when he came in the next week, he was a different man. The wall had gone well and looked great. He had filled in the trench and looked forward to growing grass. But to his dismay, the finish he put on the footing was buried, and no one would ever see it.

Take my advice: Screed the footing and leave it alone. A rougher surface holds mortar better, and nobody but the worms will ever get a chance to look at it.

LANDSCAPING WALLS

Building a running-bond brick wall

Y ou can build a wall in countless ways, all of which have the same goal—strength. Every pattern relies on the ends and corners, called leads, to create straight and true starting points. Leads are built first. They can be as high as the finished wall or you can build them in stages. Then you fill in between the leads to the center of the wall. The pattern, *right*, called running bond, gains its strength from its staggered joints—each mortar joint is bridged by a brick above and below it. On common-bond walls, the two sides of the wall are tied together by occasional rows of bricks laid perpendicular to the others. Directions for building a common-bond wall are on pages 90–92.

Use grade SW brick in freezing climates and MW or NW elsewhere.

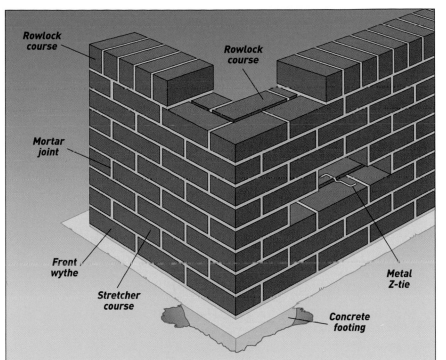

A RUNNING-BOND WALL IS NOTHING MORE THAN BRICKS STACKED ON TOP OF EACH OTHER. The bricks are offset so the joints don't line up. Because mortar is the only thing tying the two sides of the wall together, use metal Z-ties to link the two wythes. (A wythe is any continuous vertical section of a wall one masonry unit in thickness.)

TOOL TIP

USING MASON'S OR LINE BLOCKS

Mason's blocks (or line blocks) ensure that the front and the top of each brick in the course is positioned correctly. Cut a piece of mason's line the length of the wall, and tie a knot in each end. Slip the knots in the slots provided so that the line comes out through the inside corner of the L.

Hook one block on a corner of the lead while a helper hooks the other block on the opposite lead. Adjust the blocks until the line is about 1/16 inch from the surface of the wall and aligned with the top of the course you're laying. Move the blocks up the wall as you add courses.

MAKE A STORY POLE to check that courses of bricks are properly spaced. Mark the thickness of each brick on a 1×4, including the thicknesses of the mortar joints.

Cut a brick to size by marking the cut and striking the line lightly with a brick chisel and a sledgehammer. Strike the line with increasing intensity until the brick splits.

LANDSCAPING WALLS 87

Building a running-bond brick wall

DRY-LAYING RUNS

1 **LAY OUT THE WYTHES OF THE WALL.** If necessary, have a friend help you snap chalk lines on the footing to lay out the front and rear faces, or wythes, of the wall. Separate the lines by the length of one brick.

2 **MAKE A TRIAL RUN.** Dry-lay the first course of both wythes. Begin one row with a half brick so joints are staggered. Leave gaps between the bricks using plywood spacers. Leave a ½-inch gap for bricks 7½ inches long and a ⅜-inch gap for bricks 7⅝ inches long. Mark the location of the bricks on the footing.

3 **DRY-LAY A CORNER LEAD.** Mark the location of the bricks on the footing.

Hose the bricks with water for 25 minutes before laying them so they don't absorb moisture from the mortar.

BUILDING THE WALL

1 **LAY MORTAR.** Remove the bricks and spread a ¾-inch-thick mortar bed for the first three bricks at one end of the wall. To lay the mortar, load a mason's trowel with mortar and slowly turn it on edge as you drag it along the footing.

2 **SET THE BRICKS.** Push the first brick into the mortar until it sits ½ inch above the footing. Butter the next brick, patting mortar onto one end of it. Push the brick into the mortar and up against the first brick. Repeat for the third brick.

3 **CHECK FOR LEVEL.** Scrape off the excess mortar that squeezes out of joints. Check the bricks for level and tap them into place with the end of the trowel handle. Lay a second wythe of three bricks parallel to the first.

4 **BUILD THE LEADS.** Follow up with courses of bricks so each brick spans the joint below it. Begin courses with half bricks as needed. Place metal Z-ties between wythes as your local code requires. Press each tie into some mortar and spread a little more mortar on top. Check the spacing of the courses with the story pole.

5 **BUILD UP THE CORNER** and end leads of both wythes to a height of five courses, checking the bricks often for plumb and level.

6 **FILL IN BETWEEN THE LEADS.** Attach mason's blocks to the ends of the first course and run a mason's line between them, 1/16 inch away from the bricks and flush with the top edge of the course you're laying. Working from each end, throw mortar lines the width of the brick and lay the first course of the front wythe three bricks at a time. (Throwing is laying down a bed of mortar with a trowel.)

7 **LAY THE CLOSURE BRICK.** The last brick in each wythe's course is called a closure brick. If you've followed the marks you made during the dry run, the brick should fit without trimming. Test the brick's fit, then butter each end of it and the neighboring bricks and push it into place. Now finish the first course of the back wythe.

8 **WORK YOUR WAY UP THE WALL.** Build between the leads and check your progress, course by course, with mason's blocks and line, a level, and the story pole. As you work, scrape off the excess mortar from the joints. When the rest of the wall reaches the top of the leads, build the leads higher, then fill in between them.

9 **AS THE MORTAR BETWEEN BRICKS BEGINS TO GET FIRM,** press it with your thumb. If your thumb leaves an impression, run over the joints with a concave jointer. After you've laid the last course, cap the wall as explained on page 92.

Laying a common-bond brick wall

Like running bond, the common-bond design features bricks that run the length of the wall. However, it also has headers, which are bricks that run across the wall to tie the faces of the wall together.

For the pattern to work, you need nominal 4×8-inch bricks. Nominal bricks are those that are less than the stated dimension by the thickness of a mortar joint. In fact, 4×8-inch bricks actually come in two nominal sizes: If you measure a brick and find that it's off its nominal dimension by ⅜ inch, use a ⅜-inch mortar joint; if it's off by ½ inch, lay a ½-inch joint.

In addition to strengthening a wall, common bond makes for a prettier wall. It's often accented with headers that are a different color from the rest of the wall.

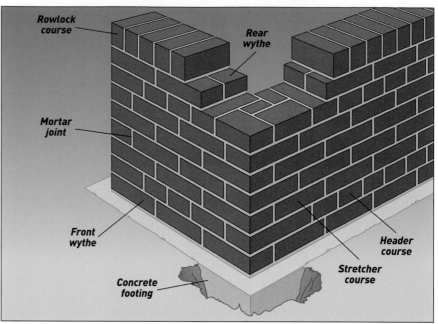

ONE OF THE MOST COMMON WAYS TO LAY BRICKS IS CALLED, fittingly enough, common bond. Both of the wall's faces begin with a row of bricks placed long edge out—masons call them stretchers. This stretcher course is followed by a course with the narrow edge out, called a header course, which ties the wall together. A header course is followed by four courses of stretchers which, in turn, are followed by another header course, and so on. The top of this wall is capped with rowlocks, which are bricks set on edge.

BUILDING END LEADS

1 LAY THE FIRST COURSE OF THE LEAD. Dry-lay two rows of bricks on the foundation, each starting with a full brick. Then spread mortar for three bricks. Butter the ends, set them, and check them for level. Repeat for the second row of three bricks.

2 START THE SECOND COURSE. Start the second course with two bricks cut to three-quarters of their length. Spread mortar lines and lay the bricks, buttering the inner edge of one just enough to close the faces, or wythes. Press the bricks into place, using a story pole to space them correctly.

3 LAY HEADERS. Butter the long edge of a full brick and push it into the mortar up against the end bricks. Lay three more header bricks the same way. The next four courses of the lead are stretchers followed by a header course. Continue building up the lead as high as you are comfortable.

BUILDING CORNER LEADS

1 **LAY THE FIRST COURSE.** Throw mortar lines and lay the first course, beginning with the front wythe. Lay a corner brick and two more along each arm. Lay two bricks along each arm of the rear wythe. Check for level along and across the wythes, adjusting bricks as needed.

2 **TRIM BRICKS FOR THE CORNER.** For the second course, cut two bricks into one-quarter and three-quarter pieces, called closures. Lay the two three-quarter closures on the front wythe. Lay the two one-quarter closures on the rear wythe, as shown. Then begin laying headers in both directions.

3 **LAY HEADERS.** Continue laying header bricks to complete the second course of the lead. Then lay the next four courses of both wythes with stretchers. Check for level and plumb after each course.

FILLING IN BETWEEN THE LEADS

Mason's block

1 **FILL IN BETWEEN THE LEADS.** Attach mason's blocks to the ends of the first course and run a mason's line between them, $1/16$ inch away from the bricks and flush with the top edge of the first course. Working from each end, spread mortar and lay the first course of the front wythe three stretchers at a time until you reach the center. Lay the last brick, called the closure brick, to finish the front wythe and then lay the rear wythe.

2 **LAY A HEADER COURSE.** The next course is made entirely of headers, or bricks laid across both wythes. Move up the mason's blocks and line, lay a bed of mortar, and butter the long edge of each brick before setting it into place.

CLOSER LOOK

GETTING CLOSURE
The last brick in a wythe is placed after you have filled in from the leads to the center of the wall. It's called the closure brick and offers you a margin for error if the joints between bricks aren't uniform. If the wythes are laid out perfectly, the closure brick will fit easily, but if the space is a little tight you can trim the closure brick to fit the opening.

Laying a common-bond brick wall

FILLING IN BETWEEN THE LEADS (continued)

3 **FILL IN BETWEEN THE LEADS OF THE FRONT WYTHE.** Once you've laid the row of headers for the second row, build up the front wythe between leads. Row two consists entirely of headers; the next four rows are stretchers, followed by a row of headers, after which the pattern repeats itself. Move up the mason's blocks and line as you go, and check your progress with the level and story pole.

4 **STRIKE THE JOINTS.** As you lay the bricks, use the trowel to scrape off the excess mortar. Test the mortar between the bricks by pressing with your thumb. When your thumb leaves an imprint, run a concave jointer over the joints.

5 **FILL IN BETWEEN THE LEADS OF THE REAR WYTHE.** When the front wythes are done, shift the mason's blocks and line to the rear wythe. Continue to build between the leads, moving up the mason's blocks and line for each course. Check often for plumb and level. When both wythes are at the heights of the leads, build the leads higher and fill between them until the wall is the desired height.

BUILDING A CAP

1 **LAY OUT THE BRICKS.** Cap the wall, regardless of the pattern you used. Use a course of rowlocks, or bricks set on edge across the wythes. First place the story pole on the last course and mark where the bricks will lie. You may have to trim one of the bricks. If so, place it a few bricks from an end or corner to hide it.

2 **WORK FROM ONE END TOWARD THE MIDDLE.** To start the cap, lay mortar for a short distance along one end and place bricks on edge in the mortar. At corners, lay mortar and place a brick at the end of one arm, then butter the face of the next and butt it against the first. Lay a few more bricks along that arm, then begin along the other arm, as shown. Slope the cap slightly to allow drainage off the top.

3 **WORK FROM THE OTHER END BACK TOWARD THE MIDDLE.** As you approach the end of the wall, skip a few bricks and lay the end brick. Then work your way back, filling in the gap. Dry-lay the last brick, or closure brick, to check its fit. Trim it, if necessary, with a masonry saw. Butter the brick and its neighbors, then tap it into place with the trowel handle.

Building a mortared stone wall

It was while restacking the stones of a dry stone wall that Robert Frost observed that "good fences make good neighbors." Better fences make better neighbors, and if you'd like a better wall, build one that's mortared together.

Buy the stone from a dealer and have it delivered—scrounging stones from a field is a tremendous amount of work. Ashlar is cut stone, rubble is uncut quarried stone, cobblestones are naturally rounded, and fieldstones are those found on the ground. The difference between stone types is largely a matter of taste and expense.

Like any other mortared wall, a mortared stone wall needs a foundation. Leave anything taller than 4 feet to the skills of a professional.

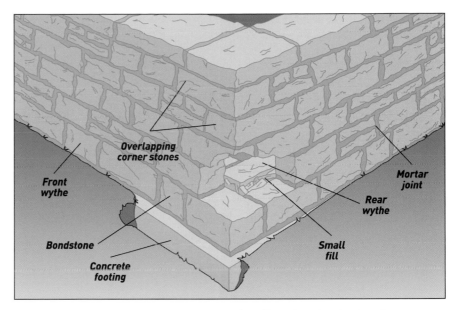

Overlapping corner stones

Front wythe

Bondstone

Concrete footing

Mortar joint

Rear wythe

Small fill

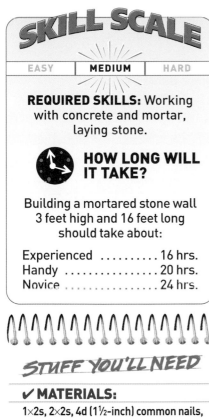

SKILL SCALE

EASY	MEDIUM	HARD

REQUIRED SKILLS: Working with concrete and mortar, laying stone.

HOW LONG WILL IT TAKE?

Building a mortared stone wall 3 feet high and 16 feet long should take about:

Experienced .... 16 hrs.
Handy .... 20 hrs.
Novice .... 24 hrs.

STUFF YOU'LL NEED

✔ **MATERIALS:**
1×2s, 2×2s, 4d (1½-inch) common nails, stones, mortar

✔ **TOOLS:**
Tape measure, chalk line, level, mason's trowel, mason's line, line level, concave jointer, scrub brush, safety glasses, work gloves

A MORTARED STONE WALL NEEDS A FOOTING (see "Building a Footing for a Stone or Brick Wall," pages 82–86). Building one is extra work, but the stones won't shift and crack once the wall is set on it. A typical mortared wall of this type has two parallel faces, or wythes, made of large stones. Smaller stones fill the gap between wythes. Bondstones, which stretch the width of the wall, are placed every 4 to 6 feet to tie the wythes together. For strength, the wall is wider at the bottom than at the top, and each side has a slope, or batter, of 1 inch per vertical foot. Stagger the mortar joints so each is bridged by a stone above and below.

BUILD A BATTER GAUGE TO CHECK THE WALL'S SLOPE. Nail two 3-foot 1×2s together at one end and separate them at the other end with a 3-inch spacer. To check the wall, hold one leg of the gauge against it and a level against the other leg. If the level reads plumb, the wall has the correct batter.

TOOL TIP

STONEMASON'S HAMMER
One of the nice things about working with ashlar is that the stones are cut with square edges, eliminating the need for you to cut them. On occasion, however, you may find that a stone is troublesome to place because of a small irregularity. Keep a stonemason's hammer on hand for such times; the pointed end of this heavy tool is ideal for trimming off small bits of stone.

Building a mortared stone wall

LANDSCAPING WALLS

DRY-LAYING RUNS

1 **LAY OUT THE WALL.** Pour a foundation as described in "Building a Footing for a Stone or Brick Wall," pages 82–86. Working with a helper, snap a chalk line on the footing outlining the front and rear faces of the wall.

2 **LAY BONDSTONES AT THE END.** At each end of the wall, lay a bondstone that is the width of the wall. The bondstones tie the front and rear wythes together. You'll need one of these stones every 4 to 6 feet.

3 **MAKE A TRIAL RUN.** Dry-lay the first course of both wythes, choosing stones that fit neatly between the bondstones at the ends of the wall.

When lifting heavy stones, bend your knees and keep your back straight.

BUILDING END LEADS

1 **LAY THE FIRST COURSE.** Remove 3 to 4 feet of stones at each end of the wall and set them aside in order. Apply a 1-inch-thick layer of mortar to the exposed section of footing and furrow it lightly. Set the first course in the mortar. Pack the joints between stones with mortar.

2 **BEGIN CONSTRUCTING LEADS.** Allow the mortar to set slightly so it isn't dislodged by subsequent stones. Dry-lay a few stones at each end of the second course to make sure they bridge the joints below. When you're satisfied with the fit, lay the stones in mortar. Fill in between the wythes with smaller stones and mortar.

3 **COMPLETE THE LEADS.** Continue building courses. After each one, check the slope, or batter, of both the wythes and the wall end with the batter gauge and a level. When the mortar is firm enough to hold a thumbprint, run a concave jointer over the joints to remove excess mortar.

BUILDING CORNER LEADS

1 **LAY THE FIRST COURSE.** Start in the corner, setting two stones at right angles to each other in each wythe. Dry-lay the rest of the stones in the first course. Remove the first 3 or 4 feet of stones, then set them in an inch of mortar. Fill the space between the wythes with rubble and mortar.

2 **LAY THE SECOND COURSE.** Test-fit the stones, overlapping them as shown. When you're satisfied with the fit, set the stones in mortar. Continue building up the lead one course at a time, test-fitting, setting them in mortar, and filling the gap between the wythes with stones and mortar.

3 **CHECK THE SLOPE,** or batter, of each wythe with the batter gauge and a level as you build up the corner lead. When the mortar is firm enough to hold a thumbprint, run a concave jointer over the joints to remove excess mortar.

BUILDING BETWEEN LEADS

1 **SET THE FIRST COURSE OF STONES.** Put the stones in a 1-inch mortar bed. Drive stakes into the ground at the ends of both wythes and run mason's lines between them at the height of the leads' second course. Dry-lay the second course of both wythes between the leads, choosing stones that sit roughly ½ inch below the lines.

2 **SET THE SECOND COURSE.** Put the stones from each wythe aside, keeping track of how they fit together. Apply a 1-inch-thick layer of mortar on the first course of stones, then lay the second course of stones. Once the course has been completed, move up the mason's lines and dry-lay the third course.

3 **CONTINUE LAYING STONES.** Build the wall a course at a time, test-fitting the stones before you set them in mortar. Fill the space between wythes with rubble and mortar. Move the mason's lines up at the start of each course to help you keep the wall level.

Building a mortared stone wall

BUILDING BETWEEN LEADS *(continued)*

4 **CHECK THE BATTER OF THE WALL.** Check your progress often with the batter gauge and a level.

5 **REPOSITION STONES AS NECESSARY.** If you make a mistake, remove the stone and scrub it with a wet brush before repositioning it. Dirt, grit, and dried bits of mortar weaken the joint.

6 **FILL THE JOINTS WITH MORTAR.** As you work, pack mortar into the joints between the stones. Scrape off the excess mortar that squeezes out as the stones are set.

7 **TOOL THE JOINTS.** When the mortar between the stones is firm enough to take a thumbprint, run over the joints with a concave jointer ½ inch deep or so.

8 **SET THE CAP.** For the cap, choose the flattest stones you can find. Line up the stones with mason's lines set at the finished height of the wall. Lay a 1-inch-thick bed of mortar and set the stones in place, tapping them with a trowel handle.

HOMER'S HINDSIGHT

STAY FOCUSED

One customer got so caught up with building his wall that he forgot to strike the mortar joints as he worked. By the time he got to the top of the wall, the mortar on the lowest stones was already hard, and the raking tool was ineffective. The result? He chipped away as best he could but, in the end, he left a sloppy-looking job. Stay focused on the process and finish each step before you move on. That's how you really save time ... and trouble!

Building a concrete block wall

A concrete block wall is a fast, inexpensive alternative to brick. Unfortunately the wall also looks like a fast, quick alternative, so you might want to consider applying a stucco finish to the blocks.

Concrete blocks measure 7⅝×7⅝×15⅝ inches. Mortar joints ⅜ inch thick bring this to a full 8×8×16 inches—use this size to figure out how many blocks you'll need. If you look at a block, you'll see that the thickness of its walls varies. Lay the blocks with the thick-walled side up—it holds more mortar.

Make sure you get the right type of mortar: Use type N for general outdoor use and type S in an area prone to strong winds. If you plan to stucco the wall, don't bother to strike the joints with a jointer. Simply cut them flush with a trowel.

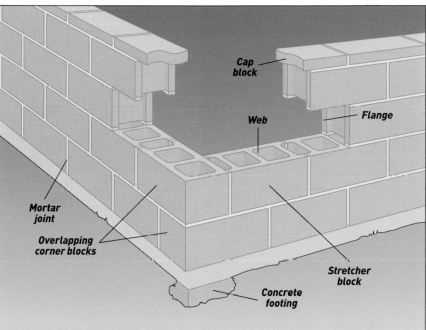

Cap block

Web

Flange

Mortar joint

Overlapping corner blocks

Stretcher block

Concrete footing

LIKE OTHER MORTARED WALLS, A CONCRETE BLOCK WALL REQUIRES A CONCRETE FOOTING that extends at least 6 inches below the frost line. (See "Building a Footing for a Stone or Brick Wall," pages 82-86.) The wall is built with several types of blocks. Stretcher blocks have flanges, or "ears," at each end to hold mortar. Corner blocks are used at corners and ends. They have one flat end and come in half and full sizes. In straight walls, half corner blocks are laid every other course to stagger joints. Cap blocks seal the top of the wall, protecting it from water.

SKILL SCALE

EASY	MEDIUM	HARD

REQUIRED SKILLS:
Mixing mortar, measuring, laying block.

🕐 HOW LONG WILL IT TAKE?

Installing a block wall 3 feet high and 16 feet long should take:

Experienced . . . . 8 hrs.
Handy . . . . 10 hrs.
Novice . . . . 12 hrs.

STUFF YOU'LL NEED

✔ **MATERIALS:**
1×4, concrete blocks, mortar, screening

✔ **TOOLS:**
Tape measure, circular saw, brick chisel, 3-pound sledgehammer, chalk line, pencil, mason's trowel, level, line level, mason's blocks, wheelbarrow, concave jointer, safety glasses, work gloves

MAKE A STORY POLE TO HELP SPACE COURSES CORRECTLY. Cut a 1×4 to the finished height of the wall. Lay out and mark the courses on the board, separating them by ⅜ inch for mortar joints.

TO TRIM A BLOCK, SCORE A CUTTING LINE with a circular saw and a masonry blade. Split the block at the scored line by striking it with a brick chisel and sledgehammer.

Building a concrete block wall

MAKING A TRIAL RUN

Half corner block

Full corner block

1 **LAY OUT THE FIRST COURSE.** Snap chalk lines on the footing to lay out the front and back faces of the wall, separating the lines by the width of a block.

2 **LAY THE FIRST COURSE WITHOUT MORTAR.** For a wall with no turns, start with a corner block, which is half the length of a regular block. Space the blocks with a ⅜-inch plywood spacer. Adjust the wall's length, if necessary, so it ends with either a full or half block. Mark the position of each block on the footing.

TO START A CORNER ON A WALL THAT TURNS, lay one full corner block, which has one flat end, then lay two stretcher blocks along each arm. Once again, follow the chalk lines, space bricks ⅜ inch apart, and mark joints on the footing.

CONSTRUCTING END LEADS

1 **LAY THE FIRST TWO BLOCKS.** Build the ends, or leads, first. Lay a mortar bed 1½ inches thick. Push the first block—in this case, a full corner block— into the mortar until it's ⅜ inch above the footing. Mortar the ears at one end of the second (stretcher block), and push it up against the corner block as shown.

2 **LAY THE THIRD BLOCK.** Mortar the ears on the next block, and set it into place. Check the level of the first three blocks from side to side and front to back. If necessary, tap the blocks into position with the end of the trowel handle. Trim away any excess mortar with the trowel.

3 **BUILD UP THE LEAD.** Lay the next few courses, with leads alternating half and full corner blocks at the end of each course. Check your work often to make sure the lead is both plumb and level.

BUILDING CORNER LEADS

1 **START WITH A FULL CORNER BLOCK.** Lay a 1½-inch-thick mortar bed along the first three blocks of each arm. Put a full corner block on the bed. Mortar the ears and place two stretcher blocks along each arm.

2 **LAY THE SECOND AND THIRD COURSES.** Build up the lead by laying a full corner block so it's at 90 degrees to the one below it. Lay stretchers until you reach the end of the lead. Repeat for subsequent courses. As you go, check that the lead is plumb and level from front to back and side to side.

3 **CHECK THE SPACING WITH A STRAIGHTEDGE** laid diagonally across the blocks at each end of the lead, as shown. If gaps occur between any of the blocks and the level, tap the errant block into place with the end of the trowel handle.

BUILDING BETWEEN LEADS

1 **STRETCH A GUIDE LINE.** Attach mason's blocks to the leads and run a mason's line level with the first course of blocks between them. Lay a mortar bed 1½ inches thick on the footing and start the first course, working from each lead to the center.

2 **LAY THE CENTER BLOCK.** Lay the first course until you reach the center of the wall. Test-fit the last block, called a closure. If you've followed the marks you made on the footing, the closure block should fit without trimming. Mortar the block and its neighbors, then set it in place.

3 **REPOSITION THE LINE.** Move the mason's blocks and line up to the top of the next course. Apply mortar to the top of the blocks in the first course. Mortar the ears and lay the second course, working from the leads inward.

Building a concrete block wall

BUILDING BETWEEN LEADS *(continued)*

4 **TOOL THE JOINTS.** Scrape off excess mortar from the joints as you go. Test the mortar every so often by pressing it with your thumb. When the mortar is firm enough to hold a thumbprint, shape the joints by running a concave jointer across them.

5 **CHECK YOUR PROGRESS.** Use a level and your story pole to make sure each course is aligned, level, and plumb. Tap blocks into position with the end of the trowel handle.

WORK SMARTER

FIBERGLASS TO THE RESCUE
Mortar has been used for decades to join concrete blocks despite the fact that it's time-consuming to butter the blocks and lay down a bed of mortar for each course. A faster alternative is to apply a commercially made surface-reinforced bonding cement. Lay the blocks with no mortar between them, then cover the wall with a ⅛-inch-thick layer of the cement and your wall is done.

IF YOU'RE LAYING CAP BLOCKS, apply a 1½-inch-thick mortar bed on the top edges of the last course of blocks. Mortar the ends of the cap blocks and set them in place. Tap them into position, leaving a ⅜-inch-thick mortar line. Make sure the caps are level and centered on the wall.

FOR A MORTAR CAP, lay wire mesh into the mortar before laying the last course of blocks. Lay the blocks, then fill the gaps between the webs with mortar to the top of the blocks. Level the mortar.

Designer Tip

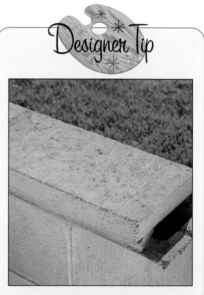

FINISHING TOUCHES
You can top off your wall with any style block you like. Ask to see the entire line at the store and get your favorite even if it requires a special order.

Stuccoing a block wall

Stucco—a mixture of portland cement, hydrated lime, sand, and water—is a durable covering for exterior walls. Simply put, it's outdoor plaster. One of the advantages of stucco is that you can create different textures (page 103) while masking minor imperfections in the wall. You also can add color to it or buy a pretinted mix.

Stucco goes on block walls in two coats: a scratch coat and a finish coat. The scratch coat is mixed to stick to the wall and gets its name because you scratch the surface when it's wet so the finish coat sticks better. For brick walls, (which require metal lathe) you'll apply three coats: scratch, brown, and finish to guarantee that the stucco will adhere solidly to the wall.

If you're building a block wall that you plan to stucco, cut the mortar joints flush with a trowel as you build the wall. If the wall already exists, clean it with soap or detergent and water before applying stucco.

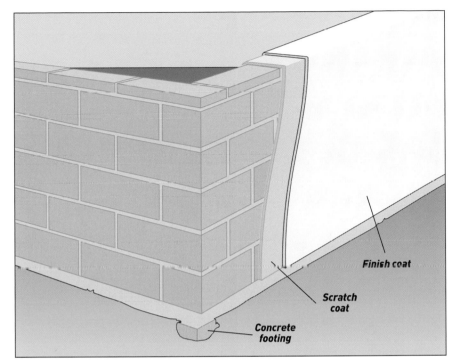

TWO LAYERS OF STUCCO ARE APPLIED TO WALLS MADE OF CONCRETE BLOCKS: a scratch coat and a finish coat. (Three coats—scratch, brown, and finish are applied to brick walls.) If you want a colored wall, buy bags of pretinted mix so the color varies as little as possible from batch to batch.

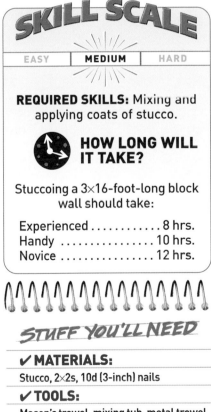

SKILL SCALE

EASY	MEDIUM	HARD

REQUIRED SKILLS: Mixing and applying coats of stucco.

HOW LONG WILL IT TAKE?

Stuccoing a 3×16-foot-long block wall should take:

Experienced . . . . 8 hrs.
Handy . . . . 10 hrs.
Novice . . . . 12 hrs.

STUFF YOU'LL NEED

✔ **MATERIALS:**

Stucco, 2×2s, 10d (3-inch) nails

✔ **TOOLS:**

Mason's trowel, mixing tub, metal trowel, texturing trowel, broom or brush, safety glasses, work gloves

Making stucco

It's easiest to make stucco from pre-mixed bags so do it whenever you can. But you also can prepare your own mixture. The basic ingredients are portland cement, lime, and sand. The only difference between the coats is the proportions.

Scratch Coat
1 part portland cement
1 part hydrated lime
2½ to 4 parts sand

Brown Coat
(for brick walls only)
1 part portland cement
1 part hydrated lime
3½ to 5 parts sand (1 part more than scratch coat)

Finish Coat
1 part portland cement
1 part hydrated lime
1½ to 3 parts sand (1 part less than scratch coat)

TO MIX STUCCO, mix the dry ingredients, then add water until the mixture is a uniform color and the consistency of a thick paste. Make only as much stucco at one time as you can apply in an hour or so. If the stucco starts to stiffen, you can retemper it once—but no more—by adding water and mixing.

Stuccoing a block wall (continued)

APPLYING A SCRATCH COAT

1 **APPLY A SCRATCH COAT OF STUCCO** ⅜ inch thick onto the wall with a mason's trowel. Spread the stucco with smooth strokes of the trowel, angling the blade slightly to keep it from catching.

2 **SCRATCH GROOVES INTO THE STUCCO.** Use a homemade tool called a scarifier (a 2×2 with 10d [3-inch] nails hammered through it at 1-inch intervals). The grooves provide grip for the next coat. Let the stucco cure for two days, misting it occasionally with a fine spray of water to prevent it from cracking.

Applying stucco to brick

A brick wall needs metal lath to hold the stucco and three coats of stucco. Fasten standard lath to the wall with self-furring nails. Such nails hold the lath a little bit out from the wall, allowing the stucco to squeeze through and lock itself in place. (You can also get self-furring lath and install it with standard masonry nails.) Whichever lath you use, apply three coats of stucco: scratch, brown, and finish.

APPLYING A FINISH COAT

1 **APPLY THE FINISH COAT.** Mix a batch of stucco for a finish coat and spread a ¼-inch layer uniformly over the scratch coat. Apply the stucco in smooth back-and-forth strokes, holding the blade of the trowel at a slight angle.

2 **SMOOTH OUT THE SURFACE.** Smooth the stucco with a metal trowel. Make broad, sweeping passes and apply even pressure, lifting the lead of the blade slightly to avoid catching an edge.

3 **SMOOTH OUT THE CORNERS.** To make crisp corners, hold a scrap board gently against one surface and sweep the trowel along the other. Texture the finish coat (opposite), if desired. Mist the wall lightly with water every few hours to prevent it from cracking while it cures.

TEXTURING A FINISH COAT

Texturing stucco takes a little practice—not to mention patience—in order to achieve the right effect consistently. Begin to texture the finish coat as soon as it begins to set.

Don't be afraid to experiment. It might take a combination of techniques to get the texture you like best.

Your texturing technique need not be complicated. You can create a coarse, uniform texture simply by making passes with a wood float. For a rougher finish, dab the stucco with a piece of carpeting that has a thick pile. Or don't texture the stucco at all—the surface created by a metal trowel is a finish coat in itself.

Textured or not, the stucco needs a few days to cure. To keep it from drying out too quickly and cracking, mist it lightly with water every few hours.

STIPPLE THE FINISH by pressing the tips of a stiff brush into the stucco without sweeping or overlapping passes. Use a wet rag to wipe off stucco that builds up on the bristles.

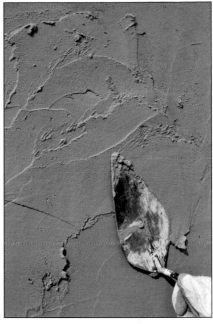

MAKE AN ENGLISH-COTTAGE TEXTURE by dabbing small amounts of stucco onto the finish coat with a round-nose trowel. Hold the trowel at an angle and twist it slightly to create ridges in the stucco.

Designer Tip

ADD SOME COLOR TO YOUR LIFE

Want something a little more exciting than white, white, and white? Use a tinted stucco. You can buy tints and make the color yourself, but it can be hard to get a uniform color. For best results, buy a premixed tinted stucco. You'll find many colors available, and the results will be more consistent than what you'd get by tinting the stucco yourself.

FOR A MARBLED FINISH, jab the smooth finish coat with a stiff brush. When the mortar begins to set, smooth out the high spots with a metal trowel, moving the tool back and forth in even strokes.

SPATTER THE FINISH by loading a paintbrush with stucco and striking it against a wood block. For a more uniform texture, repeat the process in an hour.

Maintaining walls

Nothing lasts forever, not even a well-made wall. Eventually the time will come to repair what you've built. The next few pages show you how to deal with some of the most common problems—from washing off the white, powdery substance called efflorescence to repairing joints and replacing cracked bricks, stones, or blocks. Most repairs are minor, some are labor-intensive, and some involve using muriatic acid. Whatever you're doing, wear work gloves and safety glasses to protect yourself.

SKILL SCALE

EASY	MEDIUM	HARD

REQUIRED SKILLS:
Basic masonry.

HOW LONG WILL IT TAKE?

Experienced . . . . 2 hrs.
Handy . . . . 4 hrs.
Novice . . . . 6 hrs.

VARIABLES: Repair time depends on extent of damage.

STUFF YOU'LL NEED

✔ **MATERIALS:**
Muriatic acid, mortar, brick, stone, concrete block, stucco

✔ **TOOLS:**
Garden hose, scrub brush, 3-pound sledgehammer, plugging chisel, cold chisel, screwdriver, brick chisel, mortar hook, mixing tub, mason's trowel, pointing trowel, metal trowel, concave jointer, burlap, texturing trowel or brush, safety glasses, work gloves

REPAIRING EFFLORESCENCE

1 WASH THE WALL. To wash off white, powdery mineral deposits (efflorescence), first soak the wall with a garden hose. Then scrub the surface with a stiff fiber brush and rinse.

To avoid dangerous splashes, pour acid into water. Never pour water into acid.

2 SCRUB WITH MURIATIC ACID. For efflorescence that recurs on brick or stone, scrub the surface with a solution of 1 part muriatic acid and 12 parts water. Work carefully: Muriatic acid is extremely strong. Rinse with water. On concrete blocks, use only water; acid can damage them.

REPAIRING MORTAR JOINTS

1 BREAK UP DAMAGED MORTAR. Chip away the damaged mortar with a plugging chisel and a 3-pound sledgehammer.

2 REMOVE THE RESIDUE. Rake loose mortar out of the joints with an old screwdriver. Wash out the joints with water from a garden hose.

3 **MIX THE MORTAR.** Add water a little at a time to the dry ingredients until the mortar reaches an oatmeal-like consistency that holds its shape when it's furrowed.

4 **APPLY MORTAR.** Hose the joints with water again so the bricks don't suck all the water from the mortar. Pack the joints with mortar. Scrape off excess mortar with the blade of the trowel.

5 **TOOL THE MORTAR.** Run a concave jointer over the mortar when it becomes firm enough to hold a thumbprint. Use the type and size of jointer originally used for the rest of the wall so the repair blends in well. Remove excess mortar by rubbing it with dry burlap before it dries.

REPLACING A BRICK

1 **REMOVE THE MORTAR.** Knock out the mortar around the damaged brick with a plugging chisel.

2 **REMOVE THE BRICK.** Pry out the damaged brick with a cold chisel, chipping it into pieces as necessary. Chip off remaining mortar and brush away all fragments. Flush the cavity with a spray of water.

3 **MIX MORTAR.** Mix mortar in a mixing tub with a trowel. Add water slowly, mixing well until the mortar is the proper consistency—it should cling to an inverted trowel.

LANDSCAPING WALLS

Maintaining walls

REPLACING A BRICK (continued)

4 **APPLY MORTAR.** Soak the cavity with water, then spread mortar onto the cavity's bottom and sides. Apply mortar to the top of a replacement brick.

5 **PUT THE BRICK IN PLACE.** Slide the brick into the cavity. Tap the brick gently with the end of the trowel handle until it's flush with the rest of the wall. Scrape off excess mortar.

6 **SHAPE THE JOINT.** Once the mortar is firm enough to hold a thumbprint, shape the joints with the type and size of jointer used on the original bricks so the repair blends in well. When the excess mortar is crumbly, rub it with dry burlap to remove it.

REPLACING A STONE

1 **REMOVE THE MORTAR.** Replace a mortared stone if it is badly cracked or crumbling. Chip away the mortar around the stone with a cold chisel and a 3-pound sledgehammer. Clear out particles of mortar with a mortar hook.

2 **REMOVE THE STONE.** Pry the damaged stone out of the wall, brush away remaining fragments, and flush the cavity with water. Butter the edges of the cavity and the new stone with mortar, then set the stone in place.

3 **RAKE THE JOINTS.** Once the mortar is firm enough to hold a thumbprint, scrape or rake out the joints to a depth of about ½ inch. Work with a concave jointer, as shown, or a piece of wood.

REPAIRING STUCCO

1 **CHIP AWAY THE DAMAGE.** A repair will be visible no matter how well it's done, so leave minor blemishes alone. With a cold chisel and a 3-pound sledgehammer, chip away the damaged stucco down to the wall behind it.

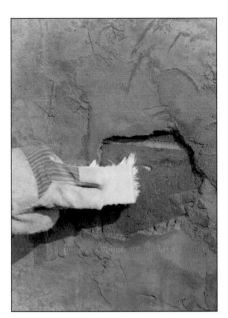

2 **CLEAN THE AREA.** Hose down the exposed wall and surrounding area with water and scrub it clean to remove loose masonry particles.

3 **MIX STUCCO PATCH.** Mix a batch of premixed stucco patching compound following the instructions on the bag. Add water slowly and blend the ingredients until the mix is thick enough to cling to the trowel.

4 **APPLY THE PATCH.** Fill the cavity with the premixed stucco patch. Fill the damaged area within ¼ inch of the adjacent surfaces. Smooth the patch with a metal trowel.

5 **SCRATCH THE SURFACE.** Make a tool called a scarifier: Drive 10d (3-inch) nails at 1-inch intervals through a length of 2×2. Use it to scratch grooves into the patched surface, making a rough area for the finish coat of stucco to grip.

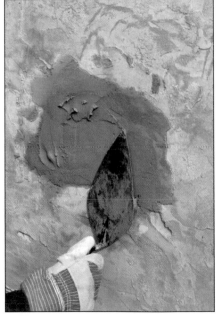

6 **APPLY THE FINISH COAT.** Keep the first, or scratch, coat moist for a couple of days while it cures. Then apply a finish coat of stucco patch and texture it to match the rest of the surface.

SHEDS

Lawn mowers, bicycles, snowblowers, basketballs, shovels, rakes, hoes, and hoses… You know you're an adult when you have more stuff than you have room for. Solving the problem may be as easy as building a shed.

But how easy is it? Building one from scratch can be an undertaking. The materials list is extensive, and the framing is as complicated as framing a garage or even a house. Unless, of course, you buy a kit.

Kit manufacturers have made shed building much easier. To begin with, you have all the pieces and hardware you need. All of the pieces are cut to the right length, and the ends are cut at the right angles. Complicated assemblies are color-coded so that Tab A fits in Slot B as it's supposed to. Best of all,

you can call a customer support number if things go wrong.

Until recently, sheds were made of either metal or wood. The differences between the two were practical as well as aesthetic. Wood rotted and metal rusted; metal came prepainted, wood didn't; wood required nails, metal required screws. Recently, however, vinyl entered the scene. It doesn't rot or rust, needs no painting, and requires no nails and only a few screws.

The choice between materials is a matter of taste, budget, and application. You may want a wood shed in the backyard to match the house, a vinyl shed beside the cottage to avoid rust, and a metal shed any number of places because it's economical and easy to build.

CHAPTER 4

Sheds tool kit 110

Materials 111

Laying out a shed 112

Installing a skid foundation 114

Installing concrete footings with
    fiber forms 115

Constructing a concrete slab foundation .. 117

Building a subfloor 121

Building a wood shed 123

Roofing a shed 131

Applying trim, hardware, and paint 133

Installing a shed window 135

Building a vinyl shed 137

Building a metal shed 144

Building a shed ramp 150

REAL-WORLD SITUATIONS

A SHED NEEDS SOMEWHERE TO SIT

Whether you choose a vinyl, metal, or wood shed, it will need a place to sit. This seat can be as simple as a couple of beams on some gravel or as finished as a concrete slab, often called a pad.

Of all the sheds, vinyl gives you the least as far as flooring options go. It is designed to sit only on a concrete slab. You screw a metal channel into the slab and mount the panels in the channel.

Metal sheds sit on a wood platform or a concrete slab. You can also buy a "foundation" kit, a metal grid that houses sheets of plywood. It requires that you dig up the sod, create a flat surface, and set the plywood and metal grid on it. (Though the frame holds the plywood slightly off the ground, use a pressure-treated ply.) Because you walk on the foundation and because it requires further anchoring, a kit is really more floor than foundation. In fact, if you buy a foundation kit, you should also buy an anchor kit, which contains cables and augers that you twist to seat in the ground.

Manufacturers of wood sheds make floor kits that are designed to fit perfectly inside the shed. Because they truly are floors, they'll need a foundation. The simplest foundation is a series of beams set and leveled on the ground. The beams act as both foundation and floor joists, reinforcing a floor that is otherwise pretty flexible.

The foundation is a good deal more permanent if you put the beams on footings that begin below the frost line and extend at least 6 inches above grade. Cylindrical forms for concrete give you a nice, neat footing that is easy to smooth and level.

A good concrete slab may outlast your shed. Slabs are durable and convenient. Getting the lawn mower off a floor at or slightly above ground level is a lot easier than pulling the lawn mower from a shed that's 8 to 12 inches off the ground. All good things come with a price, however: Of all the foundations, concrete slabs are the most labor-intensive.

SHEDS

SHEDS TOOL KIT

3-POUND SLEDGEHAMMER

CONTROL JOINTER

HAMMER

MASONRY BITS

RUBBER MALLET

STEPLADDER

BROOM

CROWBAR

HANDSAW

PENCIL/MARKER

SAFETY GLASSES

TAMPER

BULL FLOAT

DRILL, BITS, AND DRIVER

LEVELS

PLANE

SCREWDRIVERS

TAPE MEASURE

CAULK GUN

DUST MASK

LINE LEVEL

PLIERS

SHOVEL

UTILITY KNIFE

CIRCULAR SAW

EDGER

MASON'S LINE

PLUMB BOB

SPADE

WHEELBARROW

COMBINATION SQUARE

FRAMING SQUARE

MASON'S TROWEL

POWDERED CHALK

SOCKET WRENCHES

WORK GLOVES

Materials

FOUNDATIONS

A shed foundation is made of **Ⓐ beams, Ⓑ concrete footings** cast in a cylindrical form, or a poured concrete pad. If you make the foundation out of concrete, reinforce it with **6×6-10/10 wire mesh** (a 6"×6" mesh made of 10-gauge wire).

FOUNDATION AND FLOOR KITS

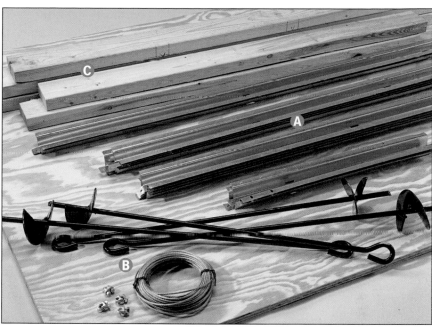

Kit manufacturers make kits that serve as either a foundation or floor in their sheds. The kits are sold separately from the sheds. **Ⓐ Metal shed foundation kits** are pieces of metal that you assemble into a grid. You'll have to buy the plywood separately that fits in the grid. **Ⓑ A separate metal shed foundation kit** is called an anchor and has guy wires and augers that you twist into the ground. **Ⓒ Wooden floor kits** contain studs and plywood that are precut to give you the right size floor.

SHED KITS

You can buy kits for three different kinds of sheds: **Ⓐ metal, Ⓑ vinyl,** and **Ⓒ wood.** Metal sheds get their strength from ribs in the siding and a frame that runs around the top, bottom, and sides of the shed. Thick walls with interior ribs give vinyl sheds their strength. Wood sheds rely on stud walls and siding.

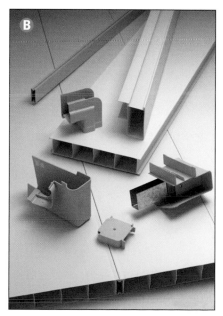

Laying out a shed

Laying out a shed is the first part of building a shed, but before that, you need to plan. Does your municipality require you to set the shed back from the property line? Does it require a building permit? Is your site easy to access? Does it use space wisely? Think it through. Once your shed is up, you won't want to move it by even a few inches.

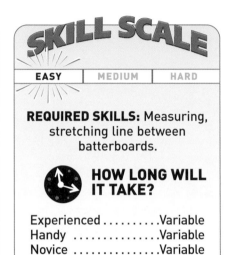

SKILL SCALE

EASY	MEDIUM	HARD

REQUIRED SKILLS: Measuring, stretching line between batterboards.

HOW LONG WILL IT TAKE?

Experienced . . . . Variable
Handy . . . . Variable
Novice . . . . Variable

VARIABLES: Time required to lay out a shed depends on size and weather conditions.

STUFF YOU'LL NEED

✔ **MATERIALS:**
2×4s, 2×2s, 10d (3-inch) nails, landscape fabric, ¾-inch gravel, perforated plastic drainpipe

✔ **TOOLS:**
Tape measure, circular saw, hammer, 3-pound sledgehammer, mason's line, line level, plumb bob, powdered chalk, shovel, tamper, 4-foot level, safety glasses, work gloves

1 **BUILD BATTERBOARDS.** Build four pairs of batterboards with 2×4 stakes and crosspieces that are about 2 feet long. Nail the crosspieces a few inches below the top of the stakes with 10d (3-inch) common nails.

2 **LAY OUT THE FIRST WALL.** Put batterboards about 2 feet past the ends of one of the walls. Tie mason's line between the batterboards along the path of the wall. Level the line with a line level.

3 **LAY OUT THE SECOND WALL.** Lay out the next wall at a 90-degree angle to the first with batterboards and a level mason's line. Square the corner using the 3-4-5 triangle method, adjusting the lines until points 3 feet and 4 feet from the intersection are exactly 5 feet apart.

4 **LAY OUT THE REMAINING WALLS.** Drive in the remaining batterboards and stretch lines to mark the locations of the third and fourth walls. Make sure you square the third wall with the second wall and the fourth wall with either the first or third.

5 **DOUBLE-CHECK FOR SQUARE.** Measure diagonally between the corners. If the measurements are equal, the layout is square. If not, recheck all the corners using the 3-4-5 triangle method and make the necessary adjustments.

6 **MARK THE SHED'S CORNERS ON THE GROUND.** Use a plumb bob and powdered chalk to mark the ground where the lines cross. To make a more permanent mark, drive a landscape spike through a small piece of paper.

7 **USING THE MASON'S LINES AS GUIDES,** mark the shed's edges on the ground with powdered chalk, sand, or fluorescent layout paint. Mark where the lines meet the batterboards and remove the lines until you need them again during construction.

LAYING DRAINPIPE

If you're building a shed on a site that drains poorly, install perforated plastic drainpipe to prevent water from pooling around the foundation. Slope the drainpipe 1 inch every 4 feet. For a 6×8-foot shed on skids or piers, lay the drainpipe across the center of the site. For a shed that develops a drainage problem after it has been built, install drainpipe around the perimeter if the shed sits on a concrete slab.

TOOL TIP

SLOPE CHECKER
To check for a slope of 1 inch over a distance of 4 feet, slip a 1-inch spacer under one end of a 4-foot level and set both on a straight 2×4. The slope is correct when the level's bubble is centered.

1 **DIG A TRENCH.** Start it at a depth of 6 to 8 inches at the top of the run and drop 1 inch every 4 feet. Continue the trench to a point where the pipe can exit the ground. Line the trench with landscape fabric, leaving enough overlap to fold it over the top.

2 **ADD GRAVEL.** Add 2 to 3 inches of gravel to the trench and tamp firmly. Lay the drainpipe and add or remove gravel until it slopes 1 inch every 4 feet. Cover the pipe with 2 to 3 inches of gravel, then fold the landscape fabric over it. Fill the trench with soil and tamp firmly.

Installing a skid foundation

The fastest way to lay a skid foundation for your shed is to set 4×6 or larger timbers on patio pavers that are set in a gravel bed. To keep the timbers from rotting, use pressure-treated wood that's rated for ground contact. If you like, bevel the ends of the timber to dress up the skids.

Once all materials are in place, shim between the pavers and the skids to level the foundation.

For frost-free ground that drains well, dig trenches 4 to 6 inches deep, fill them with gravel, and rest the timbers on the gravel.

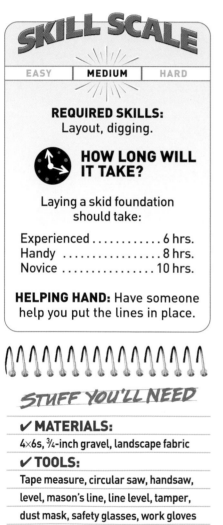

SKILL SCALE

EASY	**MEDIUM**	HARD

REQUIRED SKILLS:
Layout, digging.

HOW LONG WILL IT TAKE?

Laying a skid foundation should take:

Experienced . . . . 6 hrs.
Handy . . . . 8 hrs.
Novice . . . . 10 hrs.

HELPING HAND: Have someone help you put the lines in place.

STUFF YOU'LL NEED

✔ **MATERIALS:**
4×6s, ¾-inch gravel, landscape fabric

✔ **TOOLS:**
Tape measure, circular saw, handsaw, level, mason's line, line level, tamper, dust mask, safety glasses, work gloves

Pressure treatment doesn't get to the center of timbers, so treat cut ends with a preservative.

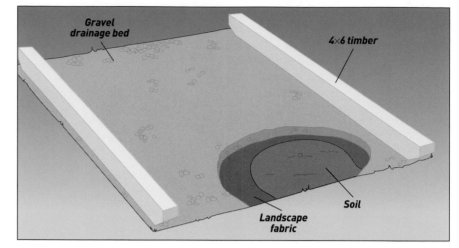

Gravel drainage bed
4×6 timber
Soil
Landscape fabric

YOUR SHED CAN SIT ON 4×6 OR LARGER PRESSURE-TREATED TIMBERS placed parallel to each other and no more than 8 feet apart on center. To provide drainage, excavate the entire site to a depth of 3 to 4 inches, lay landscape fabric, and fill to ground level with gravel. Tamp the gravel to create a firm surface and space a line of patio stones to support the skids. Level the skids with each other and from end to end and side to side.

INSTALLING SKIDS

1 **LAY A GRAVEL BED AND PATIO STONES.** Remove the grass and dig out an area 3 to 4 inches deep underneath your shed. Fill the excavation with gravel and tamp firmly to create a hard surface. For larger sheds, use a power tamper. Lay patio stones to support the timbers, spacing them 4 feet on center.

2 **LAY OUT AND LEVEL THE SKIDS.** Position and align the skids using mason's line and batterboards. Shim between the pavers and skids to level one of the skids. Put a straight 2×4 across the skids and level them with each other at one end of the shed. Shim the second skid to level it along its length.

Wear safety glasses and a dust mask when cutting pressure-treated timbers.

Installing concrete footings with fiber forms

Concrete footings provide a more stable foundation than skids. The footings support 4×6 pressure-treated timbers which are fastened to them with a metal bracket. The beams, in turn, support the shed. Lay out the shed, dig the site to a depth of 3 to 4 inches, and dig holes 10 inches below the frost line for footings. Line the holes with leveled, round fiber forms, and add about 4 inches of gravel before you pour in the concrete. Put bolts for the hardware in the concrete while it is still wet. Once the concrete cures add achoring brackets, lay down landscape fabric and a gravel drainage bed, then install the beams.

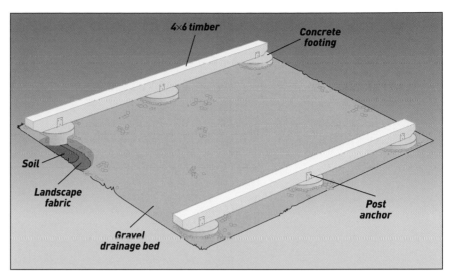

FOOTINGS EXTEND 10 INCHES BELOW THE FROST LINE and their tops protrude at least 6 inches above grade. Space the beams 8 feet apart and support them with footings spaced 4 feet apart on center. Attach to 4×6 beams with concrete anchors.

SKILL SCALE

EASY	MEDIUM	HARD

REQUIRED SKILLS: Layout, digging, pouring concrete.

HOW LONG WILL IT TAKE?

Experienced . . . . .Variable
Handy . . . . Variable
Novice . . . . Variable

HELPING HAND: Have someone help you lift and place the beams.

STUFF YOU'LL NEED

✔ **MATERIALS:**

2×2s, 2×4s, 4×6s, 10d (3-inch duplex nails, fiber concrete forms, J-bolts and anchoring brackets, ¾-inch gravel, landscape fabric

✔ **TOOLS:**

Shovel, line level, mason's line, tape measure, posthole digger, plumb bob, powdered chalk, hammer, level, safety glasses, work gloves

POURING FIBER FOOTINGS

1 **LAY OUT AND DIG FOR THE SHED.** Lay out the shed and centers of the beams with batterboards and mason's line. Mark the ground with chalk about 1 foot outside the outline of the shed. Remove the lines and dig along the chalk line and remove sod and 3 to 4 inches of soil in the entire area.

2 **DIG FOR THE FOOTINGS.** Reattach the lines for the beams to the batterboards and mark them every 4 feet with pieces of tape. Transfer the marks to the ground and dig a hole large enough to hold a concrete tube form. Dig 10 inches below the frost line and shovel 4 inches of gravel into the holes for drainage. Tamp with the end of a 2×4.

Installing concrete footings with fiber forms

POURING FIBER FOOTINGS *(continued)*

3 **PUT FORMS IN THE HOLES.** Build a triangular frame like the one shown and nail it to a tube form from inside the tube. Seat the forms over the holes. Measure to make sure each one is exactly the same distance below the layout lines (6 inches is the minimum).

4 **LEVEL THE FORMS.** Check each form for level. Shim underneath the frame to correct any problems. Double-check that each form is still at the right height.

5 **POUR CONCRETE.** Mix concrete and shovel it into the forms and holes. Work the shovel up and down in the concrete to help eliminate air pockets. Level the concrete to the top of the forms by pulling a 2×4 across the surface.

6 **SET J-BOLTS IN THE FOOTINGS.** Drop a plumb bob at each piece of tape and push a J-bolt into the wet concrete. When the concrete dries, you'll use the bolt to attach the anchoring bracket. When the concrete is cured cut away the forms above ground level.

7 **INSTALL THE ANCHORING BRACKET.** Put anchoring brackets (made to hold a 4×6) over the J-bolts and align them so you can put the beams in them. Tighten the nuts over the bolts.

8 **LEVEL THE BEAMS.** Place beams into the anchors on the footings. Level the beams from end to end and side to side and with each other by slipping shims under them as needed. Nail the beams to the anchors. Cover the excavation with landscape fabric to prevent weeds, and fill with gravel for drainage.

Constructing a concrete slab foundation

Though it isn't strictly necessary, a concrete slab makes the best foundation for your shed. Exactly how you build it varies. If your soil is firm (such as clay), remove the grass and pour the slab on grade. If your soil is unstable, excavate and pour a gravel bed, compact it, and build the slab on top. A heavy-duty shed may require a footing below the slab as shown here.

You will need a building permit for your shed. Talk to your local building inspector or zoning official to learn the local requirements for a foundation, including the need for a footing.

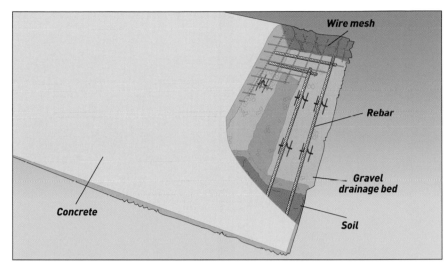

Wire mesh

Rebar

Concrete

Gravel drainage bed

Soil

SKILL SCALE

| EASY | **MEDIUM** | HARD |

REQUIRED SKILLS: Measuring, layout, digging.

HOW LONG WILL IT TAKE?

Excavating and pouring a foundation should take about:

Experienced . . . . 18 hrs.
Handy . . . . 24 hrs.
Novice . . . . 30 hrs.

STUFF YOU'LL NEED

✔ MATERIALS:

2×2s, 2×4s, 2×8s, 10d (3-inch) duplex nails, ¾-inch gravel, #4 (½-inch) rebar, tie wire, 6×6 10/10 wire mesh, wire supports (chairs), concrete, 6-mil poly, concrete release agent or vegetable oil, J-bolts

✔ TOOLS:

Hammer, tape measure, mason's line, powdered chalk, shovel, tamper, 6-pound sledgehammer, power tamper, paintbrush, wheelbarrow, bull float or darby, mason's trowel, broom, concrete edger, control jointer, knee pads, safety glasses, work gloves

BUILD A CONCRETE-SLAB FOUNDATION (CALLED A PAD) THE APPROPRIATE SIZE FOR YOUR SHED AT GRADE LEVEL on a 4- to 6-inch-thick gravel drainage bed. Make the slab a minimum of 4 inches thick and the same amount above grade. Codes and manufacturer's instructions often require footings as part of the slab to stabilize it. Footings are edges typically 12 inches deep, 8 inches wide at the bottom, and 18 inches wide at the top. Reinforce the footings at the top and bottom with continuous runs of rebar. Install wire mesh with wire supports (chairs) to reinforce the slab.

EXCAVATING AND BUILDING FORMS

1 **LAY OUT THE SHED.** Put batterboards 3 feet outside each corner, stretch mason's line, and square up the lines. (For more on layout see "Laying Out a Shed," pages 112–113.) Sprinkle flour or powdered chalk along the lines to mark the layout on the ground. Remove the mason's line but not the batterboards.

2 **EXCAVATE FOR THE SLAB AND FOOTINGS.** Dig out an area that extends 6 inches beyond the foundation on all sides. Remove the sod, then dig 4 inches deeper for the gravel bed. (If a footing is required, dig out a footing the size and depth required by code.)

Constructing a concrete slab foundation

EXCAVATING AND BUILDING FORMS (continued)

SHEDS

Footing trench

3 **LAY A GRAVEL BED.** Pour 2 inches of gravel in the footings, dampen with water to help compact it, then compact with a hand tamper. Repeat. Lay about 2 inches of gravel in the rest of the excavation. Dampen and compact with a power tamper. (Rent, don't buy.) Add, dampen, and compact gravel until the surface is at ground level.

4 **BUILD THE FORMS.** Nail together a 2×4 box that has an inside dimension the size of the pad. Restring the layout lines. Align the box with the lines and square it by adjusting until the diagonal distances are equal. Use a level to make sure the form doesn't slope.

5 **BRACE THE FORMS.** Drive 2×6 stakes at the corners and nail them in place with duplex nails. Drive and nail additional stakes every 2 to 3 feet. For extra support, add kickers made with 2×2s and 2×4s.

6 **REINFORCE THE FOOTING.** Put two runs of #4 rebar about 4 inches apart around the trench and support them with commercially sold wire frames called chairs. Tie the rebar to the chairs with tie wire. Overlap the ends of rebar at joints and corners and wire them together.

7 **REINFORCE THE PAD.** Lay down 6×6-10/10 wire mesh to reinforce the slab, keeping it 1½ inches or so from the edges. Prop the mesh on chairs so it runs through the middle of the form. Overlap sections by 4 to 6 inches and wire them together.

Installing a plastic vapor barrier

In poor drainage areas, lay a vapor barrier of 6-mil plastic on the gravel drainage bed to keep moisture from working its way into the concrete. Overlap strips of plastic by at least 12 inches, being careful to avoid tears and punctures. If the vapor barrier isn't continuous, the slab may curl upward or develop high spots.

BUYER'S GUIDE

Rebar is sold by the number. #2 rebar is ⅜ inch thick; #3 is ⅜ inch thick, and #4, the most common, is ½ inch thick.

Mesh is sold by size and wire gauge: 6×610/10 has 6-inch squares, all sides of which are made of 10-gauge wire.

8 **BRUSH ON A RELEASE AGENT.** Apply a commercial release agent or vegetable oil to the forms so concrete won't bond to them. Though once a popular substitute for a release agent, motor oil leaches into the soil and causes damage. Use a release agent instead.

9 **HANG TWO RUNS OF REBAR AT THE TOP OF THE TRENCH** about 2 inches below the wire mesh. Suspend the rebar from the mesh with wire and tie the ends at joints and corners so the runs are continuous.

SHEDS

POURING AND FINISHING CONCRETE

1 **POUR THE CONCRETE.** Build a sturdy ramp over the form so the wheelbarrow won't move the forms. Start in a corner and dump each load of concrete against the one before it. If you spread the concrete too much with a shovel or rake, the ingredients separate.

2 **REMOVE THE AIR POCKETS.** Work a shovel or rake slowly up and down the concrete to rid it of air pockets. Tap the outside of the forms with a hammer so the edges of the concrete don't become honeycombed by trapped air.

3 **LEVEL THE TOP.** Enlist a helper to level the concrete with the top of the forms using a 2×4 as a screed. Rest the screed on the forms and pull it forward with a side-to-side sawing motion. Make a second pass at 90 degrees to the first.

Wear long sleeves, safety glasses, and gloves to protect yourself from contact with concrete.

Constructing a concrete slab foundation

POURING AND FINISHING CONCRETE (continued)

4 **FLOAT THE SURFACE.** Smooth the surface with a bull float if the slab is large, moving it in broad, sweeping arcs with a slightly side-to-side sawing motion. Float with a darby if the slab is small and easy to work from the edges. Stop floating when water appears on the surface.

5 **BROOM THE SURFACE.** Push a broom made for concrete work across the surface. The resulting surface will be nonslip, but brooming will not cover any flaws, so be sure to use a float or darby first, as described in Step 4.

6 **SEPARATE THE PAD AND FORMS.** With a trowel, cut carefully along the inside edges of the forms to separate the concrete from them. This makes the forms easier to remove after the concrete cures.

Anchoring the shed

7 **ROUND OVER THE EDGES.** If you leave the edges square, they will chip. Round them over with a tool called an edger, guiding it along between the form and the pad.

8 **CUT CONTROL JOINTS EVERY 4 FEET.** If your pad is more than 8 feet long in any direction, cut control joints with a control jointer to help prevent cracking. Get a jointer that will cut one-quarter of the way through the pad. Put a 2× across the pad, resting it on the forms. Guide the control jointer against the 2× to cut the joint. Cover the slab with 6-mil poly that does not touch the concrete until the slab has cured.

Put ½-inch J-bolts into the concrete before it sets so you can attach the shed to the pad later. Sink the bolts 1¾ inches from the edges, leaving 2½ to 3 inches of the threads exposed. The bolts will pass through the midpoint of the shed's 2×4 soleplates that are set flush with the slab edges. Starting 6 to 8 inches from a corner, space the bolts about 4 feet apart.

Building a subfloor

Most shed kits don't come with a floor, so you have to decide what you want and build it yourself. The subfloor that is shown here sits on wood skids, but the assembly on beams and piers is identical.

If you're building on a concrete slab, a subfloor is optional: The concrete is its own subfloor. If you choose to build a subfloor over a concrete pad, anchor it to the slab with angle irons, lag screws, and anchor shields.

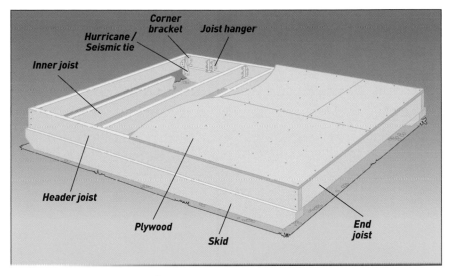

BUILD A SUBFLOOR MADE OF ¾-INCH EXTERIOR-GRADE PLYWOOD on a frame of pressure-treated 2×6s. Strengthen the corners with corner brackets and anchor them to the foundation—in this example, wood skids—with hurricane/seismic ties. Hang the inner joists with joist hangers at 16-inch intervals. Place the plywood so joints are staggered and fall at the center of joists.

EASY	**MEDIUM**	HARD

REQUIRED SKILLS: Building a subfloor requires basic carpentry skills.

 HOW LONG WILL IT TAKE?

Building a subfloor for an 8×10-foot shed should take about:

Experienced . . . . 8 hrs.
Handy . . . . 12 hrs.
Novice . . . . 16 hrs.

STUFF YOU'LL NEED

✔ MATERIALS:
2×6s, 8d (2½-inch) nails or #8 2½-inch deck screws, 10d (3-inch) nails, corner brackets, hurricane/seismic ties, joist hangers, ¾-inch exterior-grade plywood

✔ TOOLS:
Tape measure, circular saw, clamps, hammer, combination square, cordless drill and bits, safety glasses, work gloves

Cut end joists 3 inches shorter than the frame dimension to account for the thickness of header joists.

FRAMING A SUBFLOOR

1 CUT THE JOISTS. Cut 2×6s to make the four sides of the platform. They're called end and header joists. The headers are the ones that all the other joists nail into.

2 BUILD AND SQUARE THE FRAME. Nail the end and header joists together with 10d (3-inch) common nails. Set the frame in place on the foundation. Check for square by measuring across opposite corners. Adjust the frame as needed until the two diagonal distances are equal.

Building a subfloor

FRAMING A SUBFLOOR (continued)

3 **ATTACH METAL HANGERS.** Nail a corner bracket at each corner of the frame to reinforce the joint. Attach the frame to the skids with hurricane/seismic ties. Recheck the corner for square.

Wear safety glasses when cutting lumber and driving nails.

4 **LAY OUT THE JOISTS.** Mark joist positions every 16 inches on the opposing header joists. Extend the lines down the inside face of the header joists with a combination square.

5 **ATTACH THE JOIST HANGERS.** Center a joist hanger at each mark. Drive nails through the flange on only one side of each hanger so you can insert the joists easily.

6 **CUT THE JOISTS.** Cut 2×6 joists to length and set them in the hangers. Press each hanger closed, nail the other flange to the header joist, then nail the hanger to the sides of the joist.

7 **LAY THE SUBFLOOR.** Lay ³/₄-inch exterior-grade plywood on the joists. Trim panels so joints are at the center of joists, but stagger the joints so no joint runs into another joint. Leave a gap of ¹/₈ inch between edges to keep the panels from buckling.

8 **NAIL THE SUBFLOOR IN PLACE.** Fasten the panels to the joists with 8d (2¹/₂-inch) nails or #8 2¹/₂-inch deck screws. Space the fasteners every 6 inches along the edges of panels and 12 inches elsewhere.

SHEDS

Building a wood shed

A shed is basically a small house with stud walls, windows, doors, and a roof. Shed kits are for do-it-yourselfers who want a shed without the hassle of building a house, no matter how small. The parts come precut and ready to nail. If six pieces are supposed to be exactly the same length, they are. If a piece is supposed to be notched, it is. If a roof truss is supposed to be cut at a special angle, it is.

With the details taken care of, you're left with just the fun of building. Nothing is ever foolproof, but kits are foolproof enough that you can tackle some things you otherwise might not try, such as the gambrel roof on the shed shown on the following pages.

Wood sheds include neither floor, roofing, nor paint—allowing you to choose a wood or concrete base and shingles that match the paint scheme you choose.

Kits vary from manufacturer to manufacturer and model to model. This one starts with the construction of the rear wall. Follow the directions that come with your kit.

BUILDING THE FLOOR

You can build the floor for your shed in one of three ways: You can buy a floor kit made to go with the shed you're using; you can build your own wood floor; or you can pour a concrete floor. If you buy a floor kit, make sure it's made to go with the make and model of the shed you're building. If you build a wooden floor, follow manufacturer's recommendations so it will fit inside the shed you're building. If you're pouring a concrete slab, attach 2×4 sill plates to the floor with masonry screws, which drive directly into the concrete, or lag screws. If you're using lag screws, drill into the concrete to set anchors for the lag screws, then attach the 2×4 sill plates to the slab. The kit directions should provide dimensions for the sill.

ONCE THE SLAB HAS CURED, LAY OUT AND ATTACH THE SILLS. Concrete screws are designed especially to anchor the sills securely into the slab. Drill a pilot hole slightly smaller than the size of the screw.

Building a wood shed

BUILDING THE REAR WALL (continued)

1 **NAIL THE REAR CROSSBRACE TOGETHER.** The heart of the back wall framing in this shed is a T-shape assembly in the center of the wall. Fit the two pieces together, then nail them together with 2-inch nails.

2 **NAIL THE OUTER STUDS IN PLACE.** Measure to find where the outside studs are attached to the crossbrace. Nail each in place with 10d (3-inch) nails.

3 **APPLY A WIDE PANEL.** The back wall is made of four panels: two wide panels and two narrow extension panels. Nail in one of the wide side panels as directed. On this shed, the panels stick out beyond the bottom of the framing, creating a flange that you'll nail to the floor framing later.

4 **APPLY A NARROW EXTENSION PANEL.** Put a narrow extension panel in place next to the wider panel. Prop an edge of the extension on a spare piece of framing to help support it while you nail.

5 **INSTALL THE REMAINING PANELS.** Repeat the process to cover the unpaneled section of the back wall.

BUILDING THE FRONT WALL

The front wall also is made of two wide pieces and two narrow extensions. The wide pieces attach to each other via a gusset nailed across the center seam. The extensions are attached to the wider pieces with a piece of framing that spans the joint between the two.

Read over and familiarize yourself with the manual that comes with your shed before you begin assembly. The order of work as outlined is usually the easiest way to guarantee a successful installation.

1 **NAIL IN THE GUSSET.** Lay one of the wide pieces on the ground. Support it with a wall extension brace on one side and a spare piece of framing on the other. Slide the gusset under the panel, positioning it as directed. Nail it in place.

2 **NAIL IN THE EXTENSION BRACE.** Position the extension brace so half of it is under the panel and half of it is exposed. Make sure the panel overhangs the bottom of the brace as directed, then nail the brace in place.

3 **NAIL IN THE EXTENSION PANEL.** Put the extension panel over the brace and snug it up against the wide panel. Nail the extension panel to the gusset.

4 **INSTALL THE REMAINING PANELS.** Put the remaining wide panel in place so it overlaps the gusset and is tight against the first panel. Nail it to the gusset, then toenail through the trim to tie the two wide panels together. Nail in the remaining extension brace and attach the remaining extension panel as before.

5 **NAIL IN THE INSIDE BRACE AND NAIL THE DOORS IN PLACE.** On this shed, a crossbrace travels the width of the shed above the door to help support the front wall. Position the brace as directed and slip framing not yet in use under an edge to keep the panel from rocking. Nail the crossbrace in place.

Position the doors as directed, then screw temporary braces across the opening between them to prevent them from opening while you work.

Building a wood shed

BUILDING THE SIDEWALLS

Unlike the framing on the front and back walls, the framing on the sidewalls is a fairly traditional stud wall. The bottom of the panel once again extends beyond the studs so you can nail it to the floor framing. The paneling extends beyond the corner of the framing, too, for easy nailing into the front and back walls.

If your arm gets tired of driving nails into studs, rent a pneumatic nailer and air compressor from your local home center to make the job easier. Lower-tech, slower solutions include drilling pilot holes or lubricating the nails with soap.

1 **LAY OUT THE WALL.** Put the top plate on a flat surface and put a stud against it. (The exact location will depend on the make and model of your shed.) Put your foot on the stud and nail through the top plate into the stud. Attach the remaining studs, positioning them as directed.

2 **POSITION A SIDE PANEL.** Put a side panel on the framing, positioning it as the manufacturer directs. On this shed, one edge of the panel is cut to lie on the corner of the shed; the other is cut to lie in the middle of the shed. The panel extends beyond the end of the top plate and below the bottom of the studs. These areas get nailed to other parts of the shed later. Double-check that everything is properly aligned.

3 **NAIL THE PANEL TO THE CENTER STUD AND TOP PLATE.** Nail the edge of the panel to the center stud, leaving half the stud exposed. Nail the entire edge in place, spacing the nails as the manufacturer directs. When you're done, nail the top edge to the top plate.

4 **NAIL THE PANEL TO THE REMAINING STUDS.** Measure between the end of the center stud and the next stud to make sure they're still properly spaced. Once you're sure, nail the panel to the stud. Repeat for any remaining studs.

5 **REPEAT FOR THE REMAINING PANELS.** Put the remaining panels in place as directed, positioning them to get the proper overhang and making sure the corner edges are where they belong. Nail the paneling to the center stud and top plate, check the position of the next stud, then nail the paneling to it. Repeat for remaining panels until you've covered the framing.

RAISING THE FRONT AND SIDEWALLS

With the walls assembled, you're ready for the modern-day equivalent of a barn raising. Get a couple of friends to help you put the walls in place and nail them. The sidewalls get nailed in place first, followed by the front wall. What you nail them to depends on what you've chosen for a floor. If you have a concrete floor, you'll nail to the 2×4s you've attached to it. If you have a wooden platform, you'll nail the walls to its sides.

Wearing gloves while you're hammering nails may seem a bit cumbersome at first, but they'll protect your fingers, especially when you're working in tight spaces.

1 **RAISE THE FIRST SIDEWALL.** Have a couple of helpers put the wall in place on the floor so the paneling overhangs the framing. Nail through the paneling into the framing. Support the wall while the helpers toenail through the studs and into the floor framing.

2 **RAISE THE SECOND SIDEWALL.** Install the second sidewall the way you installed the first one: Put the wall in place, nail through the siding, then toenail through the studs.

3 **RAISE THE FRONT WALL.** Put the front wall in place with the paneling overhanging the floor framing. Nail through the wall into the top plate of the side walls. Nail or screw through the bottom of the wall into the floor framing as directed. Once the wall is firmly attached, toenail through the braces into the floor framing.

4 **REMOVE THE DOOR BRACES.** Now that the front wall is in place, remove the braces that hold the doors shut by unscrewing the screws that hold the braces in place.

A+ WORK SMARTER

WORKING WITH FRIENDS

When you ask friends to help you with a project, you're asking a big favor. Make the job as easy as you can by having a solid understanding of the project and how you want your friends to assist. Nothing is more frustrating for people than standing around on a Saturday afternoon while you solve problems or figure out how something is supposed to fit together. The more problems you've solved before everyone gathers in the backyard, the more pleasant their volunteer experience will be. Prioritize! You're more likely to need your friends for tasks you can't handle by yourself, so don't waste valuable labor by asking someone to hand you a few nails.

Building a wood shed

ASSEMBLING THE TRUSSES

With three walls up, you'd think it was time to install the fourth. Some manufacturers, however, recommend that you assemble the trusses first. The floor makes a good work surface, and the absence of the back wall gives you easy access to it. Placing the ends of the trusses against the sidewalls helps align the trusses and ensures that they will be the right width. In this kit, the trusses come partially assembled, and the ends are color-coded to help you put them together in the right order.

Even if the trusses come partially assembled, it's up to you to finish the job properly. Otherwise you'll have problems when it's time to put on the roof.

1 **LAY OUT THE PIECES.** Put the pieces for one of the trusses on the floor of the shed. In this kit, half of each truss is preassembled. Put the black ends against the wall and the red ends against each other in the center of the shed.

2 **APPLY CONSTRUCTION ADHESIVE.** Slip a section of newspaper under the center seam to protect the floor. Put the gusset temporarily in place and trace around it. Apply construction adhesive to the mating ends of the trusses and to the surface to be covered by the gusset.

3 **ATTACH THE GUSSET.** Put the gusset in place, pushing it into the adhesive. Nail according to the pattern the manufacturer recommends.

4 **TURN THE ASSEMBLY OVER.** Hold on to the peak of the truss while a helper holds on to the lower section. Turn the gusset over. Put a section of newspaper under the peak to catch any construction adhesive that squeezes out.

5 **NAIL ON A SECOND GUSSET.** Attach a gusset to this side of the truss the same way you attached one to the other side. Clean up any construction adhesive on the floor with paint thinner—it will be nearly impossible to remove once it dries. Assemble the remaining trusses.

RAISE THE REAR WALL

Once the rear wall is in place, the walls are relatively stable, and you can begin nailing on trim and ultimately the roof trusses. Putting the rear wall in place is essentially no different from putting the front wall in place, and you will need some helpers to get the wall into position and make sure it's square. Once again, the siding should overlap the sidewalls and the floor framing. When the wall is in position, nail the siding to the top plate in neighboring walls, then nail the paneling to the floor framing. Next comes the trim. Nailing on the trim before you install the roof makes the job easier because you won't have to reach around obstacles to get into corners.

1 **PUT THE REAR WALL IN PLACE.** Have helpers put the rear wall in place. Make sure the siding overlaps the floor framing as well as the sidewalls.

2 **NAIL THE SIDING TO THE TOP PLATES.** Drive nails through the siding of the back wall into the top plates in the sidewall.

3 **NAIL PANELING TO THE FLOOR FRAMING.** Working from the outside, drive nails through the siding into the floor framing. Working from the inside, toenail the vertical braces to the floor.

4 **ATTACH THE ROOF TRIM.** Clamp the roof trim in place, aligning it per the manufacturer's directions. Drive screws from the inside to hold it in place or attach as directed.

5 **ATTACH THE CORNER TRIM.** Put the corner trim on the corner, butting it against the bottom of the roof trim. Nail through the trim into the paneling. Repeat for the remaining corners.

Building a wood shed

RAISING THE ROOF *(continued)*

Yes, you're ready to raise the roof and all that that means. You'll begin by resting the trusses on the top plates and toenailing them in place. Toenailing supplies minimal support, so don't climb on the roof yet. Wait until all the panels have been nailed in place. Cover the roof with tar paper and then apply shingles—neither of which comes with the roof.

SAFETY ALERT

The structure may look secure once the walls are up and the trusses are in place, but it's still relatively fragile. Do not climb on the roof until all panels have been nailed in place. Otherwise the structure could collapse, and you could get hurt.

1 NAIL A TRUSS IN PLACE. Have helpers hold a truss in place. Toenail through each end of the truss into the top plate. Repeat to attach the remaining trusses.

2 NAIL A ROOF PANEL IN PLACE. Put a lower roof panel in place and nail the corners of one end to the side wall. Align the other end of the panel with the other end of the shed, pushing against the wall, if necessary, to pull it into alignment. When the panel and wall are properly in place, nail the corners.

3 NAIL THE PANEL TO THE TRUSSES. Measure to make sure the first truss is the correct distance from the wall and parallel to it. Drive a nail through the top of the panel into the truss. Repeat on the remaining trusses. When you're finished, install the lower panel on the other side of the shed.

4 NAIL THE UPPER PANEL IN PLACE. Put the upper panel in place and nail down two corners. Rack the panel as needed to align the other end properly, then nail those corners in place. Nail the top edge to the trusses, making sure they are spaced properly. Repeat on the other side of the shed.

5 DRIVE NAILS EVERY 8 INCHES. Once all the panels are properly in place and nailed along the edges, drive nails every 8 inches into the trusses or trim beneath the panels.

SHEDS

Roofing a shed

When it comes to keeping out water, roofing is an art. Most of this is done in layers: Roofing felt overlaps the sheathing, and shingles overlap the paper. Each row of shingles overlaps the one below, and a full shingle overlaps the joint between the sides of the shingles below it. In one way or another, each seam is sealed by another shingle. Any water that wants to get in will have to do what it is least inclined to do—flow uphill.

Unfortunately, roofing supplies don't come in a shed kit. Here's what you'll need:

■ Enough 15-pound roofing felt to cover the roof.

■ Drip edge to cover the eave and rake edges of the roof (also known as the bottom and ends of the roof).

■ Enough shingles to cover the roof. Multiply the width in feet by the length in feet of each slope of the roof. (There are four on this shed: the two lower panels and the two upper panels.) Write down the amounts, and ask a salesperson to help you purchase the right amount.

■ Hot-dipped galvanized roofing nails. (Electroplated nails have a thinner coating and don't last as long.) Roofing pros suggest you buy nails long enough to go ¾ inch into the deck. If the deck is thinner than ¾ inch, get nails that go through and stick out at least ⅛ inch.

■ Staples. They hold down the roofing felt until you cover it with shingles .

WORK SMARTER

KEEP THOSE SHINGLES COOL
Don't roof your shed in full sunlight on a hot day. When asphalt shingles get hot, they become so malleable that you can damage them simply by walking on them. Start early in the morning and do as much as you can before midday, then take a well-deserved break until the next day or the evening, when it's cooler.

APPLYING ROOFING

1 **INSTALL DRIP CAPS ALONG THE BOTTOM EDGES OF THE ROOF,** called the eaves. Nail at 10-inch intervals into the roof sheathing, using 2d (1-inch) roofing nails.

2 **STAPLE 15-POUND BUILDING PAPER TO THE SHEATHING.** Start with a double layer along the eaves and work up toward the ridge—the peak of the roof. Overlap strips by about 2 inches at the edges and by 4 inches at the ends.

3 **INSTALL DRIP CAPS ALONG THE RAKES** on top of the roofing paper. Drive 2d (1-inch) roofing nails every 10 inches.

4 **INSTALL A STARTER COURSE OF SHINGLES.** Cut the tabs off a shingle. Nail the shingle in place with four nails so the shingle overlaps the drip cap on the end and bottom of the roof by ½ to ¾ inch. Continue nailing cut shingles along the bottom row to create a solid strip of shingles at the bottom of the roof.

Roofing a shed

APPLYING ROOFING (continued)

5 **SNAP A CHALK LINE.** Measure up the width of a full shingle from the drip edge and make a mark at each end of the roof. Snap a chalk line between the marks.

6 **NAIL A ROW OF FULL SHINGLES ON TOP OF THE STARTER COURSE.** Align the upper edge of the shingle carefully with the chalk line. Nail in place with galvanized roofing nails long enough to come out the bottom of the roof panel. Follow manufacturer's instructions for nails.

HOMER'S HINDSIGHT

A LITTLE DAB WON'T DO YOU
For some reason, the myth that you need to dab roofing cement over each nailhead when roofing persists. Whenever I see customers walking out with cans of cement, I try to set the record straight. Asphalt shingles have a self-sealing adhesive that bonds each shingle with the row below. It probably doesn't hurt to dab roofing cement over each nail, but it doesn't help either. In fact, roofing cement is a thick, sticky, tarlike substance, and anyone who works with it is bound to get a substantial coating on their hands. Roofing cement? Forget about it. Roofing is dirty enough work as it is.

7 **START THE SECOND ROW.** The tabs of the second row overlap the solid portion of the first row. Snap a chalk line to mark the upper edge of the row. Begin the row by trimming 6 inches off the end of the first shingle. This positions the shingles so a tab covers the joints in the row below. Lay the rest of the row with full shingles.

8 **WORK YOUR WAY UP THE ROOF.** Trim the first shingle of every row so it is 6 inches shorter than the first shingle of the previous row. Start the seventh row with a full shingle, then begin shortening the first shingles in 6-inch increments again. Work your way all the way up the roof, then shingle the other side of the roof, using the same technique.

9 **SHINGLE THE RIDGE.** Roof the ridge with 12-inch squares cut from standard shingles. Bend each edge over the ridge and drive nails 1 inch from each edge and 5½ inches from the butt.

Applying trim, hardware, and paint

1 **APPLY TRIM OVER THE DOOR.** Clamp in place the trim piece that goes over the door. Measure to make sure the overhang is equal on each side of the door. Screw the trim in place from inside the shed.

2 **INSTALL DOOR STIFFENERS.** The doors will flex unless you reinforce them with battens. Clamp the battens in place and measure to make sure they are directly in line with the crosspieces on the doors. Screw through the battens into the crosspieces.

3 **INSTALL A DOOR LIP.** Sheds with double doors have a strip of wood that covers the gap between the doors screwed to one of the doors. Screw it in place as directed.

4 **PUT IN A BARREL BOLT.** When locking double doors, one of the doors needs to lock to both the shed and the other door. Install a barrel bolt on the inside of the door to lock the door to the shed (refer to manufacturer's instructions).

5 **ATTACH A HASP.** Attach a hasp to the outside of one of the doors so you can close them. Put in a padlock so you can lock the shed when not in use.

Applying trim, hardware, and paint *(continued)*

6 **CUT THE SIDE VENT.** The shed must be ventilated, especially if you will store gas-powered equipment in it. Lay out a vent on the lower front corner of a sidewall or as directed by the manufacturer. Drill holes inside the layout lines at each corner and cut along the lines with a jigsaw.

7 **CUT THE REAR VENT.** Lay out the rear vent toward the top of the rear gable or as directed by the manufacturer. Drill holes and cut out as before.

8 **CAULK THE SEAMS.** Use a long-lasting, paintable acrylic caulk to caulk all the seams in the shed. Be sure to caulk between the trim and the wall, as well as around all the door trim.

9 **PAINT THE SHED.** Paint helps keep moisture from causing rot that could eventually destroy the shed. Paint all the outside surfaces, including the top and bottom of each door, the top edge of the trim, and the bottom edge of each wall.

10 **SCREW THE VENTS IN PLACE.** Put a vent in each of the cutouts and screw it in place.

11 **CHECK FOR PROTRUDING NAILS.** Look for nails that protrude (other than roofing nails; the protruding end of roofing nails help keep the shingles in place) on the inside and outside of the building. Bend them over with a hammer or cut them flush with a pair of diagonal cutters.

Installing a shed window

I f you often find yourself fumbling around the shed for the snowblower on cold winter mornings or putting away tools on a late summer evening, sooner or later you're going to want more light. Electricity is one solution; a window and the light it sheds is a lower-tech solution.

In addition to cutting a hole in the siding and putting in a window, you'll need framing to support the window; and if the window is more than about 14 inches wide, you'll need headers and framing to replace the studs you'll have to cut out of the way.

The key to installing a window is making sure it sits level and square in the opening. A noticeably out-of-level window will be disconcerting from inside the shed and embarrassing when viewed from the outside. An out-of-square window, on the other hand, won't open. Because it's so important to get it right, standard practice is to build an oversize opening, called the rough opening, and shim the window to get it where you want it.

Top plate

Stud to be removed for rough opening

Rough window placement

Sole plate

WINDOW FRAMING EXPLAINED. Because windows are in exterior walls, which are always load-bearing, they have built-up **headers** consisting of 2×4s or 2×6s sandwiched around a piece of ½-inch plywood and 2×4 **rough sills** to hold the bottom of the window. They are supported by cripple studs, which hold the frame of the window in place and help support the weight of the roof.

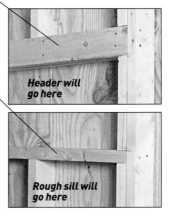

Header will go here

Rough sill will go here

1 MEASURE FOR NEW STUDS. The opening for a window is always slightly larger than the window and is called the rough opening, which will be noted in the directions that come with the window. You will need to remove at least one existing stud and cut at least one or two new studs depending on the location of the window. Measure between the soleplate and the top plate and cut the new studs (called king studs) to fit between them.

R.O.
WINDOW

2 TOENAIL THE KING STUDS IN PLACE. Put the king studs between the soleplate and top plate, spacing them so that the inside surfaces are separated by the width of the rough opening. Plumb them and double-check the distance between them. Toenail them in place. Mark the studs to show where the top and bottom of the window will be and make a second set of marks showing the top and bottom of the rough opening.

Installing a shed window (continued)

3 **NAIL CRIPPLE STUDS TO THE KING STUDS.** Cut three supports 3½ inches shorter than the distance between the rough opening and the top plate and nail them to the king studs. Cut two more supports, each 1½ inches shorter than the distance between the rough opening and the soleplate. Cut any studs that fall between either set of supports to the same length. Toenail the cripple studs in place.

4 **INSTALL THE ROUGH SILL AND HEADER.** Cut three 2×4s to fit between the king studs. Nail one in place as the rough sill. Put ½-inch plywood between the other two. Nail the sandwich together and nail it in place as a header across the top of the opening. Cut a 2×4 to fit on each side of the opening and nail them in place.

5 **CUT AN OPENING FOR THE WINDOW.** Working from inside the shed, drill ½-inch-diameter holes at the four corners of the rough opening. Working from the outside, cut between the holes with a jigsaw to remove siding and create a hole for the window.

6 **PUT THE WINDOW IN THE OPENING.** Slide the window into the rough opening. Put shims underneath to level the window in the opening and above the window to fill in the space. Shim to the sides of the window to hold it in place. Check to make sure the window operates and is square. Reshim as needed.

7 **NAIL THE WINDOW IN PLACE.** Drive 6d nails into the window frame, through the shims, and into the framing, leaving a bit of the nail exposed so you can remove it if necessary. Verify that the window works and remove the nails and reshim if needed. Nail the flange to the framing per the window manufacturer's instructions.

8 **APPLY WINDOW TRIM.** Cut a 1×4 to fit around the window and to cover the nailing flange. Nail the 1×4 pieces in place. Caulk, taking special care to fill any voids created by the siding.

Building a vinyl shed

HOMER'S HINDSIGHT

LOCATION IS EVERYTHING!
Everyone has had a laugh about painting themselves in a corner, but it isn't just inside where people get into trouble. I've talked to folks who did the same thing in their back yards. The decision about placement is really important because once the slab is in place, you're stuck. It's not just about where the door goes, it's also about clearance on both sides and maybe even about how close the structure is to that big tree. Take some time deciding where you want the shed to go before you pour the slab.

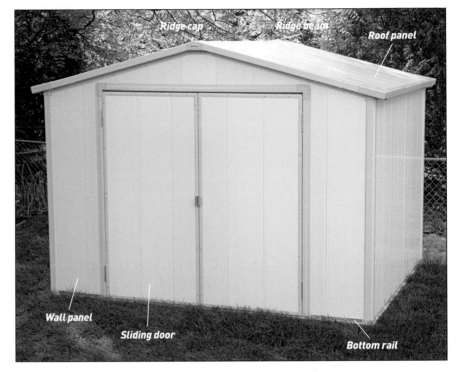

BECAUSE VINYL SHEDS ARE RATHER BASIC in terms of design, they're relatively easy to assemble. They also provide almost indestructible storage. Properly situated and cared for, a vinyl shed will shelter your garden tools for decades.

Vinyl sheds are the low-maintenance solution to your outdoor storage problems. The thick vinyl panels that make up the shed are durable and will neither rust nor rot. The color you buy is the color you get—no painting required.

Building a vinyl shed is completely different from building a wood shed. It requires no framing, no siding, no nails. Vinyl panels about 2 inches thick do the job of both framing and siding. The edges of the panels are grooved, and splines slip into the grooves to tie neighboring panels together.

While this simplifies construction, be prepared for a couple of hidden problems. First, the edges of the panels can be surprisingly sharp. Wear work gloves while assembling the shed. Second, beware of the wind. The panels are both wider and lighter than wood. In fact, they're light enough to get caught in the wind but heavy enough to knock you over as they sail across the yard. Work on days when the wind is calm.

Flooring and foundations for a vinyl shed

Vinyl shed kits do not include a floor. Most are designed to sit on a concrete pad. A metal channel screws to the concrete, and the vinyl panels are held in place by the channel. You won't need to drill and install anchors. Masonry screws, which screw into holes in the concrete, are strong enough. Manufacturers recommend that you make the pad somewhat larger than the shed, but they give no specific guidelines.

Pour the pad before you start installation and position it so each side has at least 4 feet of clearance—you'll need the room to put on the roof. (See "Constructing a Concrete Slab Foundation," pages 117–120.)

Building a vinyl shed

MOUNTING THE CHANNELS

1 **PUT IN THE REAR CHANNEL.** Put the rear channel in place. Measure to make sure it's centered from side to side. Attach a corner block to each end.

2 **ATTACH THE SIDE CHANNELS.** Put side channels into the corner blocks. Use a framing square to make sure they're square. If the side channel is made of more than one piece, use one of the vinyl panels as a guide to make sure they're in a straight line.

3 **DOUBLE-CHECK FOR SQUARE.** To make sure the sides are square with the back, measure the diagonals. If the diagonals are equal, the sides are square. If not, adjust them until they are and double-check with the framing square.

4 **ATTACH THE FRONT CHANNELS.** Put corner blocks on the side channels and put the front channels in the blocks, leaving room for the door. Measure to make sure the opening is the right size and layout for any screws that will hold the threshold. Some kits have a special tape that shows where the screws go.

5 **SCREW THE CHANNELS TO THE FLOOR.** Check again for square—you'll find it virtually impossible to assemble the shed if it's out of square. Trace the screw holes in the channels to mark the concrete and drill pilot holes one size smaller than the screws you'll be using. Screw the channels in place with phillips-head masonry screws that don't need anchors.

MOUNTING THE PANELS

1 **PUT PIECES FOR THE REAR CORNER IN THE TRACK.** Put a sidewall panel in the track at the corner. Put a rear panel in the rear track (all of the side panels are usually the same, but the tops of the rear panels follow the slope of the roof and are different lengths). Make sure you have the right panels.

2 **INSTALL THE CORNER POST.** Slide a corner post over the two panels. Slide it all the way down and seat it in the corner block.

Keep all the pieces in order so you don't install the wrong piece in the wrong place.

3 **WORK YOUR WAY ACROSS THE BACK WALL.** Once the corner is in, put in the next panel of the back wall. Align the grooves and join the two panels by sliding a connector into them.

4 **WORK YOUR WAY ALONG THE WALL.** Make sure the panel follows the roofline. When you reach the middle, a panel with two square ends supports the vent. Install the panel and work your way across the rest of the wall.

5 **INSTALL THE VENT.** Put the vent in its opening in the wall and put the vent panel over it. Slide connectors to hold it in place.

WORK SMARTER

EASIER SLIDING
Vinyl is a relatively high-friction material, which can make assembling a vinyl shed tricky because the connectors may not slide in easily. This is especially true as you complete more of the assembly and the structure becomes more rigid. Some manufacturers recommend lubricating the connectors with dishwashing detergent before you slide them between the panels. And, of course, the more square the assembly, the easier it is to connect.

Building a vinyl shed

BUILDING THE FRONT WALL

1 **INSTALL THE CORNER PANEL.** Put the shortest front panel in place in the corner and slide a corner post over it. Repeat on the other side of the shed.

2 **INSTALL THE REMAINING PANELS.** Put the next longest panel in place and attach it with a connector. Work your way to the doorway and repeat on the other side of the shed.

3 **PUT IN THE HINGE POSTS.** The doorposts are reinforced with metal, and the hinges already mounted on them. Put one on each side of the door and attach it to the adjacent panel with a connector.

4 **HANG THE UPPER DOOR FRAME.** The upper door frame also is reinforced with metal. Put the frame at the top of the doorway and gently slide each end into the sockets in the hinge posts.

5 **INSTALL THE UPPER DOOR PANELS.** Put the panels that form the peak of the roof in place on the beam and attach them with connectors.

INSTALLING THE MAIN ROOF BEAM AND THE DOORS

1 **SLIDE THE CAPS ONTO THE MAIN BEAM.** Slide the mounting caps onto each end of the main roof beam. Screw the caps in place.

2 **HANG THE BEAM.** With a helper, put the beam in place. Align it with the marks on the panel and screw each end in place.

3 **HANG THE DOORS.** Lift the half hinge on the door above the half hinge on the shed and slide the hinge pin into the hinge barrel. Repeat on the other side.

4 **ALIGN THE DOORS.** Eye the top edge of the doors to see if the top edge of one and the top edge of the other form a straight line. If not, push gently on the appropriate side of the shed to bring the doors into alignment.

5 **CHECK THE GAP BETWEEN THE DOORS.** If the gap between the doors isn't parallel, neither are the sides of the shed. Correct the problem at the bottom of the shed. Put a piece of wood against the appropriate side along the bottom and tap with a hammer until the space between the doors is uniform.

Building a vinyl shed

INSTALLING THE ROOF

The roof is made of several panels that slip into grooves on the beam and the walls. At the front and back of the shed, the panels fit into the trim too. Work from one end toward the center of the roof, then work from the other end toward the center. This gives you wiggle room when working with the end panels.

Have a helper stand inside the shed to feed the panel into the groove on the beam. Then have the helper use a drill with a phillips-head bit to drive a single screw into the panel and the beam. This will prevent the panel from falling down while you work on the next panel. Once all the panels are in place, drive several screws into each panel to secure them.

1 INSTALL ROOF GUIDES. Put a roof guide over one of the exposed ends of the rear wall so the channel faces the inside of the shed. Repeat for the other exposed end of the rear wall and the front wall.

2 INSTALL THE SIDE MOLDINGS. These moldings go over the tops of the sidewalls. Put one on each wall with the angled flange on the inside of the wall.

3 PUT IN THE FIRST ROOF PANEL. Have a helper work inside the shed while you work from the outside. Put a roof panel into the main beam and against one of the roof guides. Attach with a connector and screw the connector to the inside of the main beam.

4 WORK YOUR WAY TOWARD THE CENTER OF THE SHED. Put in as many panels as it takes to get to the center of the shed, connecting them and screwing the connectors to the main beam as you go.

5 START ON THE OTHER END OF THE SHED. Once you reach the center, go to the opposite end of the roof, install a panel against the side molding, and screw it in place. Work your way back across the roof, screwing the connectors in place as you go. Attach the two center panels with a connector, and screw the connector in place. Repeat on the other slope of the roof.

6 **ATTACH THE ROOF TRIM.** Snap the roof trim to the lower edge of the roof. You'll screw it in place later.

7 **ATTACH THE CORNER COVER.** Snap the corner trim over the gutter. You'll screw it, too, in place later.

8 **DOUBLE-CHECK THE ALIGNMENT OF THE DOORS.** If the doors are out of alignment, one or more of the sides is out of plumb. To check, close the doors against a thin strip of wood such as a stir stick; then remove the stick without moving the doors. Next see if the gap is the same at the bottom. If not, correct as before: Push against the side of the shed to align the tops and tap against the bottom to make the door edges parallel.

9 **SCREW THE SHED TOGETHER.** Once the shed is properly aligned, drive screws into the connectors as directed by the manufacturer. Screw the gutter in place.

10 **HANG THE DOOR HARDWARE.** Screw the doorstop, the door handles, and the latch in place.

11 **APPLY CAULK.** Apply caulk between the ends of the panels and the metal channels, working from the inside. Use a clear, long-lasting silicone caulk.

Building a metal shed

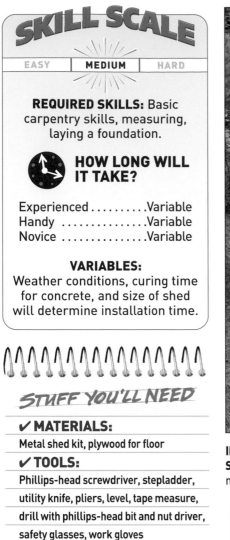

SKILL SCALE

EASY | **MEDIUM** | HARD

REQUIRED SKILLS: Basic carpentry skills, measuring, laying a foundation.

HOW LONG WILL IT TAKE?

Experienced . . . . .Variable
Handy . . . . .Variable
Novice . . . . .Variable

VARIABLES:
Weather conditions, curing time for concrete, and size of shed will determine installation time.

STUFF YOU'LL NEED

✔ **MATERIALS:**
Metal shed kit, plywood for floor

✔ **TOOLS:**
Phillips-head screwdriver, stepladder, utility knife, pliers, level, tape measure, drill with phillips-head bit and nut driver, safety glasses, work gloves

When you're working outside weather is always an issue. Obviously it's no fun to assemble a shed in the rain but wind poses a more serious problem. Metal walls can literally sail away on a windy day and not only do you risk damaging the panels, sharp edges can result in serious injuries. On a really windy day tackle another project or wait for better weather.

INSTALLING A METAL SHED KIT REQUIRES LITTLE MORE THAN THE ABILITY TO DRIVE A SCREW or tighten a nut. Make sure you square the assembly as directed by the manufacturer and don't work on windy days. Metal panels fly like kites and cut like knives.

Metal sheds are an economical, relatively simple way of storing things in your yard. If you can use a screwdriver, you can build a metal shed. One of the handier things about metal sheds is that you don't necessarily need to pour a pad or build a platform for it. Cut up a few sheets of plywood and screw them to a metal grid (sold as a foundation kit), and you've laid all the foundation a metal shed needs. (If you prefer a concrete or wooden platform, you can buy hardware that simplifies attaching the shed to these materials.)

The siding and roof of a metal shed are prepainted, unlike wood sheds, so once the shed is up, you're done. The only maintenance concern is rust. Get some touch-up paint from the manufacturer and paint nicks and scratches as soon as they occur. Brush leaves off the roof with a soft-bristled broom. If you really want your shed to shine, periodically wash—and wax—it.

Flooring and foundations

Like all other sheds, you can build a metal shed on a wood platform or concrete pad, and most manufacturers sell accessory kits that simplify attaching the shed to the foundation.

Many kits, however, come with their own foundation kit. When assembled, the foundation is a grid of beams to which you screw several pieces of plywood to make a floor. Foundation kits are the simplest way to put down a base for your shed. If your shed comes without such a kit, you can usually purchase one separately.

The time at which you attach the shed to the foundation depends on which type of foundation you are using. Follow the manufacturer's directions.

ASSEMBLING THE FRAME PARTS

The first step in building your shed is to put together the frame around which the structure is built. For the first hour or so, you won't assemble anything you can easily recognize, and most of what you build you'll set aside until later.

Fortunately, the framing for a metal shed is less extensive than the framing for a wood shed. You'll find a floor frame, a rim that goes around the top of the shed, and a parallel frame that goes around the middle. The roof requires a couple of beams too.

The framing gives the shed shape and horizontal rigidity. The rest of the shed's strength comes from the siding. Ribs bent into the siding during manufacture keep it from buckling and give it strength to support the roof.

Assembly, fortunately, is easy. Everything is either screwed or bolted together.

SAFETY ALERT

Wear gloves to protect your hands from sharp metal edges.

1 ASSEMBLE THE PARTS FOR THE BOTTOM FRAME. The bottom frame is the sill upon which you build the entire shed. For now, assemble front, back, left, and right frames separately, then set them aside.

2 ASSEMBLE THE PARTS FOR THE TOP AND THE MIDDLE FRAMES. The main frame on this shed is a right angle, called a wall angle, that goes around the top of the walls and reinforces them. The middle frame is called a wall channel and is attached to the walls midway between the floor and roof. You will have a wall angle and a wall channel for each wall. Put them together and set them aside for now.

3 ASSEMBLE THE ROOF BEAMS. The roof beams run between the front and back walls and support the roof. Assemble each of the beams and set them aside.

4 ASSEMBLE THE DOOR BEAM. Put together the parts that will form the track that the door slides on. Put the slides in the track.

5 ASSEMBLE AND SQUARE THE BOTTOM FRAME. Put the four sides of the bottom frame together with screws. Make sure the assembly is square by measuring the diagonals. If one is longer than the other, push gently on the frame until the diagonals are equal, at which point the frame is square.

Building a metal shed

ASSEMBLING THE WALLS

1 PUT IN A CORNER PANEL. Put a corner panel in the left rear corner of the bottom frame. On this shed, the wider face of the panel goes on the side of the shed. Put a washer over a screw, and screw the panel into the floor frame. Support the panel with a ladder.

2 SCREW A WALL PANEL TO THE CORNER PANEL. Rest a panel on the bottom frame so it overlaps the narrow part of the corner panel. Brace it as shown to hold it in place while you work. Put a washer over a screw and screw the two panels together, then put in the rest of the screws and washers that connect them.

3 REPEAT IN THE REMAINING CORNERS. Put in another corner panel and screw a flat panel to it. Repeat on the remaining corners, bracing each one as you work.

SAFETY ALERT

Don't work with metal panels on windy days.

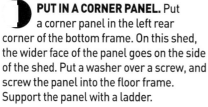

4 FASTEN THE REAR WALL ANGLE. Screw the rear wall angle, which you assembled earlier, to the top of the rear wall.

5 FASTEN THE REAR WALL CHANNEL ASSEMBLY. Screw the rear wall channel, which you assembled earlier, across the middle of the wall.

6 **REPEAT ON SIDEWALLS.** Fasten the sidewall angle and sidewall channels the same way you attached the assemblies to the rear wall.

7 **ASSEMBLE THE DOOR TRACK OVER THE DOOR OPENING.** Fasten the door track assembly across the top of the front wall. You'll fasten the doorjambs later.

8 **LAY OUT THE WALL PANELS.** The wall panels are usually not identical. Check the part numbers against the directions and lay out the panels in order along the shed's perimeter. Double-check that you have the panels in the right places: if so, the holes on each panel will align with those on its neighbor.

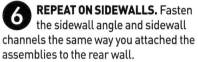

9 **ATTACH THE PANELS.** Put each panel in place so the rib on the edge of the panel fits over the rib of an installed panel. (On this shed, one of the ribs is crimped and should always be covered by an uncrimped rib.) Screw the panel in place at the top and bottom, then screw the middle of the panel to the wall channel.

10 **INSTALL THE REMAINING PANELS.** Work your way around the shed, installing neighboring panels one at a time.

11 **FASTEN THE DOORJAMB.** Screw the front wall channel in place. Put the doorjamb in place and bolt it to one adjacent wall panel. Screw through the jamb to attach it to the floor frame, wall channel, and door track. Repeat on the other side.

Building a metal shed

ATTACHING THE GABLE AND ROOF

1 **ATTACH ROOF BEAM SUPPORTS.** Use brackets to attach the roof beams to the gables. Screw them in place before you put the gables in place.

2 **FASTEN GABLE PANELS TO SHED.** Each gable is made of two panels. Fasten the panels to the front and to the back of the shed.

SAFETY ALERT

Don't put your full weight on the roof.

3 **BOLT THE GABLE PANELS TOGETHER.** At the back of the shed, shown here, attach a brace to the panels while fastening them together. At the front, attach supports for the door track while fastening the gable panels together.

4 **ATTACH THE ROOF BEAMS.** Fasten the main beam following the directions supplied by the manufacturer. Once it's in place, fasten the smaller beams as directed.

5 **INSTALL LEFT AND RIGHT REAR ROOF PANELS.** Roof systems vary from shed to shed. On this shed, you screw the left and right rear panels in place first. Follow the directions supplied by the manufacturer.

6 **INSTALL LEFT AND RIGHT FRONT ROOF PANELS.** Once you've installed the back panels, install the front panels. Then return to the back of the shed to install the wide panels.

7 **ATTACH THE RIDGE CAP.** Attach weather stripping to the roof panels as you work. The weather stripping should be continuous, so don't cut it between panels. Screw a section of ridge cap over the weather stripping.

8 **INSTALL THE REMAINING PANELS.** Put the next two panels in place using the manufacturer's instructions as a guide. Cover with weather stripping and put the ridge cap in place. Continue until the roof is installed.

INSTALLING THE DOOR

1 **SCREW IN BRACES.** Several screwed-in braces stiffen the door. Attach them and the door hardware per the manufacturer's instructions.

2 **TILT INTO PLACE.** Put the bottom of the door in place and tilt it so the holes in the door align with the holes in the door slides. Screw the door to the slides.

Anchoring the shed

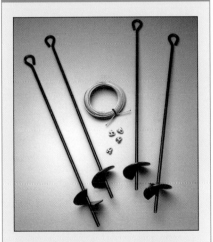

Shed manufacturers suggest you anchor a metal shed to protect it from the huffing and puffing of the wind. If your foundation is a wooden platform, screw through the floor frame into the platform. If the platform is concrete, drill into the concrete and install anchors for lag screws. You can also anchor the shed to wood posts set into the ground or use special tie-downs. Ask the manufacturer of your shed what accessories are available for anchoring.

Building a shed ramp

After you've lugged your lawn mower into your shed a few times, you'll definitely be ready to build a ramp to get over the lip. Make it wide enough for the equipment you need to move: 3 feet should be sufficient. To build a ramp, you'll nail 2×6s onto a frame. To attach it, rest the ramp on a ledger and nail it in place. For a sturdier ramp, anchor it on a concrete footing.

SKILL SCALE

EASY | **MEDIUM** | HARD

REQUIRED SKILLS: Building a shed ramp requires basic carpentry and basic masonry skills.

HOW LONG WILL IT TAKE?

Experienced . . . . 4 hrs.
Handy . . . . 6 hrs.
Novice . . . . 8 hrs.

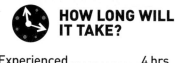

STUFF YOU'LL NEED

✔ MATERIALS:

2× lumber, ⅜ × 3-inch lag screws, ½-inch J-bolts, concrete, duplex nails, galvanized 8d (2½-inch) and 10d (3-inch) nails or #8 2- and 2½-inch deck screws

✔ TOOLS:

Hammer, socket wrenches, circular saw, tape measure, combination square, pencil, square-point shovel, crowbar, plane, drill, level, 3-pound sledgehammer, safety glasses, work gloves

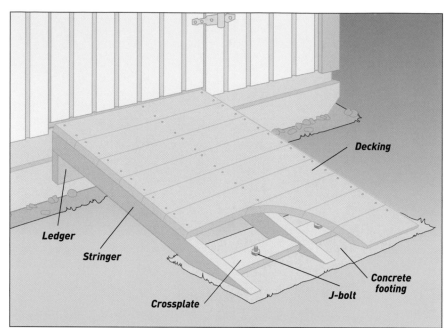

Labels: Decking, Ledger, Stringer, Crossplate, J-bolt, Concrete footing

THE SURFACE OF A RAMP IS SUPPORTED BY THREE STRINGERS—one on each side and another in the center—and a ledger that ties the ramp to the shed. Pour a concrete footing for the base and nail the upper end of the ramp to the ledger. Anchor the foot of the ramp to the concrete with J-bolts.

INSTALLING A RAMP

1 **CUT A 2×6 LEDGER EQUAL TO THE RAMP WIDTH** and cut the top edge so it is beveled at the ramp angle. Drill three ⅜-inch holes in the ledger, level the ledger so it's 5 inches below the floor, and hold it in place with a couple of nails. Drill ⁵⁄₁₆-inch holes in the shed through the existing holes in the ledger. Attach with ⅜ × 3-inch lag screws. If attaching the ledger to concrete, use anchor shields.

2 **CUT STRINGERS.** Measure the height of the floor at the door. For a comfortable slope, make the length of the ramp about eight times this height. Cut three 2×4 stringers to this length.

3 **CUT THE ENDS OF THE STRINGERS.** Rest the 2×4 stringers on the ledger and make a plumb mark with a combination square. Cut along the line with a circular saw so the ends of the stringers will lie flat against the shed. Cut the other ends of the stringers so they will lie flat on the ground.

4 **POUR THE PAD.** Build a 2×6 form 18 inches wide and 12 inches longer than the width of the ramp. Dig a 6-inch-deep hole for the form, level the form in the hole, and drive in stakes. Mix and pour concrete; screed it level. Set two J-bolts in the wet concrete at the center of where you will install cross plates.

5 **SCREW THE STRINGERS IN PLACE.** Allow the footing to cure for two or three days, then remove the forms. Fasten the top of each stringer to the ledger by driving #8 2½-inch deck screws through the stringer at an angle.

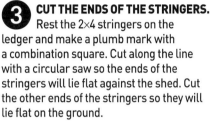

6 **ATTACH THE SURFACE.** Cut 2×6s the same length as the ledger. Leaving a ¼-inch gap between each 2×6, drive 8d (2½-inch) nails or #8 2-inch deck screws through each board into the stringers. Wait to attach the last two boards.

7 **BOLT TO THE CONCRETE.** Cut two 2×4 cross plates to fit between each side of the center stringer and the outer ones. Then mark the J-bolt locations on the cross plates and drill holes ⅛ inch larger than the bolts to allow for error. Drive screws at an angle through the cross plates and into the stringers, then fasten the cross plates with nuts and washers.

8 **ATTACH THE REMAINING 2×6s.** Rip a bevel on the last board to make the transition from ground to ramp smoother, then nail or screw the last two boards to the stringers.

TRELLISES AND ARBORS

A rose-draped arbor is easy on the eyes, but from a builder's point of view, its strength lies underground. The general rule proclaims that the holes for arbor posts should be half as deep as the arbor is high. An 8-foot-tall arbor belongs in holes that are 4 feet deep. The poles need to be 12 feet long overall—enough to anchor the arbor against wind, top-heavy vines, and 10-year-olds playing baseball. While the lattice, braces, and rafters enhance the structure's attractiveness, they add little strength. Like roses, the arbor has its roots in the ground; what one sees is mostly there for appearance.

An arbor stuck in the middle of a featureless lawn seems out of place no matter how well-built or how healthy the plants. The landscaping at the foot of an arbor planter makes it seem part of its surroundings. Siting this arbor at an angle to the house visually connects the porch with other plantings. The pink roses that arch over this arbor lead the eye to a red Japanese maple. The green leaves lead the eye back to the green trim of the house. Select the plants you want to grow on your arbor with care. For extra color, combine varieties of flowers; to attract hummingbirds, pair honeysuckle or trumpet vine with colorful flowers at the base of the arbor.

Sometimes an arbor is more than you need or want to build. Climbing plants such as morning glory and clematis will fill out a trellis and thrive. Roses will grow on a trellis, too, though the trellis won't support plants as large as those shown here. Build and install your trellis or arbor in the late fall or early spring to give yourself a full growing season for whatever you choose to plant.

CHAPTER 5

Trellises and Arbors tool kit 154

Materials 155

Building a trellis panel 156

Hanging trellises 159

Building an arbor 163

Building an arched-top arbor 172

Availability of certain products and materials varies by region. Your local home improvement center can guide you to the right alternative product or, in some cases, arrange for special orders.

REAL-WORLD SITUATIONS

TRELLISES AND ARBORS

A ROSE BY ANY OTHER NAME

Like fence posts, arbors and trellises face a special challenge: For reasons of stability, one-third of such a structure must be underground. While the upper section has to withstand wind, rain, and perhaps freezing temperatures, the bottom portion has to withstand the rigors of an underground life.

Plan for the bottom section of your arbor or trellis. Whether you opt for cedar, redwood, pressure-treated wood, or vinyl above ground is merely a matter of taste; what you use underground is a matter of survival. The almost constant exposure to water makes buried wood a prime candidate for rot and carpenter ant and termite attacks.

The best candidate for an arbor or trellis is pressure-treated wood—usually a southern pine (longleaf, shortleaf, loblolly, or slash pine) soaked under pressure in a combination of preservatives. (The specific solutions are alkaline copper quat [ACQ] and copper azole [CA]. Copper chromium arsenate (CCA) is no longer available for residential use).

But not all pressure-treated woods are equally hardy. They fall into three categories depending on how much of the preservative they have absorbed: aboveground use, soil and freshwater use, and permanent-foundation. Aboveground is fine for fence panels, and soil and freshwater works well for raised-bed gardens. But if you want wood to last underground, use permanent-foundation pressure-treated wood.

As its name implies, it is manufactured for use in foundations, and of the three classes, it's the only one that holds up underground. The three types look identical, and the only way to tell them apart is to locate an inked stamp on the wood. The rating is stamped in capital letters that are centered in the upper portion of the stamp.

Above ground, you have a wider range of choices. Pressure-treated wood and redwood both boast excellent above-ground durability; cedar is rated as good; and vinyl outlasts them all and needs no paint.

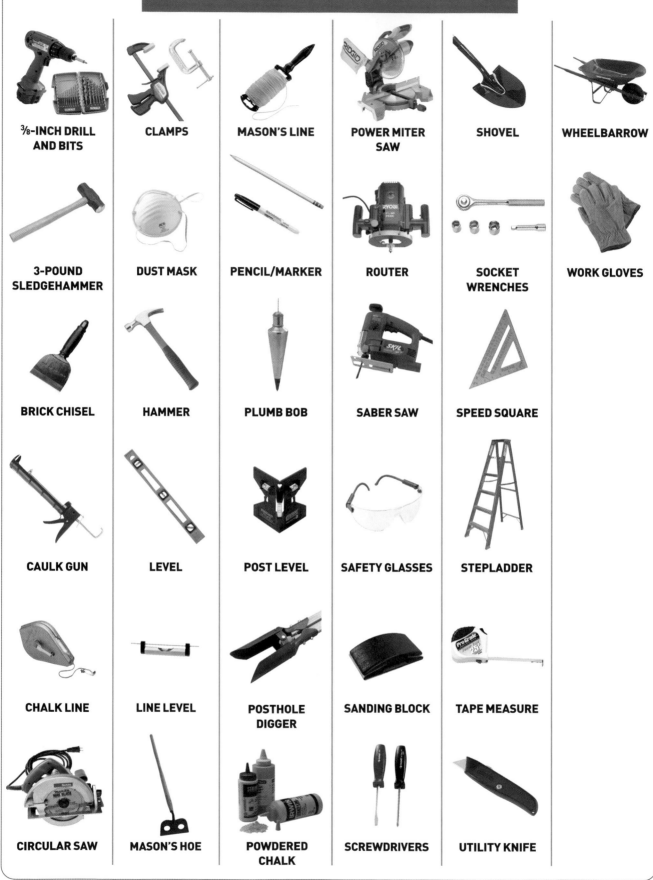

TRELLISES AND ARBORS TOOL KIT

⅜-INCH DRILL AND BITS

CLAMPS

MASON'S LINE

POWER MITER SAW

SHOVEL

WHEELBARROW

3-POUND SLEDGEHAMMER

DUST MASK

PENCIL/MARKER

ROUTER

SOCKET WRENCHES

WORK GLOVES

BRICK CHISEL

HAMMER

PLUMB BOB

SABER SAW

SPEED SQUARE

CAULK GUN

LEVEL

POST LEVEL

SAFETY GLASSES

STEPLADDER

CHALK LINE

LINE LEVEL

POSTHOLE DIGGER

SANDING BLOCK

TAPE MEASURE

CIRCULAR SAW

MASON'S HOE

POWDERED CHALK

SCREWDRIVERS

UTILITY KNIFE

Materials

Trellises and arbors are exposed to the elements year-round and need to be made from materials that will last. Common species of naturally rot-resistant wood are **A** **redwood** and **B** **cedar.** A less-expensive alternative is **C** **pressure-treated wood,** which is chemically treated to prevent it from rotting. Frame custom-made panels with prefabricated **D** **U channels**—get vinyl channels for vinyl, and wood channels for wood. You can buy prefabricated lattice panels made of **E** **wood** or **F** **vinyl** to make your trellis or cover your arbor. Lattice isn't the only material you can use to cover your arbor; **G** **shade fabric** and **H** **reed** or bamboo make attractive as well as practical alternatives. (Both products are not available in all parts of the country and may have to be special ordered.) Anchor the posts of your arbor in the ground with **I** **pre-mixed concrete. J** **Cardboard forms** help create a level surface to work from.

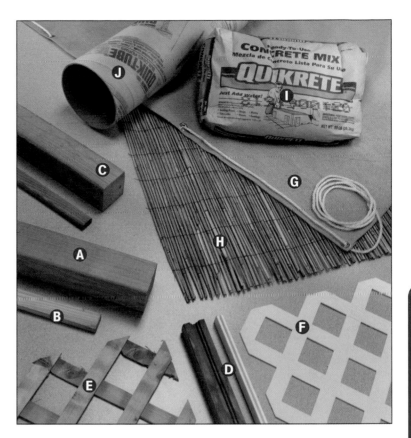

Building trellises and arbors that last is easy with the right fasteners and hardware. Make strong wood joints with **A** **galvanized carriage bolts** instead of nails or screws. Hang a trellis on wood with **B** **lag screws.** For a masonry wall, you'll also need **C** **lag shields.** Reinforce corners with **D** **angle brackets.** **E** **Hurricane/seismic ties,** also known as rafter ties, secure the top of your arbor to the beams—and may be required by your local building codes. **F** **Post/beam connectors** allow you to secure beams on the top of posts. Three basic types of post anchors are available to secure posts to concrete piers. **G** **Flanged-style post anchors** and **H** **rebar-style post anchors** can do the job, but they aren't adjustable once the concrete sets. You'll want the leeway to make minor positioning corrections that are possible with **I** **platform-style post anchors,** which are secured to **J** **J-bolts** placed in the wet concrete. **K** **Reinforce holes used for hanging shade fabric with grommets** to keep the fabric from tearing.

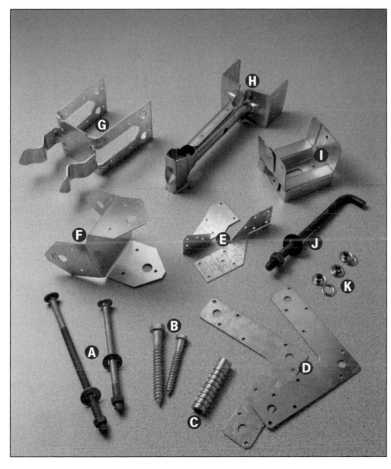

Aluminum products are NOT recommended for use in contact with pressure-treated wood. Fastener and connector manufacturer's recommend hot-dipped galvanized, polymer-coated, or stainless-steel fasteners and connectors.

Building a trellis panel

TRELLISES AND ARBORS

Unsupported, a trellis panel is flexible, and thinner ones are downright flimsy. Consequently, the first step in any trellis project is to strengthen it with a frame. The frame begins as a 2×4; a prefab channel that you nail to it holds the trellis in place. Vinyl channels are for vinyl trellis. They're U-shape and about ½ inch thick and 1 inch wide. Wood channels are beefier, and the groove is stepped in order to handle panels of different thicknesses.

Wood trellis comes in two thicknesses—⁷⁄₁₆ inch and ⁵⁄₈ inch. Get the ⁵⁄₈ inch—it's more durable. Vinyl panels are a standard thickness.

REINFORCE A TRELLIS PANEL BEFORE YOU BUILD WITH IT. Make a frame with mitered corners and hold the trellis in place with prefabricated U-channels. Trellis is available in both wood and vinyl, and thicknesses vary. Buy U-channel made of the same material as the trellis; it will have the right size groove in it.

SKILL SCALE

EASY	MEDIUM	HARD

REQUIRED SKILLS: Cutting miters, cutting lattice, assembling miter joints.

HOW LONG WILL IT TAKE?

Experienced . . . . 1 hr.
Handy . . . . 1.5 hrs.
Novice . . . . 2 hrs.

STUFF YOU'LL NEED

✔ MATERIALS:
U-channels, 2×4 for frame, galvanized deck screws, wood or synthetic lattice panels

✔ TOOLS:
Circular saw, power miter saw, clamps, drill and bits, utility knife, screwdriver, dust mask, safety glasses

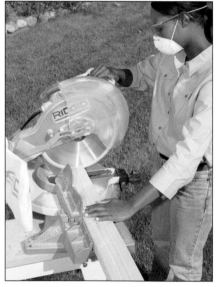

1 CUT THE FRAME PIECES SO THEY'RE A BIT LONG. To determine the size, add at least twice the width of the frame to the desired length of the piece. For example, if you have a 2×4 frame and want a finished frame that is 6 feet square, cut pieces that are 6 feet plus 2×2, or 6 feet 4 inches. (A 2×4 is really 1½ inches thick. Using the full 2 inches in the formula gives you an extra margin of error.)

2 SCREW U-CHANNEL TO THE FRAME. Cut pieces of U-channel to the same length as the frame pieces. Drill holes in the channel that are slightly wider than the shank of a #8 galvanized deck screw. Screw through the holes to attach the channel to the frame. If the channel is wood, tighten the screws so they're snug. If the channel is vinyl, leave them slightly loose so the channel can expand and contract with changes in temperature.

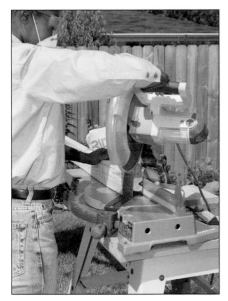

3 **CUT ONE END OF EACH FRAME PIECE.** Set your power miter saw to cut a 45-degree angle. Put an assembled frame-and-channel piece in the box so the groove is against the fence. Cut one end of all the pieces you'll need.

SAFETY ALERT

When cutting lattice with a circular saw, make sure the blade doesn't hit any staples.

4 **MITER THE SECOND CORNER OF EACH PIECE.** Measure out the length you want on one of the pieces and mark the edge of the wood with a sharp pencil. Lay out the miter with the help of a combination square. Repeat the process on an adjoining side. Cut the pieces to length with the power miter saw.

If you enjoy home improvement projects, a power miter saw is a great investment. The tool is versatile and easy to use. Just be sure you learn to operate it safely.

5 **LAY OUT THE REMAINING FRAME PIECES.** Use the first two pieces as a pattern for laying out the remaining two. Put the finished pieces on top of the unfinished ones. Have a helper carefully align the mitered ends and hold them together. Trace along the other end of the finished piece with a sharp knife to lay out the remaining miters.

6 **MITER THE REMAINING PIECES TO SIZE.** To ensure that you hit your mark right on the money, ease into the cut by starting about ½ inch longer than the mark but lower the blade only enough to begin the cut. Slide the piece slowly toward the knife mark until the saw is positioned accurately, then finish the cut.

7 **TRIM A PREFABRICATED LATTICE PANEL TO FIT INSIDE THE FRAME.** Measure the opening, add the depth of both grooves, and subtract ¼ inch to allow for expansion in humid weather. Clamp a piece of 1×2 to the lattice to serve as an edge guide while you make the cut. Work slowly to keep the slats from splintering.

Building a trellis panel *(continued)*

8 **PREDRILL FOR SCREWS.** Start by putting the pieces next to each other to form the frame. Lay out three holes in each corner: two through one frame piece, one through the other. To prevent splitting, keep the holes at least 1 inch from the tip of the miters. Drill oversize holes through the marked pieces but not into wood behind them.

9 **SCREW THE FIRST CORNER TOGETHER.** Have a helper hold two sides of a corner in position, or clamp them to a work surface. Drive galvanized deck screws through the holes and screw the pieces together.

10 **ASSEMBLE THE FRAME.** Screw a third piece to the other two, creating a U-shape assembly. Slide the sheet of lattice into the assembly. Have a helper hold the fourth side in place while you screw it to the others.

11 **ANCHOR THE LATTICE.** Lattice is flexible and could pop out of the frame if someone were to lean against it or bump into it. To anchor wood lattice, drive 1½-inch deck screws at an angle through the lattice and into the body of the U-channel.

IF THE LATTICE IS VINYL, drill holes along the top so the screws will go through the lattice. Screw the lattice in place. On the sides and bottom drill holes so that they go through channel but not the lattice which needs room to expand and contract with seasonal changes in weather.

TOOL TIP

HOW OVERSIZE IS OVERSIZE?

Driving screws near the end or edge of a board can cause the board to split. The oversize holes in this project help prevent splitting. The holes you make through the first piece should be big enough that the threads won't grip and small enough that the head won't slip through. To drill the right size, hold the shank of a drill behind the threads of the screw. The right size bit will just peek out beyond the threads. Better yet, use a combination bit that drills the oversize hole in the first piece and a slightly smaller hole for the threads in the second piece.

Hanging trellises

You can purchase wooden trellises in kits that are easy to assemble and mount on the side of your house. Mounting depends on the wall itself and the size of the trellis. If you have wood siding, you can fasten furring strips, called ledgers, to studs in the wall with lag screws and attach your trellis to them. Putting a ledger on a masonry wall requires anchor shields. Both vinyl and aluminum siding will dent easily. Mount the trellis on hinged posts as shown on page 160.

SKILL SCALE

EASY	MEDIUM	HARD

REQUIRED SKILLS:
Basic carpentry skills.

HOW LONG WILL IT TAKE?

Building a trellis should take:

Experienced .... 1 hr.
Handy .... 2 hrs.
Novice .... 3 hrs.

STUFF YOU'LL NEED

✔ MATERIALS:
Wooden trellis kit, pressure-treated 2×s, 4×4s, ¼×3-inch lagscrews, washers, anchor shields, #8 2½-inch deck screws, pre-mixed concrete, hinges, hook-and-eye fasteners

✔ TOOLS:
Tape measure, ⅜-inch drill and bits, masonry bits, circular saw, socket wrenches, level, hammer, screwdriver, mason's line, stepladder, 3-pound sledgehammer, line level, plumb bob, powdered chalk, posthole digger, wheelbarrow, mason's hoe, pencil, safety glasses, work gloves

Use the siding joints and fasteners as guides to finding wall studs.

ATTACHING A TRELLIS TO SIDING

BECAUSE THE TRELLIS FRAME MAY NOT FALL OVER ANY STUDS, it's usually necessary to screw a ledger to the studs, then nail the trellis to the ledger. Drill the holes in the ledger slightly larger than the bolt diameter to make it easier to align the holes with those you drill in the studs.

1 ASSEMBLE AND PAINT THE TRELLIS THEN HANG THE LEDGER STRIP. Find studs and mark their locations. Place a 2× against the wall at the marks, level it, and transfer the marks to the 2×. Bore ⁵⁄₁₆-inch holes through the 2×, and ³⁄₁₆-inch holes into the studs at the marks.

2 HANG THE LEDGER. Slip washers over ¼×3-inch lag screws and drive them through the holes in the ledger and the studs. Tighten the lag screws with a ratchet and socket wrench. Repeat, installing a ledger to support the trellis at the opposite edge.

3 HANG THE TRELLIS. Put the trellis against the ledger strips. Plumb the trellis against an edge or center upright. If necessary, have a helper hold the trellis in place while you nail or screw it.

Hanging trellises

ATTACHING A TRELLIS TO MASONRY

ATTACHING A TRELLIS TO A MASONRY WALL is similar to hanging it on a wall with siding. The only difference is that you'll need to install anchor shields in the masonry for the lag screws. Make the ledger easier to align by drilling the holes in the ledger so they are slightly larger than the ¼-inch lag bolts.

1 DRILL HOLES. Drill ⅜-inch holes into a 2× ledger for the lag screws. Place and level each furring strip, marking for anchor shields in the mortar. Drill holes (typically ½ inch) in the wall with a masonry bit and insert the shields. If a hole is too big, put anchoring cement in it, then insert the shield. The cement will expand as it sets.

2 HANG THE LEDGER. Position each furring strip on the wall, aligning the holes with the anchor shields. Put a washer over a ¼-inch lag screw and drive the screw into the shield with a ratchet and socket wrench. Fasten the trellis to the furring strips with nails or screws.

INSTALLING A TRELLIS ON HINGES

HANGING A TRELLIS ON 2×4 POSTS lets you fold the trellis out of the way for cleaning or painting the wall. Space the posts equal to the width of the framed panel and set them in concrete. Buy hook-and-eye fasteners beforehand so you set the posts at the right distance from the wall.

1 PUT THE POSTS IN HOLES. Dig the holes. Cut two 2×4 posts about 6 inches above ground. (Half the exposed height of the post will be below ground.) Join the two sections of each post with a hinge and a temporary cleat. Screw the frame to the posts and remove the cleats.

2 ATTACH THE TRELLIS. Screw supports a few inches from the top of the posts to hold them out from the wall. Offset the screws to prevent splitting. Position hook-and-eye-fasteners, screwing the hooks into the posts and the eyes into the wall. Plumb and brace the posts, then fill the holes with concrete. (See page 19.)

ATTACHING A TRELLIS TO POSTS

Hanging a trellis on posts is a step short of building an arbor. While the structure is less complicated, it can still serve much the same purpose: You can grow vines on it or use it to break your yard into smaller areas.

The biggest task in putting a trellis on posts is actually putting in the posts, but this is a relatively simple undertaking. Set posts in holes that are half as deep as the post is high. For example, a post that extends 8 feet above ground needs to extend another 4 feet underground for stability. Fill the holes with concrete to further anchor the posts.

Dealing with the inevitable calluses and blisters that come from digging postholes isn't fun. Wearing gloves will help you avoid sore hands.

Lattice panel

Concrete

4×4 post

YOU CAN MOUNT TRELLIS PANELS BETWEEN POSTS TO PROVIDE A PRIVATE CORNER IN YOUR BACKYARD. Set the posts in holes that are half as deep as the exposed height of the posts. Screw the panels to the posts, then plumb the posts and fill the holes with concrete. Install post caps or trim the tops of the posts at an angle so water will drain off them.

1 LAY OUT THE CORNER. Lay out a corner with mason's lines and batterboards set a foot or so past where the end posts will go. Level the lines, then square them with a 3-4-5 triangle: Mark one line 3 feet and the other 4 feet from where they meet. Slide them on the batterboards until the distance between the marks is exactly 5 feet.

2 LAY OUT THE POSTS. Measure from the corner to find out the location of the other posts. Put tape on the mason's line to show where each post will be. Transfer the taped points to the ground with a plumb bob and powdered chalk. Mark where the lines are tied to the batterboards, then untie them. You'll put the lines back later.

3 DIG THE HOLES. With a posthole digger, dig holes that are half as deep as the post will be high. Placing the dirt you remove from the posthole on a tarp or garbage bag will make disposal easier.

Hanging trellises

ATTACHING A TRELLIS TO POSTS (continued)

4 **RESTRING THE LAYOUT LINES.** Reattach the mason's lines to the batterboards and slide them along the crosspieces until they mark the outer edges of the posts. Set the posts into the holes, plumb them, and brace them.

5 **INSTALL THE TRELLIS PANELS BETWEEN THE POSTS** at the height you want. Make sure each panel is level and sits at least a few inches above the ground. Fasten the panels with #8 2½-inch deck screws. Plumb each post again after screwing into it.

6 **MIX CONCRETE.** Mix bagged concrete in a wheelbarrow. Add water a little at a time, blending the ingredients with a mason's hoe until the concrete clings to the hoe when you lift it from the wheelbarrow.

7 **FILL THE HOLES.** Fill each posthole with concrete, working a 2×4 up and down in it to eliminate air pockets. Allow the concrete to cure for two or three days before removing the braces.

A+ WORK SMARTER

ANCHOR OPTION

Metal anchor spikes are a quick way to set posts. Drive the spike into the ground, then install the post in the anchor. Posts set in anchor spikes provide less support than posts anchored in the ground with concrete, but they're much easier to install.

TRELLISES AND ARBORS

Building an arbor

Building an arbor is a big job. It's a big job made of several smaller ones, however, including setting posts, trimming them, attaching beams, and attaching rafters. Double-check your work as you go. A small error at ground level can make a big difference at the top of a post.

Building starts with the posts. You can install them in the ground and fill the hole with concrete, or you can pour a concrete pier and rest the posts on top of it.

REQUIRED SKILLS: Good carpentry and measuring skills; working with power tools, wood, and concrete.

HOW LONG WILL IT TAKE?

Construction time will vary with the complexity and size of the arbor.

Experienced . . . . Variable
Handy . . . . Variable
Novice . . . . Variable

STUFF YOU'LL NEED

✔ MATERIALS:

4×4s, ¾-inch gravel, fiber tube forms, 1×4s, 2×4s, 2×8s, 1×2s, 1×1s, lattice, duplex nails, #8 2½- and 3-inch deck screws, pre-mixed concrete, post anchors, reed, bamboo, or shade fabric as necessary

✔ TOOLS:

Tape measure, mason's line, line level, chalk line, 3-pound sledgehammer, plumb bob, post level, powdered chalk, clamps, posthole digger, shovel, level, wheelbarrow, mason's hoe, hammer, socket wrenches, circular saw, drill and bits, stepladder, speed square, saber saw, pencil, dust mask, safety glasses, work gloves

AN ARBOR ADDS AN ELEGANT AND FORMAL TOUCH TO A LANDSCAPE. Place your arbor to take advantage of focal points in your garden or in a spot which provides a striking view of the general landscape. Arbors can have built-in or removable seating.

YOU CAN EITHER BURY POSTS IN THE GROUND OR SET THEM ON CONCRETE PIERS. If you're setting the posts in the ground, dig each hole either 10 inches below the frost line or half as deep as the exposed height of the post plus 10 inches (whichever is deeper). Widen the holes at the bottom, set each post on a bed of gravel, then fill the holes with concrete.

To set the posts on a concrete pier, dig holes 10 inches below the frost line, add 4 inches of gravel, and pour a concrete footing and pier. Put a post anchor in the concrete while it's still wet. Once it's dry, you can attach the post to the anchor.

ARBOR CONSTRUCTION IS TYPICAL OF WHAT YOU MIGHT FIND IN BUILDING A DECK. The 4×4 posts rest on concrete footings that provide stability. Beams made of 2×8s are bolted to the posts, and 2×6 rafters sit on top of the beams. The rafters support 1×2 slats that provide shade. Braces reinforce the beams, and end rafters provide stability. Lattice panels along the sides enclose the arbor and provide structure for climbing plants.

Building an arbor

LAYING OUT THE POSTS

1 **INSTALL BATTERBOARDS.** Drive batterboards into the ground 2 to 3 feet beyond each post's position. Stretch mason's line between the batterboards, outlining the edges of the arbor. Level the lines with a line level.

2 **SQUARE THE CORNER.** To square a corner, mark one of the mason's lines 3 feet and the other 4 feet from where the lines cross. Slide the lines on the batterboards until the distance between the points is exactly 5 feet. The corner is now square.

3 **MARK THE GROUND.** At each corner, drop a plumb bob and mark the ground below it with powdered chalk or sand. Mark the position of the mason's lines on the crosspieces. Untie the lines, but leave the batterboards in place.

SETTING POSTS BELOW GRADE

1 **DIG POSTHOLES.** Use a posthole digger or power auger to dig holes at the marked spots. Dig at least 10 inches deeper than half the exposed height of the posts. For example, a post that's 8 feet tall needs to sit in a hole that's 4 feet 10 inches deep. Shovel in 4 inches of gravel, tamp it, pour in a 6-inch layer of concrete, and let it dry.

2 **ALIGN THE POSTS.** Retie the mason's lines and slide them on the crosspieces to mark the outside edges of the posts. Set each post into its hole, plumb it with a fence post or regular level, and brace it with 1×4s and 2×4 stakes.

3 **FILL THE HOLES WITH CONCRETE.** Pour the concrete and work a 2×4 up and down in it to remove air pockets. Slope the top of the concrete so water drains away from the posts. Let the concrete cure for two to three days.

SETTING POSTS ON A PIER

1 **PLACE THE FORMS.** Dig postholes 10 inches below the frost line, pour in 4 inches of gravel, and tamp. Retie the mason's lines and center fiber tube forms in the corners. Nail pieces of wood to opposite sides of each form so the form sits at least 6 inches above the gravel. Put the form in the hole and level it.

2 **MIX CONCRETE.** Mix bagged concrete in a wheelbarrow. Start by making a crater in the dry ingredients. Pour in about half the water recommended by the manufacturer. Mix with a mason's hoe, then slowly add the remaining water until the concrete has the consistency of oatmeal.

3 **FILL THE FORMS.** Shovel concrete into the forms. The concrete will form a footing by spreading out into the 6-inch gap between the form and the bottom of the hole. Keep adding concrete, filling the forms to the top.

Coat the J-bolt threads with petroleum jelly or soap so concrete will not stick to them.

4 **RELEASE ANY TRAPPED AIR.** Work a 2×4 or shovel up and down in the concrete to release any trapped air. Pull a short section of 2×4 across the top of the form as a screed to level the concrete with the top of the forms.

5 **MARK THE CENTER.** Reset the mason's lines and drop a plum bob to mark the centers of the posts. Sink 6-inch J-bolts into the concrete.

6 **REMOVE THE FORMS.** Allow the concrete to cure for two to three days, then strip off the forms and fill in around the concrete with soil. Tamp the soil with your feet.

Building an arbor

SETTING POSTS ON PIERS *(continued)*

7 **INSTALL POST ANCHORS.** Put a post anchor over the J-bolt. Put a washer over the bolt. Fasten with a nut.

8 **ATTACH THE POSTS.** Attach rot-resistant 4×4 posts to the post anchors with hanger nails.

Cut a recess in the side of the post, if necessary, to fit it into the anchor.

TRIMMING THE POSTS

1 **LAY OUT THE CUTS.** Mark the final height on one post and tack mason's line to it at that point. Run the line to the next post, level it with a line level, and mark the height on the post. Repeat the process for the remaining posts.

2 **MAKE A CUTTING GUIDE.** Clamp a speed square to the post at a measurement that compensates for the distance between the edge of the circular saw's base and the blade so the cut will be on your mark.

3 **CUT THE POSTS.** Set the saw's base plate against the cutting guide and cut into the post. The blade won't cut all the way through, so finish the cut with a handsaw. (The cutoff will fly off wildly if you finish the cut with the circular saw.) Cut the other posts the same way.

INSTALLING BEAMS

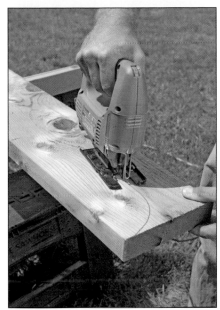

1 **CUT THE BEAMS TO LENGTH.**
Before installing beams, check with your local building department for code specifications. Usually 2×8s are installed, one on each side of the posts. If you want a decorative effect, extend the beams beyond the post and cut a shape in them. Make a cardboard pattern of the shape, trace it onto a board, and make the cut with a saber saw. Use the board as a template to cut the other beams and the rafters.

2 **SCREW THE BEAMS IN PLACE.** With a helper, screw a beam in place on one side of the posts so it's flush with the top of the posts. Place a second beam on the other side. Fit two 4×4 spacers between the double beams as reinforcement and screw them in place on both sides with 3-inch screws. (See Step 1, page 168 for reference.)

(See Step 1, page 168 for reference.)

WORK SMARTER

CAN'T TAKE THE PRESSURE
The chemicals that pressure-treating exposes wood to travel from the outside surfaces of the board toward the middle. Unfortunately they never make it all the way to the center.

Usually this isn't a problem. The bug that can gnaw through enough pressure-treated wood to get to the untreated core of a board has yet to be born. Once you cut a board to length, however, you've exposed the core. Every bug known to man (plus several fungi) will be ready to feast on the freshly cut end.

Treat cut ends with a preservative recommended by the manufacturer of the board. The warranty requires it, as does common sense.

3 **DRILL FOR BOLTS.** Drill two ¼-inch holes per post that run through a beam into the post and out through the second beam. Offset holes to avoid weakening the wood. Put a washer over a carriage bolt, put the bolt through the hole, slip on a washer and a nut, and tighten.

4 **ADD A TEMPORARY SUPPORT.** Tack a board to the post under each end of the double beam. Level the board and tack it to the adjacent post. The two boards will serve as a temporary support for the other double beam and ensure that the two beams are square and level.

5 **INSTALL THE SECOND SET OF BEAMS.** Rest the second set of beams one at a time on the supports. Drill and counterbore holes as before, then install carriage bolts. Remove the temporary support once the second beam has been installed.

TRELLISES AND ARBORS

Building an arbor

ADDING RAFTERS

1 **LAY OUT THE RAFTERS.** Start with the end rafters, positioning them so the outside edges align with the outside edge of a post. Measure, then space the rest of the rafters between the end rafters at 16 inches on center.

2 **CUT THE RAFTERS TO LENGTH.** Cut the rafters 24 inches longer overall than the distance between beams. Cut any desired design at the ends of the rafters. Place an end rafter on the beams and adjust it so the overhang is equal at both ends.

3 **SCREW THE RAFTER IN PLACE.** Drill starter holes for the screws at an angle through the rafter, making the holes a bit smaller than the diameter of the screw. Repeat on the other end.

4 **STRETCH A LINE BETWEEN THE ENDS OF THE RAFTERS.** Tack a nail to each end of the end rafters and pull a mason's line taut between the nails. The lines will help align the ends of the rest of the rafters.

5 **ATTACH THE REMAINING RAFTERS.** Place the rafters one at a time, spacing them according to the marks you made on the beams. Align the ends of each rafter with the mason's lines, then drill starter holes and toenail the rafter in place with 3-inch deck screws. Repeat, screwing all the rafters in place.

6 **INSTALL BRACES.** Cut miters on both ends of short 2×4s to make braces for the rafters. Drill ⅜-inch-diameter holes through each brace, then drill through the brace with a ¼-inch-diameter bit to create a pilot hole. Drive ⅜×3-inch lag screws through the holes. Seal any gaps at the joints with exterior caulk.

INSTALLING ROOF SLATS

1 **CUT THE SLATS TO LENGTH.** Cut 1×2 slats to length by clamping several together at a time and cutting them with a circular saw.

2 **MARK THE CENTER OF THE ARBOR.** Locate the centerpoint of the rafters and snap a chalk line across them.

3 **INSTALL THE SLATS.** Align the center of the first slat with the chalk line on the rafters. Drill holes into the slat with a combination countersink bit and screw the slat into place with #8 2-inch deck screws. Use a slat as a spacer to lay out the next slat and screw it in place. Repeat across the entire roof.

Working with galvanized hanging hardware

Using galvanized hangers makes installing beams a little easier. They're stronger than nails, and using them is easier and more effective than toenailing. This means you'll get a better connection and the structure will come together faster. However, there is a potential downside from a design perspective: Nails are effectively invisible; hangers are not. In general, construction hangers are usually hidden from view; consequently, designers give little thought to how they look. The truth is they're not very pretty. So decide whether seeing the hangers will bother you once the structure is complete. If so, use nails. But check your local building codes: In regions subject to high winds and earth tremors, rafter ties—also known as hurricane/seismic ties—may actually be required.

NAIL A POST/BEAM CONNECTOR ON TOP OF THE POST and you'll find that the problem of holding heavy beams in place while you work has largely been solved.

PUT RAFTER TIES ON TOP OF THE BEAMS TO HOLD THE RAFTERS, and the problem of toenailing disappears. Rafter ties also are sold as hurricane/seismic ties. They make great all-purpose hangers even if you don't live in an area that is prone to earthquakes or high winds.

Building an arbor

ATTACHING LATTICE PANELS AND POST TRIM

1 ATTACH RAILS. Screw 2×4 top and bottom rails to the posts with galvanized #8 2½-inch deck screws. Place 1×1 stops along the outside edges of the posts and rails to support the lattice panel. Secure the stops with galvanized #8 2½-inch deck screws.

2 INSTALL THE LATTICE. Place the lattice panel against the stops and install 1×1 stops along the other side, sandwiching the panel.

3 ATTACH TRIM. As a decorative touch, add four mitered 2×2s around each post directly below the beams. Cut the pieces to size, then drill pilot holes and nail each piece to the post with galvanized #8 2½-inch finishing nails.

COVERING WITH WOVEN REED OR BAMBOO

1 BUILD A FRAME. Construct a frame of 2×2s and screw it to the rafters with #8 2½-inch deck screws. Nail 2×2 supports every 2 feet inside the frame so they're at right angles to the rafters. Unroll the material onto the frame and tack two adjacent corners to the frame.

2 INSTALL THE COVERING. Cut 1×2s to fit over the 2×2s. Lay the 1×2s in place. Have a helper pull the material tight while you screw the first 1×2 to the rafters with #8 2-inch deck screws. Pull the material tight and screw in the next 1×2, continuing this way to the other end.

A woven reed or bamboo covering provides shade but is less durable and less sturdy than slats. To install reed or bamboo, nail a frame of 2×2s to the rafters, then tack the covering to it. Add 1×2s on top of the covering to help hold it in place.

APPLYING SHADE FABRIC

① BUILD A FRAME. Build a four-sided frame from 2×2s to sit on top of the rafters. (Unlike the frame for bamboo, this frame needs no crosspieces.) Screw the frame to the top of the rafters with #8 2½-inch deck screws. Cut a piece of shade cloth so it's the same size as the outside dimensions of the frame.

Shade fabric is a meshlike material that lets in air but keeps out sun. Fabric that provides 60 percent shade is best for plants. For people, buy fabric that provides 80 percent. Shade fabric comes in rolls with unfinished edges. Make your own border or roll up the edges before installing grommets. Secure the fabric with cord and eye screws on a 2×2 frame.

② LAY OUT THE GROMMETS. Roll the edges of the fabric under about 2 inches and pin them in place. Put a grommet in place at a corner and trace around the inside to mark where the hole will be. Repeat in each corner and every 16 inches along the edges.

③ SET THE GROMMETS. Cut a hole in the fabric with the hole cutter that comes in a grommet kit. Set up the grommet punch as shown, with the top-hat-shape half of the grommet on the bottom and the flat grommet piece on the top. Strike with a hammer to drive the grommet halves together.

④ ATTACH SCREW EYES. Put the fabric loosely in place. Lay out holes on the frame for screw eyes, positioning them to align with the grommets. Drill holes one bit size smaller than the screw shank and screw the screw eyes in place.

⑤ TIE THE FABRIC IN PLACE. Lace a strong, weather-resistant cord long enough to secure the fabric on all sides through the grommets and screw eyes. Pull the cord tight to stretch the fabric taut across the frame. Tie the cord securely and cut off the excess.

Building an arch-top arbor

Arch-top arbors are classic and beautiful, especially when roses are climbing up the sides and over the top. The challenge is building the arches. Each arch is constructed from three pieces of 1× lumber that are laminated together to provide thickness and strength. Making them is easier than it sounds, and you'll get a chance to use a router to cut them out. The router will eliminate lopsided arcs and uneven lines. You'll use a jig that turns the router into a big compass to cut a template. The template will be your guide for cutting the arches themselves. Once you have cut the pieces to shape with a saber saw and glued them together, you'll use the router again to trim the arches to their finished shape.

The holes for the posts should be half as deep as the structure is high (excluding the arched top). The base of this arbor is 6 feet tall, so the holes should be 3 feet deep and the posts 9 feet long overall. Make sure you use posts rated for ground burial and weather-resistant lumber for the entire structure.

THIS ARBOR HAS 4×4 POSTS THAT ARE 6 FEET HIGH and spaced 47½ inches apart from side to side and 3 feet apart from front to back. To simplify alignment, the posts are anchored in concrete after the arches are attached. Horizontal 1×3 slats brace the structure and provide a climbing surface for plants.

top plate

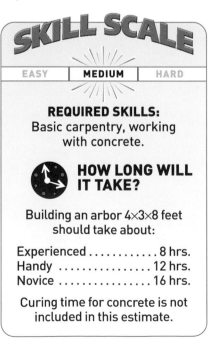

SKILL SCALE

EASY	MEDIUM	HARD

REQUIRED SKILLS:
Basic carpentry, working with concrete.

HOW LONG WILL IT TAKE?

Building an arbor 4×3×8 feet should take about:

Experienced . . . . 8 hrs.
Handy . . . . 12 hrs.
Novice . . . . 16 hrs.

Curing time for concrete is not included in this estimate.

STUFF YOU'LL NEED

✔ MATERIALS:
Pressure-treated 1×8s, 4×4s, 1×2s, 1×3s 2×4s, tempered hardboard, ½-inch plywood, construction adhesive, galvanized 6d (2-inch) and 10d (3-inch) nails, #8 2-inch deck screws, sandpaper, ¾-inch gravel, pre-mixed concrete

✔ TOOLS:
Tape measure, mason's line, utility knife, circular saw, saber saw, router and bits, caulk gun, hammer, sanding block, mason's hoe, wheelbarrow, shovel, level, ⅜-inch drill and bits, screwdriver, pencil, dust mask, safety glasses

A+ WORK SMARTER

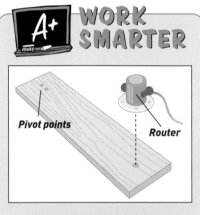

Pivot points

Router

CUTTING ARCHES WITH A ROUTER JIG
Drilling pivot points and mounting a router on a piece of 1×8 guarantees that you will cut a perfect circle or arch everytime. If this will be your first experience with a router, read the directions carefully and practice so you can get used to the tool and operate it safely.

MAKING AN ARCH ROUTER JIG

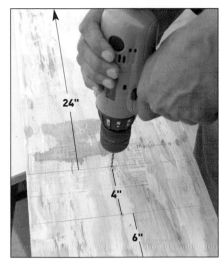

1 **MAKE A TEMPLATE WITH A ROUTER JIG.** Make a template of the arch with the help of a jig that turns your router into a giant compass. Cut a 40-inch piece of ½-inch plywood to a width of 10 inches. Drill two ¹⁄₁₆-inch-diameter holes in it: one centered 6 inches from the end and the other centered 4 inches from the first hole. Drill a centered ½-inch-diameter hole 24 inches from the first hole.

2 **DRILL FOR THE ROUTER.** Unscrew the router base, put a ½-inch bit in the router, and put the bit in the ½-inch hole. Put a pencil through the screw holes in the router base and mark the plywood. Drill stepped holes at each mark: Drill ³⁄₈-inch-diameter holes ¼ inch deep, then drill ⅛-inch holes that go all the way through the plywood in the center of the first holes.

3 **ATTACH THE ROUTER TO THE JIG.** Screw the router to the jig through the holes you just drilled, propping up the unsupported end of the jig to make the job easier. (You may need to replace the original screws with longer ones.) If the screw heads stick out above the surface of the plywood, make the holes slightly deeper.

CUTTING A TEMPLATE

1 **ATTACH HARDBOARD TO A WORK SURFACE.** Screw the corners of a sheet of tempered hardboard to a sheet of inexpensive ½-inch plywood. Draw a line across the center of the hardboard, dividing the sheet into two 48-inch squares. Accurately drill a ¹⁄₁₆-inch hole in the center of the line. Drive a #8 drywall screw through either of the holes in the jig into the ¹⁄₁₆-inch hole in the hardboard until just snug so that the jig will turn smoothly but not wiggle.

2 **ROUT ONE EDGE OF THE ARCH.** Lower the router bit to barely cut through the hardboard. Swing the jig so the bit is just to the left of the edge of the hardboard. Turn on the router and swing the jig across the hardboard in a slow arc.

3 **ROUT THE OTHER EDGE OF THE ARCH.** Put the screw in the other hole and screw the jig back in place. Drive in a couple of drywall screws to hold the arch in place once you cut it free. Make sure the router won't hit any of the screws, then rout out the arch. Cut the ends of the arch along the pencil lines you drew in Step 1.

Building an arched-top arbor

BUILDING THE ARBOR

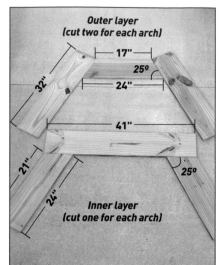

① CUT STOCK FOR THE ARCHES. For stability, each arch is made of three layers, each made of 1×8s and trimmed to shape. Lay out an inner layer and two outer layers for each arch using the dimensions given above. The angles are 25 degrees if cut on a tablesaw or power miter saw and 65 degrees if you use a protractor.

Outer layer (cut two for each arch)
17"
25°
32"
24"
41"
21"
24"
25°
Inner layer (cut one for each arch)

② ASSEMBLE THE STOCK FOR THE ARCHES. Stack up the parts for each arch and lay out the arch on each stack. Glue the layers together with construction adhesive, then nail the layers together with 4d finishing nails placed well away from the layout lines.

③ CUT OUT THE ARCHES. Cut along the layout lines with a saber saw. Cut slowly and carefully, skimming the outside edge of the line as you go. You'll clean up the cut later with your router and a flush trim bit.

Get a bit with a flush bearing on top that is long enough to cut through all three layers of wood.

④ ATTACH THE TEMPLATE. For the smoothest possible curve, rout the arch to shape using the template you made earlier as a guide. Wipe the dust off the arch, cover it with two-sided carpet tape, and press the template firmly in place over the tape. Drive finishing nails at the top and sides to secure.

⑤ ROUT THE ARCHES. Put a flush trim bit in the router—a bit with the bearing on top will be easiest to use. Clamp the arch so it overhangs a work surface and guide the bearing along the template to trim edges of the arch. Leave the ends of the arch as the saw cut them—if you try to rout them, the wood will split.

⑥ SUPPORT THE POSTS. The arch will be somewhat flexible until it's anchored in concrete. To support it, cut some leftover plywood into 3×4-foot panels and screw the panels to the posts.

Designer Tip

SLATS OR LATTICE? IT'S ALL UP TO YOU

As an alternative to putting horizontal slats on the sides of the arbor, you can place lattice panels between the posts. This design is particularly useful if you do not plan to grow tall vines or climbing plants on your arbor. The lattice panels still offer some degree of privacy and give the arbor a more finished look. Add a small lattice gate and the arched arbor becomes a Victorian-style entrance to your backyard.

7 ATTACH THE TOP PLATES AND SLATS. Measure the width of the side, subtract the combined thickness of the arches, and cut a 2×4 top plate to this length. Screw it to the tops of the posts as a support for the arches, as shown. Cut 1×3 slats to length and screw each end to the posts with two screws, spacing the slats 8 inches apart on center. Repeat on the second side.

8 ATTACH THE ARCHES AND SLATS. Remove the plywood. Put an arch in place and screw it into the 2×4 top plates. Measure to make sure the legs are parallel, then screw a brace across them. Attach the other arch and attach the slats.

If you're assembling the arbor with a cordless drill, set up the charger so a fresh battery is always ready to go.

9 LAY OUT AND DIG HOLES FOR POSTS. Dig the holes 3 feet 4 inches deep. Shovel 4 inches of gravel into the holes, tamp, then put the posts in the holes. Check that the posts are plumb, then brace them.

10 MIX CONCRETE. Prepare pre-mixed concrete in a wheelbarrow following the directions on the bag. Add water a bit at a time and mix with a mason's hoe until the concrete clings to the hoe when you lift it.

11 FILL THE HOLES. Shovel concrete into the postholes. Work a 2×4 up and down in the concrete to eliminate air pockets. Slope the top of the concrete so water drains away from the posts. Allow the concrete to cure for two or three days before removing the braces.

6 ELECTRICAL

Electricity can play an important part in your landscaping. At the most basic level, you may want power to run a hedge trimmer or a drill that you're using on one of your outdoor projects. You may want a pump for the water garden, an outlet for a bug zapper, or a light outside the garage.

Lighting can play a big role in your landscaping plan: An overhead light near your parking area makes it easier to unload the groceries at night and provides security. A series of floodlights can call attention to the landscape at night. Lights close to the ground guide you from curb to front door.

An outdoor lighting project often requires nothing more than taking down an old fixture and putting in a new one. Getting power to another part of the yard, however, means digging a trench for the wire and somehow getting power to it. Most new homes have at least one outdoor outlet, and tapping into it to run power elsewhere is relatively easy. It's slightly more complicated if you have to bring the power from inside the house, especially if the walls are masonry.

But it doesn't have to be difficult: Low-voltage lighting systems can simplify the job. A transformer steps the voltage down to a level low enough that you don't have to dig a trench; the transformer that powers the light can be plugged in almost anywhere. The wiring is simple too. You just clamp the lights onto the cable.

CHAPTER 6

Electrical tool kit 178

Materials 179

Making wire connections 181

Extending a circuit 183

Adding a GFCI circuit 190

Running conduit and cable 192

Mounting electrical boxes 196

Installing a GFCI outlet 198

Installing switches 200

Installing automatic control devices 202

Installing outdoor light fixtures 204

Installing low-voltage lighting 208

REAL-WORLD SITUATIONS

INSTALLING ELECTRICS OUTDOORS

Even if you're an old hand at indoor wiring, you'll soon find that electrical code is a bit more stringent outdoors than indoors. Safety, of course, is the primary concern in all wiring, and because more can go wrong outside, the requirements for 110-volt wiring are stiff.

■ Cable running underground must be encased in plastic conduit, or it must be UF cable, which is approved for burial.

■ Underground cable must be buried at the depths required by national and local codes.

■ Exposed cable must be housed in conduit within code specified feet of the ground.

■ All electrical boxes must be approved for outdoor use. They must have gaskets and watertight fittings.

■ Outlets must be GFCI protected. GFCI protection is installed with a special breaker at the breaker box or with a GFCI outlet. Outlets are usually simplest. A protected outlet has a sensor in it that cuts the power if electricity runs directly into the ground, whether the path has a short or a person standing in a puddle.

As you'll see, none of the requirements is beyond the skill of most homeowners. In fact, unless you're able to tap into an existing outdoor outlet, you'll probably spend most of your time indoors, running a new circuit and getting the wiring through the wall and on its way to the great outdoors.

ELECTRICAL

ELECTRICAL TOOL KIT

CABLE RIPPER	DIAGONAL CUTTER	HAMMER DRILL	NEON CIRCUIT TESTER	SAFETY GLASSES	VOLTAGE METER
CAULK GUN	DRILL AND BITS	INSULATED SCREWDRIVERS	PERCUSSION BIT	SCREWDRIVER	WIRE CUTTER
CHALK LINE	FISH TAPE	LINEMAN'S PLIERS	PLASTIC PIPE CUTTER	SHOVEL	
COMBINATION STRIPPER	HAMMER	NEEDLE-NOSE PLIERS	POSTHOLE DIGGER	UTILITY KNIFE	

ELECTRICAL

TOOL TIP

A BELT'S A BELT, RIGHT?

Electrical projects will go smoother if you're wearing a tool belt. Though a basic carpentry tool belt will keep your electrical tools close at hand, an electrician's tool belt is specially designed for keeping often-used electrical items within easy reach. Even if you work on only a half-dozen boxes and devices, a belt will save time. They are available in many styles; two are shown at right.

Materials

Cable is the heart of any electrical project. The most common cable is NM (nonmetallic jacket) cable, used indoors. Outdoors you'll want to use UF (underground feed) cable, which is weathertight.

Cable comes in various sizes and is color coded: When it comes to indoor (NM) cable, **A** **12-2G, or 12-gauge cable** with two conductors and one ground, is yellow; and **B** **14-32, or 14-gauge cable** with two conductors and one ground, is white. All **C** **UF cable** is gray. Stick with 12-gauge cable; 14-gauge wire carries less wattage and amperage. Black wires carry power, white are neutral and carry power back to the box, and grounding wires take power to the ground if there is a short. At least part of an outdoor run has to be in **D** **plastic conduit;** the section that's above ground can be encased in **E** **metal conduit.** The cover on a waterproof **F** **LB fitting** is removable to make fishing wire easier when the cable turns a corner. Connect plastic conduit with **G** **primer, PVC solvent cement,** and **H** **couplings.** Use **I** **metal fittings** on metal conduit. Attach conduit to the house with **J** **conduit straps.** Cover exposed wire ends with **K** **wire nuts.** Attach cable to joists with **L** **cable staples.** For extra security, wrap wire nuts with **M** **electrical tape** and wrap a few turns around the wire, too, to keep the nut from working loose. Low-voltage systems have **N** **crimp-on connectors.**

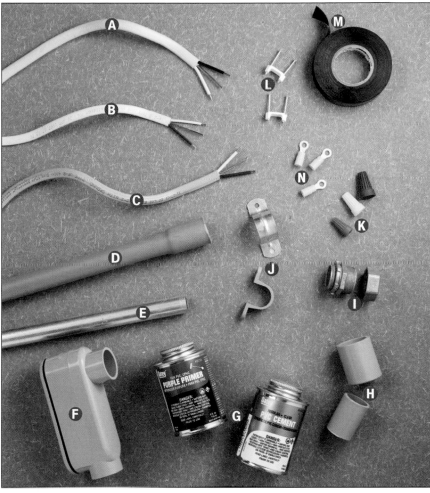

Selecting the proper size cable

WIRE GAUGE	AMPERAGE	MAX LOAD
14-gauge	15 amps	1,440 watts (120 volts)
12-gauge	20 amps	1,920 watts (120 volts)

The higher the number of a wire's gauge, the less current—or amperage—it can carry. When you install a new circuit, make sure the wire you use has an amperage rating that matches that circuit.

Planning for voltage drop

AMPERES	VOLT AMPERES	No. 14	No. 12	No. 10	No. 8
5	600	90	142	226	360
10	1,200	45	71	113	180
15	1,800	30	47	75	120
20	2,400	22	36	57	90
25	3,000	18	28	45	72
30	3,600	15	23	38	60

As electricity travels through a wire, it loses some of its strength. A voltage drop of 2 percent is acceptable, but anything more than that will affect the performance of whatever is plugged into the circuit. This chart shows the maximum number of feet a length of cable carrying a certain amount of amps can run while maintaining acceptable voltage. For example, if you want to run a circular saw that draws 15 amps 60 feet from your house, you can't use No. 12-gauge wire (maximum: 47 feet). Choose No. 10-gauge cable (maximum: 75 feet).

Materials *(continued)*

Ⓐ A ground fault circuit interrupter (GFCI) outlet provides protection against electrical shock and is required by code for outdoor outlets. You can substitute **Ⓑ an indoor outlet** if it's protected by a **Ⓒ GFCI breaker** installed in the breaker box. **Ⓓ A single-pole switch** controls a light from a single location and has two terminals. It can be used outdoors, but like switches, it must be mounted in a waterproof box made of either **Ⓔ metal** or **Ⓕ plastic.** Waterproof boxes have **Ⓖ gaskets** and **Ⓗ cover plates** to keep out the weather. Lights and other fixtures are controlled by various automatic switches, including **Ⓘ a motion-sensor switch, Ⓙ a photoelectric eye, Ⓚ a timer switch,** and **Ⓛ a time-delay switch.**

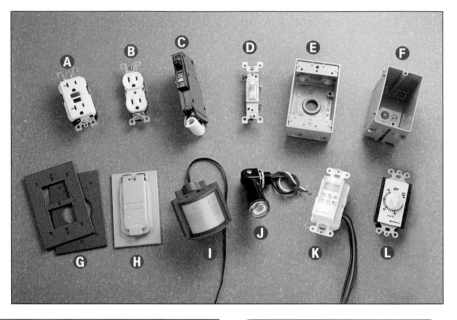

For years, your only choices for lighting up the yard were **Ⓐ floodlights** and **Ⓑ porch lights.** You'll find a wider variety of lighting in stores these days. **Ⓒ Mercury-vapor lights** produce a bluish-green light, and **Ⓓ halogen lights** provide an intense white light. You also can buy **Ⓔ low-voltage lighting,** which uses an outdoor version of lamp wire to power a network of small lights. Because it works on low voltage, this network doesn't require you to dig a trench for the wire, and the fittings are very simple. **Ⓕ A transformer** that reduces regular 120 volts A.C. to 12 volts A.C. powers low-voltage lights. You can buy low-voltage lighting piece by piece, but you'll save money if you buy the entire system as a kit.

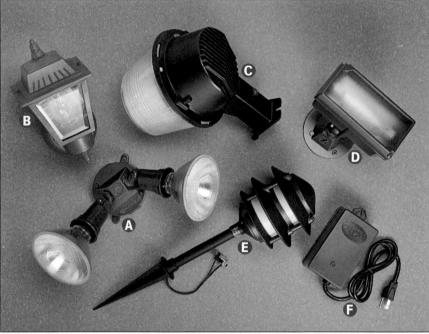

Amperage drawn by different motors

HORSEPOWER	120 VOLTS	240 VOLTS
⅙	4.4	2.2
¼	5.8	2.9
⅓	7.2	3.6
½	9.8	4.9
¾	13.8	6.9
1	16	8
1½	20	10
2	24	12
3	34	17
5	56	28
7½	80	40
10	100	50

When you want to use outdoor equipment, remember: The higher the horsepower, the more amperage the circuit draws. A 3-horsepower tablesaw, for example, running on 120 volts draws 34 amps. The circuit you plug into must accommodate the motor you plan to run. This chart applies to motors running at usual speeds and with normal torque characteristics.

ELECTRICAL

Making wire connections

No matter what type of electrical job you're going to do, it will most certainly entail the connection of wires. Start by stripping off 8 to 10 inches of exterior sheathing. Then strip ½ to ¾ inch of insulation from the wires inside. A wire that is black or red is called hot, or live, because it is meant to carry current. A white wire is neutral. A grounding wire may be green or bare copper. Be careful not to damage the wires while stripping them. If you do, start the process over. Make sure all bare wires are covered after connections are made.

SKILL SCALE

EASY	MEDIUM	HARD

REQUIRED SKILLS: Using a combination stripper and screwdriver.

HOW LONG WILL IT TAKE?

Connecting a receptacle or switch should take about:

Experienced .... 1 min.
Handy .... 2 min.
Novice .... 3 min.

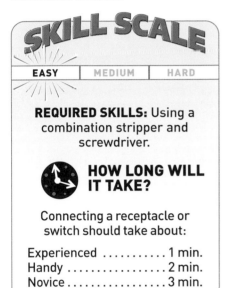

STUFF YOU'LL NEED

✔ MATERIALS:

Cable, wire nuts

✔ TOOLS:

Cable stripper, utility knife, wire cutter or combination stripper, lineman's pliers, needle-nose pliers, screwdriver

SAFETY ALERT

Make sure the power is off at the main power circuit before doing any electrical work.

STRIPPING CABLE

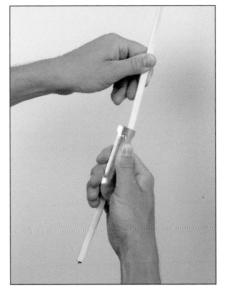

1 STRIP OFF THE SHEATHING. Strip 8 to 10 inches of sheathing off the end of the cable with a cable stripper or utility knife. Squeeze the stripper until it cuts into the sheathing, then pull it to slice open the cable.

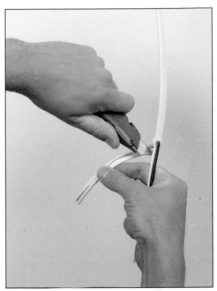

2 CUT OFF THE SHEATHING. Peel back the cable's sheathing to expose the wires. Cut off the excess sheathing with a utility knife.

STRIPPING WIRE

1 PUT THE WIRE IN A COMBINATION STRIPPER. Strip ½ to ¾ inch of insulation off each wire with a wire cutter or combination stripper. Fit the wire into the stripper slot that matches its gauge, then squeeze and turn the tool around the wire to cut the insulation.

2 REMOVE THE INSULATION. Keep the jaws closed and slide the combination stripper to the end of the wire to pull off the insulation.

Making wire connections

CONNECTING WIRES

1 **TWIST THE WIRES TOGETHER.** Hold the wires you're connecting parallel to each other and twist the bare ends together clockwise with lineman's pliers. Once you've twisted the wires together, snip the ends so they're even.

2 **SCREW AND TAPE ON A WIRE NUT.** Screw a wire nut onto the end of the twisted wires. Tug gently on each wire to be sure the connection is secure. Redo the connection if any bare wire is exposed. For extra strength and safety, wrap electrical tape around the nut and wire.

CONNECTING WIRES TO SCREW TERMINALS

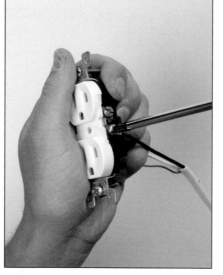

1 **MAKE A LOOP.** Shape the end of the wire into an open loop with needle-nose pliers. Create the loop by stepping the pliers toward the end of the wire, making progressively smaller bends with each step.

2 **SCREW ON THE WIRE.** Loosen the terminal screw. Hook the wire end clockwise around the terminal and tighten the screw. Looping the wire this way causes it to tighten around the terminal when you turn the screw. If the wire end doesn't loop at least three-quarters of the way around the screw or if bare wire is exposed, dismantle, snip the extra wire, and start over.

Making pigtail connections

When more than one wire is intended for a screw terminal, code requires a jumper wire. A jumper is about 6 inches long and matches the gauge of the wires it joins. Connect the jumper and the wires with a wire nut, then connect the jumper wire to the terminal. It's good practice to use a pigtail whenever you have more than one wire going to either side of an outlet or fixture. Check local codes.

Don't use the push-in connection option

Using push-in terminals on outlets is not recommended, even though the receptacle will allow you to do so. Wires can slip out of the terminal breaking the circuit which disrupts power to the outlet. Electricians prefer the screws because the connection is more secure and the wire is far less likely to slip out. Checking each outlet to find the source which one's the culprit isn't a great way to spend a Saturday afternoon so screw those wires to the terminals.

Extending a circuit

To get power outdoors, you can either add a new circuit or tap into an existing one. Outlets, light fixtures, and junction boxes are all good places to tap into. Before you tap into a circuit, make sure what you're doing meets code. You can have no more than eight devices (ceiling lights, receptacles, etc.) per 20-amp breaker. If the circuit meets that requirement, add up the amperage drawn by each device on the circuit. If what you plan on adding to the circuit brings the total amperage to more than 80 percent of the amperage of the fuse or breaker, choose another circuit.

The way you tap into a box depends on where it falls in the circuit. An end-of-the-run box—which has only one cable coming into it—is connected slightly differently from a middle-of-the-run box, which has at least two cables coming into it. Both are explained here.

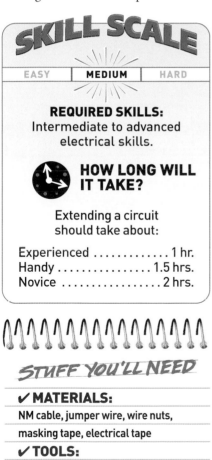

SKILL SCALE

EASY	**MEDIUM**	HARD

REQUIRED SKILLS:
Intermediate to advanced electrical skills.

HOW LONG WILL IT TAKE?

Extending a circuit should take about:

Experienced . . . . 1 hr.
Handy . . . . 1.5 hrs.
Novice . . . . 2 hrs.

STUFF YOU'LL NEED

✔ **MATERIALS:**
NM cable, jumper wire, wire nuts, masking tape, electrical tape

✔ **TOOLS:**
Screwdriver, neon circuit tester, cable stripper, wire cutter or combination stripper, lineman's pliers, needle-nose pliers

MAPPING CIRCUITS AND LOADS

1 TURN OFF THE POWER. To identify the electrical devices on a circuit, turn off a breaker for the circuit at the service panel. Turn on switches and fixtures to find those no longer receiving power. Check outlets by plugging a working lamp into each receptacle.

2 ADD UP THE EXISTING WATTAGE. Add the wattage ratings of all devices on the circuit and those you plan to install. Divide the total by 120 volts to get a result in amps and compare it to the rating for the circuit stamped on the breaker. To prevent overloading a circuit, don't exceed 80 percent of its rating.

JOINING INTO AN END-OF-THE-RUN OUTLET

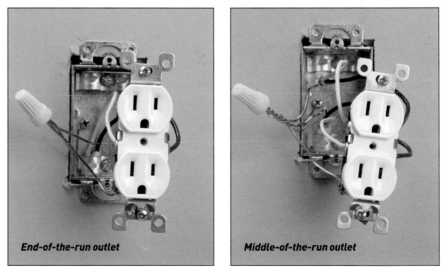

End-of-the-run outlet   *Middle-of-the-run outlet*

AN END-OF-THE-RUN OUTLET HAS ONE CABLE THAT ENTERS THE ELECTRICAL BOX.
The black hot wire is connected to a brass screw, the white neutral wire is connected to a silver screw, and the grounding wire is connected by jumpers to the grounding screws on the outlet and the box. To extend the circuit, begin by threading a new cable into the box. Connect the new black wire to the other brass screw on the outlet and connect the new white wire to the silver screw. Make pigtails to join the grounding wires to the grounding screws.

Extending a circuit

JOINING INTO AN END-OF-THE-RUN OUTLET

① **CUT OFF THE POWER.** Determine which circuit the outlet is on and shut off the breaker for that circuit at the service panel. Post a sign to alert others that you are working on the circuit.

② **REMOVE THE OUTLET.** Remove the outlet cover plate, then remove the screws that hold the outlet in the box. Without touching any wires, gently pull the outlet out of the box.

③ **DOUBLE-CHECK FOR POWER.** Check that the power is off with a circuit tester. Working with one hand, to reduce the risk of an electrical shock touch one probe to the wired brass screw and the other probe to the wired silver screw. The tester shouldn't light. If the tester does light, go to the service panel and shut off the correct circuit.

Although not required it's a good idea to wrap electricians tape around the terminals after making the connections.

Calculating box capacity

TYPE OF BOX	BOX SIZE	NUMBER OF CONDUCTORS		
		No. 10	No. 12	No. 14
Switch	3"×2"×2¼"	4	4	5
	3"×2"×2½"	5	5	6
	3"×2"×2¾"	5	6	7
	3"×2"×3½"	7	8	9
Square	4"×1¼"	7	8	9
	4"×1½"	8	9	10
	4"×2⅛"	12	13	15
	4¹¹⁄₁₆"×1¼"	10	11	12
Octagonal	4"×1¼"	5	5	6
	4"×1½"	6	6	7
	4"×2⅛"	8	9	10

Electrical boxes are made for a specific number of wires. Add up the existing and new wires to see if the box is big enough. Count all grounding wires as one wire, no matter how many there are. Each outlet, switch, fixture nipple, or any internal clamp counts as one wire. If the box isn't big enough for another cable, change it or choose another location.

Reprinted with permission from NFPA 70-1996, the National Electric Code®, Copyright© 1996, National Fire Protection Association, Quincy, MA 02269. This reprinted material is not the complete and official position of the National Fire Protection Association on the referenced subject, which is represented only by the standard in its entirety.

WORK SMARTER

WHICH SIDE IS UP? **You can install an outlet with the hole for the ground at either the top or the bottom.** One advantage of installing the outlet with the grounding hole at the top is that if something falls directly on the plug, it will hit the ground instead of the hot and neutral, and the outlet won't short out. But the main consideration is consistency—not alternating between hole-up and hole-down from one outlet to another—and making sure the position of the hole allows the plug you plan to install to drape down rather than stick up.

ELECTRICAL

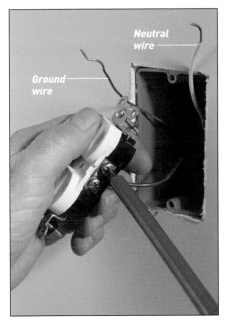

Ground
wire

Neutral
wire

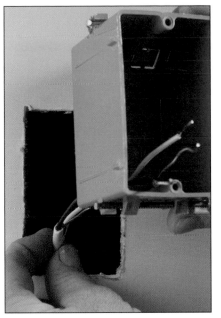

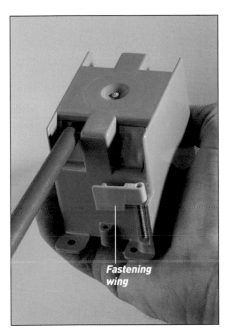

Fastening
wing

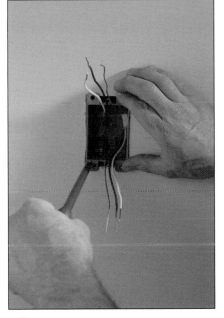

4 **DISCONNECT THE WIRES.** Once you're sure the power is off, unscrew the terminals and disconnect the wires from the outlet. Uncap the grounding wire connection and remove the jumper.

5 **REMOVE THE OLD BOX.** Remove the nails holding the box to the stud in the wall. Slip a hacksaw blade between the box and the stud and cut through the nails. Pull the box free and remove the cable. You will replace this box with a remodeling box that has screw-driven wings to hold the box firmly against the wall.

6 **BREAK THE TABS FOR THE CABLE IN THE NEW REMODELING BOX.** Run cable for the new part of the circuit. Break the tabs in the remodeling box to provide openings for the old and new cables. Run the new cable from the end of the new circuit to the box, feeding about 8 inches of it—or enough to work comfortably—into the box through the new knockout. Feed the old cable back into the outlet.

7 **INSTALL THE REMODELING BOX.** Insert the box in the opening. Tighten the box firmly to the wall by screwing the wings into place. Strip 8 to 10 inches of sheathing off the cable and ½ to ¾ inch of insulation off the wires.

WORK SMARTER

NO SHOCKS
A plug-in receptacle analyzer is a handy device for checking outlets. It features lights that tell you if a wire is hot and if a circuit is wired correctly. You also can use a penlike tester that you pass along the wall. The device beeps whenever it's near a power source.

If you have difficulty removing the old box, or if you damage it on removal, replace it with a remodeling box. Remodeling boxes have screw-driven wings that snug the box flush against the wall without having to use nails or screws.

Gotta clamp it!

If a metal box is without a built-in clamp, you'll need to install a two-piece external clamp. Slip the connector onto the sheathed cable and tighten it, then feed the cable into the box. Thread the locknut onto the connector from inside the box and tighten it by pushing against the lugs with a screwdriver.

ELECTRICAL

Extending a circuit

JOINING INTO AN END-OF-THE-RUN OUTLET (continued)

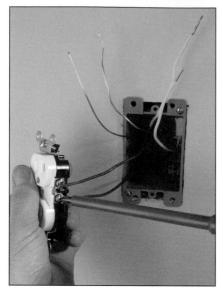

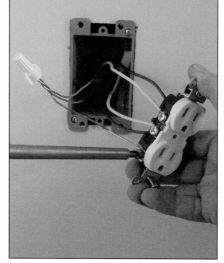

8 **CONNECT THE WIRES.** Connect the black and the white wires of the existing and new cables to different sets of terminals on the outlet: black wires to brass screws and white wires to silver screws. Make a loop in each wire, wrap it clockwise around its terminal, and tighten the screw with a screwdriver.

9 **CONNECT THE GROUND.** Make two 6-inch grounding jumpers from the grounding wire in an extra piece of cable. Connect the jumpers to the grounding wires with a wire nut. Attach one of the jumpers to the grounding screw on the outlet.

10 **REINSTALL THE OUTLET.** Gently fold the wires into the electrical box and position the outlet. Screw the outlet onto the box, then screw on the cover plate.

Use the right wire nut. Check the outlet's package to make sure the wire nut is large enough for the gauge of wire you're working with.

JOINING INTO A MIDDLE-OF-THE-RUN OUTLET

If you find two (or more) cables entering the electrical box, the outlet is in the middle of the run. Extending the circuit is likely to require a larger box to accommodate the new cable and wires (see "Calculating box capacity," page 189). In this case the total number of wires for the extension is nine (four black, four white, and one ground) so you will need a box at least 3 ½ inches deep to accommodate the new wires. Because only one wire is allowed to connect directly to a screw terminal, two of the black wires and two of the white wires require pigtails.

Before

After

IN MIDDLE-OF-THE-RUN OUTLETS, the black wires are connected to brass screws, the white wires are connected to silver screws, and the grounding wires are connected by jumpers to the grounding screws on the outlet and the box. Add the new cable, then connect all the black wires to a jumper and connect the jumper to a brass screw. Join the white wires the same way to a silver screw. Connect the grounding wires to the grounding screws with jumpers.

ELECTRICAL

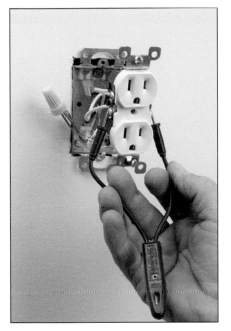

1 DOUBLE-CHECK FOR POWER.
Check that the power is off with a circuit tester. Working with one hand, touch one probe to the wired brass screw and the other probe to the wired silver screw. The tester shouldn't light. If the tester does light, go to the service panel and shut off the correct circuit.

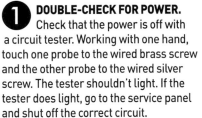

2 DISCONNECT THE OUTLET. Undo the wires and remove the outlet. Unclamp the cables and remove the electrical box. Pry out knockout holes for three cables in a new box. Run a new cable from the end of the new circuit to the box. Clamp the new cable and the two existing cables to the box.

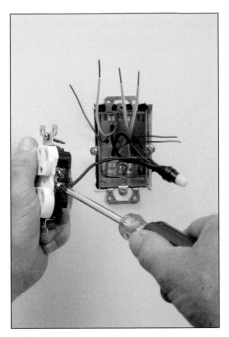

3 CONNECT THE BLACK WIRES.
Fasten the electrical box to the stud in the wall. Twist the black wires together with a jumper and screw on a wire nut. Tape it in place with electrical tape. Attach the jumper to a brass screw.

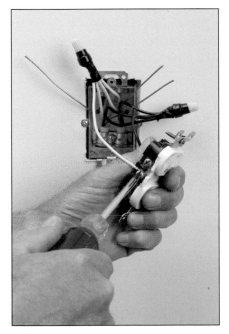

4 CONNECT THE WHITE WIRES. Twist the white wires together and screw on a nut. Tape the nut in place. Screw the jumper to a silver screw.

5 CONNECT THE GROUND WIRES.
Twist together the grounding wires with two jumpers and screw on a wire nut. Connect one jumper to the grounding screw on the electrical box and the other jumper to the grounding screw on the outlet.

6 REINSTALL THE OUTLET. Gently fold the wires into the electrical box. Screw the outlet to the box, then install the cover plate.

Extending a circuit

TAPPING INTO A LIGHT FIXTURE

One way to get power for a new circuit is to tap into an existing light fixture and run wire for a new circuit from it. This method works well when you're adding new lights, as opposed to a receptacle used for a tool that draws a lot of current.

Start by shutting off power to the circuit at the service panel, then unscrew the fixture. Support the fixture with a length of coat hanger. Don't touch bare wires until you're sure power is off. Double-check with a voltage tester.

In the box, you will most likely find a white wire connected to a black wire. This wire goes to the switch—label it "hot" by wrapping it with black electrical tape at both ends of the circuit. Disconnect the wires from the light fixture and label all the wires. Set the fixture aside. Unclamp the cables and remove the box—the extra cable will require a larger box. See the chart on page 184 for the right size.

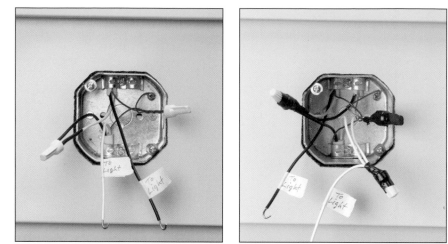

WHEN YOU REMOVE A LIGHT FIXTURE, YOU'LL SEE A BOX WITH A BLACK WIRE CONNECTED TO THE LIGHT'S BLACK WIRE and a white wire connected to the light's white wire. Another white wire (which goes to a switch) also connects to a black wire. To extend the circuit, connect the new black wire to these two. Connect the remaining white wires to the light. Connect all grounding wires and the grounding jumper with a nut and attach the jumper to the grounding screw.

SAFETY ALERT

Shut off all power to the circuit at the service panel before working on the fixture.

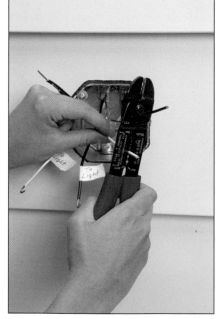

1 **INSTALL A NEW BOX AND CABLE.** Turn off the power and label and disconnect the wires. Install a new box and feed in the existing wires. Strip 8 inches of sheathing off the new cable, feed it into the box, then strip ½ to ¾ inch of insulation off the wires. Clamp the cables in place using the clamps built into the box.

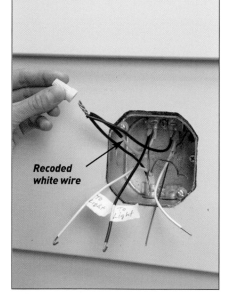

Recoded white wire

2 **CONNECT THE BLACK WIRES.** Twist the black fixture wire and the black wire originally connected to it back together and cover with a wire nut. One of the white wires was originally connected to a black wire—wrap black tape around it to "recode" it. Twist the recoded wire to the remaining black wires and screw on a wire nut.

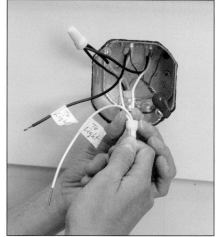

3 **CONNECT THE REMAINING WIRES.** Twist the white wires together and connect with a wire nut. Connect all the grounding wires to a jumper, cover with a nut, and connect the jumper to a grounding screw. Wrap tape around all the caps and the wires running into them. Gently fold the wires into the electrical box and reinstall the light fixture. Install the new fixture on the new cable you ran.

ELECTRICAL

TAPPING INTO A JUNCTION BOX

A junction box—an electrical box where cables that run through exposed joists or studs have been connected—is another opportunity to extend a circuit. Shut off power to the circuit at the service panel, then unscrew the box's cover plate. Don't touch bare wires until you're certain the power is off. To make sure the power is off, touch one probe of a voltage tester to the black wire connections and the other probe to the box.

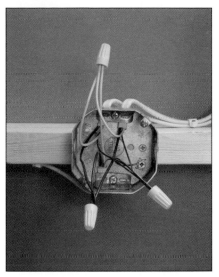

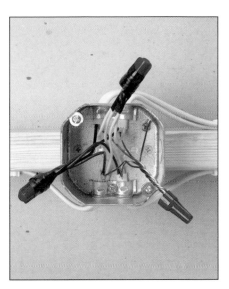

THREE CABLES ENTER THIS JUNCTION BOX, BUT YOURS MAY VARY, DEPENDING ON THE CIRCUIT. All the black wires are connected to black wires; all the white wires are connected to white wires. The grounding wires are jumpered to the box's grounding screw. To tap into the box, add a new cable to the box. Attach its black wire to those in the box. Attach its white wire to the white wires in the box. Connect all the grounding wires to the box with a jumper.

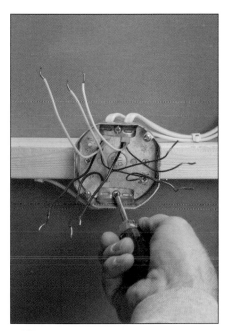

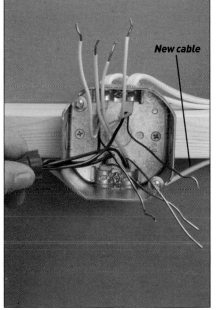

New cable

1 WITH THE POWER OFF, UNDO ALL THE WIRE CONNECTIONS. Remove the box and replace it with a larger one if necessary. Check the chart on page 184 for the proper size. Prepare the new cable and fasten all the cables into the box with built-in clamps.

2 TWIST THE BLACK WIRES TOGETHER CLOCKWISE and screw on a wire cap suitable for the gauge and number of wires. Connect all the white wires the same way.

3 CUT A GROUNDING JUMPER ABOUT 6 INCHES LONG and connect the grounding wires to it. Loop the jumper clockwise onto the grounding screw and tighten it. Wrap electrical tape around each cap and the wires that run into it. Gently fold the wires into the box and screw the cover back on the box.

ELECTRICAL

Adding a GFCI circuit

If your service panel has a free slot (one that doesn't have a breaker in it), you can run a new circuit from the panel to take electricity outdoors. Code requires you to protect an outdoor circuit with a ground fault circuit interrupter (GFCI). This device monitors the flow of electricity and automatically shuts off the circuit in the event of a problem. Installing a GFCI breaker at the service panel provides this safety protection to the entire circuit, as well as all of the electrical devices wired into it. Alternatively, you can install a regular breaker and start the circuit with a GFCI outlet, which protects all electrical devices following it on the circuit.

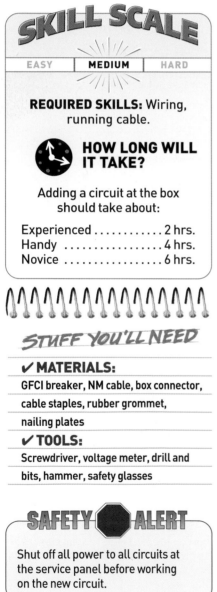

SKILL SCALE

EASY	**MEDIUM**	HARD

REQUIRED SKILLS: Wiring, running cable.

HOW LONG WILL IT TAKE?

Adding a circuit at the box should take about:

Experienced . . . . 2 hrs.
Handy . . . . 4 hrs.
Novice . . . . 6 hrs.

STUFF YOU'LL NEED

✔ **MATERIALS:**
GFCI breaker, NM cable, box connector, cable staples, rubber grommet, nailing plates

✔ **TOOLS:**
Screwdriver, voltage meter, drill and bits, hammer, safety glasses

SAFETY ALERT

Shut off all power to all circuits at the service panel before working on the new circuit.

Neutral bus bars

Ground bus bar

Hot bus bar

GFCI circuit breaker

TO ADD A GFCI CIRCUIT AT THE SERVICE PANEL, REMOVE ONE OF THE KNOCKOUTS IN THE SIDE OF THE BOX AND PUT A BOX CONNECTOR IN THE OPENING. Feed the new cable through the box connector, then begin connecting the wires: Connect the cable's grounding wire to the panel's neutral bus bar, a metal strip that grounds the neutral and ground wires of each cable. Install the cable's black wire and white wire into the GFCI breaker. Connect the GFCI breaker's white wire to the panel's neutral bus bar.

JOINING INTO THE SERVICE PANEL

1 RUN THE NEW CABLE. Feed cable from the end of the new circuit to the service panel. Drill holes through wood studs or joists. If the studs are metal, insert a rubber grommet to protect the cable. Fasten the cable to the sides of studs or joists with cable staples every foot and 8 inches above and below the box. Each cable needs its own staples. Protect the cable by securing nailing plates to the studs before you close up the wall. (See page 195.)

2 SHUT OFF THE POWER. Turn off the main disconnect switch to shut off power to all the circuits.Then turn off the circuits one by one so all the circuits won't come on at once when you restore power. Unscrew and remove the panel cover. Don't touch anything inside the panel until you're sure the power is off.

3 **MAKE SURE THE POWER IS OFF.** With a voltage meter or circuit tester, touch one probe to the front screw on the breaker and the other probe to the panel's ground or neutral bus bar. (In some panels the ground and neutral will be attached to the same bar.) If the tester lights, have an electrician rewire the box.

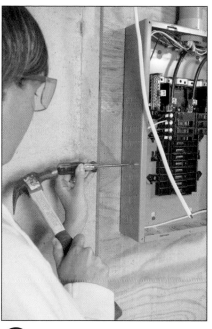

4 **REMOVE A KNOCKOUT.** Once you're sure the power is off, remove a knockout from the side of the panel. Install a box connector in the knockout and feed in 8 to 10 inches of cable (enough to connect the wires comfortably) through it. Tighten the connector.

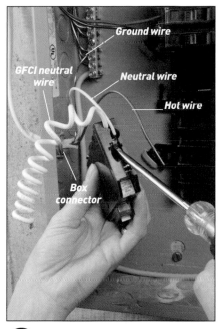

5 **WIRE THE BREAKER.** Strip the cable leaving at least one inch of sheathing inside the box. Screw the (bare) ground wire into the panel's neutral bus bar. (If your box has a separate bar for the grounding wires, attach the wire there.) Insert the white wire to a screw terminal marked "load neutral" and tighten the screw. Screw the GFCI's white wire to the panel's neutral bus bar.

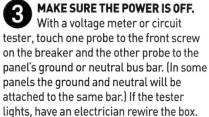

6 **CONNECT TO THE GFCI.** Insert the cable's black (hot) wire into the terminal marked "line" on the GFCI. Tighten the screw to secure the connection.

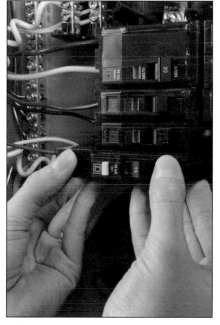

7 **SNAP THE GFCI IN PLACE.** Put the circuit breaker into an empty slot in the panel. Press the breaker until it snaps into place.

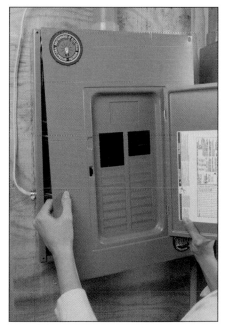

8 **REPLACE THE PANEL.** Remove a knockout for the circuit breaker in the cover of the panel. Position the cover on the panel and screw it in place.

Running conduit and cable

Though you can run cable to an outdoor light or outlet several ways, the easiest is with UF cable, which is waterproof and can be buried directly in the ground. Code requires that you protect the cable above ground, so you'll have to do some basic conduit work where the cable enters and exits the ground.

Other methods require you to enclose wiring in conduit for the entire length of the trench. You won't have to bury the cable quite as deeply, but you will have to fish wires and cut conduit. It's best to stick with UF.

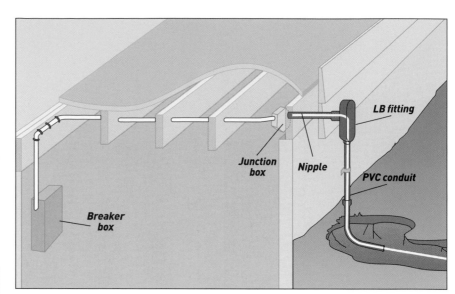

SKILL SCALE

EASY	**MEDIUM**	HARD

REQUIRED SKILLS: Wiring, working with conduit, digging a trench.

HOW LONG WILL IT TAKE?

Experienced . . . . 2 hrs.
Handy . . . . 4 hrs.
Novice . . . . 6 hrs.

STUFF YOU'LL NEED

✔ **MATERIALS:**
Caulk, PVC conduit, metal conduit, nipple, compression fittings, rubber bushing (as necessary) wood screws, anchor shields, metal screws, LB fitting, PVC solvent cement, plastic cable staples, plastic straps, electrical tape

✔ **TOOLS:**
Shovel, hammer, insulated screwdrivers, fish tape, hammer drill, plastic pipe cutter, percussion bit, caulk gun, safety glasses

INSIDE THE HOUSE, CABLE RUNS FROM THE BREAKER BOX TO A JUNCTION BOX NEAR THE FOUNDATION WALL. Inside the junction box, each wire in the cable is attached to a corresponding wire in a UF (underground feeder) cable. A length of conduit, called a nipple, protects the cable's run through the wall. Outside, attach the nipple to an LB fitting—an L-shape fitting with a removable plate that turns the cable toward the ground. The fitting attaches to conduit that goes down the house wall into an 24-inch-deep trench. The conduit then stops, and the cable continues along the bottom of the trench. At the end of the trench it reenters conduit and is routed up to the fixture it will power.

INSTALLING PVC CONDUIT

① DRILL A HOLE where you want the wire to enter the house, at a point just above the foundation. Measure and make sure the hole will go through the rim joist and not into the foundation or first floor. Make the hole wide enough to accommodate a short section of conduit, called a nipple, that protects cable.

② INSTALL AN LB FITTING. Cut a PVC nipple to length so it extends 1 inch into the basement and test the fit. Glue it to the LB fitting and push the assembly into the hole until the fitting is against the wall of the house.

3 **DIG A TRENCH.** Dig a trench for the cable below the LB fitting. Make the trench about the width of a shovel and 24 inches deep. Code requires this depth for UF cables buried without conduit.

4 **ATTACH A PIECE OF CONDUIT TO THE LB FITTING.** Cut a piece of conduit to reach from the fitting to an elbow at the bottom of the trench. Spread PVC solvent cement onto the conduit and push it into the fitting.

5 **ATTACH THE ELBOW.** Glue the elbow in place. The lower end should be at the bottom of the trench. UF cable will come out the opening and travel directly along the bottom of the trench until it reaches the other end.

BUYER'S GUIDE

USING CONDUIT

Code lets you bury UF cable directly in the ground, but you also can run conduit the length of the trench. If you do, you won't have to bury the cable quite as deep—12 inches instead of 24 inches in residential applications. You will, however, have to fish cable through the conduit. Running UF or other cable through conduit meets code, but cable adds expense and the sheathing may make it difficult to fish. Most electricians feed three single wires, known as TW wires, through the conduit instead. If you do this, run the conduit first, and glue the sections together. Once the conduit is in place, fish all three wires at once.

Using metal conduit above grade

Although PVC is flexible, rustproof, and easy to work with, some local codes won't allow PVC more than 6 inches above ground. Metal conduit, which is more durable and less likely to be damaged accidentally, is required instead. With metal conduit, all connections must be made with compression fittings, which have a compression ring (like plumbing fittings do) to keep out water. Thin-walled tubing, called EMT (electrical metallic tubing), is the easiest conduit to use. A nipple connects an interior junction box to an exterior metal LB fitting. Metal conduit extends down from the fitting to 6 inches above grade, where a compression fitting is screwed to a plastic transition fitting. An elbow is added at the bottom and then the cable runs along the bottom of the trench to the area requiring power.

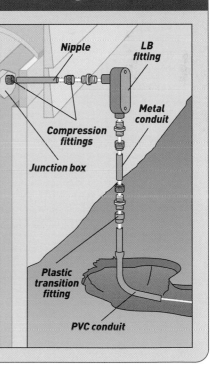

Nipple

LB fitting

Compression fittings

Metal conduit

Junction box

Plastic transition fitting

PVC conduit

Running conduit and cable

INSTALLING PVC CONDUIT *(continued)*

Cutting conduit

Running lengths of conduit often requires a fair amount of cutting. Begin by clamping the conduit in a vise. Cut PVC conduit with a hacksaw that has a 32-teeth-per-inch blade. Then remove any burrs with a utility knife and bevel the outside edges to fit the couplings. For metal conduit, use a pipe cutter or hacksaw that has an 18-teeth-per-inch blade. Wrap a piece of masking tape around the area that is to be cut to prevent the blade from slipping. Remove any burrs with a half-round file.

6 **ATTACH THE CONDUIT.** Fasten the conduit to the house wall with plastic straps. Drill holes in the foundation -tapping masonry screws and screw the straps in place.

7 **APPLY CAULK.** Caulk the gaps between the siding and the conduit to create a watertight seal.

RUNNING THE CABLE

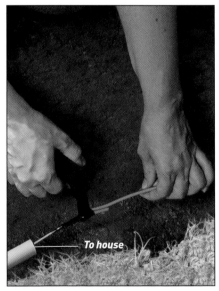

To house

1 **LAY CABLE.** Remove the cover from the LB fitting. Install the fixture at the other end of the trench and uncoil enough UF cable to reach up from the trench to the fixture—plus approximately 2 feet—and leave it at the end of the trench. Then work your way back toward the house laying cable in the trench as you go.

2 **FISH THE TAPE THROUGH THE CONDUIT.** Pushing wire through a conduit by itself is next to impossible, so use fish tape—a flat, springy length of metal in a roll. Insert the end into the fitting and push the tape until it reaches the end of the conduit.

3 **TAPE THE CABLE TO THE FISH TAPE.** To hook the cable onto the fish tape, bend the cable to form a hook and interlock it to the fish tape. Use black electrical tape to bind the fish tape and the cable together. Then pull the tape and the cable through the conduit elbow. Use conduit lubricant to make pulling easier and to prevent damage to the cable.

ELECTRICAL

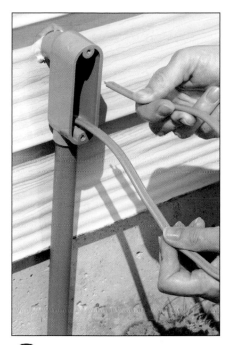

TAKE THE PATH OF LEAST RESISTANCE

electricians always look for the most efficient way to complete a job. It's not because they're looking for the easy way out; it's because they know that the least amount of drilling, demolition, and pounding will yield the least amount of damage to the structures in which they're working.

For instance, instead of running cable through the foundation, you may be able to tap into an existing outdoor light or junction box. It's worth checking out because all you need to do is replace one of the screw-in seals with a fitting and conduit. Run the conduit to where you want the new outlet, then fish the cable and make the connections. The one drawback: If the new circuit is wired to a porch light, the light will have to be on to get power.

5 **ATTACH A JUNCTION BOX TO THE END OF THE NIPPLE.** Go inside the house and attach a junction box to the nipple that runs from the LB fitting. Connect the UF cable coming in from outside with NM cable that will run to the service panel. Staple the cable along the joists with plastic cable staples spaced a maximum of y 4½ feet apart. If you use metal staples don't drive the staple too hard or it could crush the cable.

4 **PULL THE CABLE AND FEED IT INTO THE HOUSE.** Pull enough cable through the conduit to reach through the wall and terminate at the junction box, plus about 8 inches. Then remove the fish tape and feed the cable into the house through the nipple.

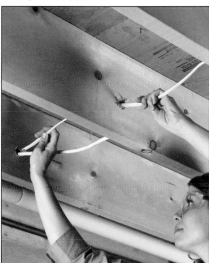

6 **IF YOU HAVE TO FEED CABLE THROUGH JOISTS,** drill holes in the middle of the joists to avoid weakening them. Connect the cable to the box as described on page 189.

Mounting tricks

To protect your cable from accidentally being punctured during future renovations, nail metal straps to the joists directly underneath where the cable passes through or directly in front of where it passes through a stud.

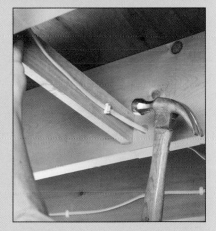

Cables tend to droop from one joist to another. To keep them running in straight lines, nail 1×2 runners between the joists and staple the cables to the runners.

Mounting electrical boxes

The outdoors is not a great place for an electrical box. Rain, snow, and sleet can blow into the box and cause a short. To help prevent this, boxes for outdoors have gaskets and fittings that keep the inside of the box—and the electrical wires—dry. Code also requires you to install a GFCI receptacle to help protect against shock.

It's possible to mount electrical boxes just about anywhere outdoors and on any type of siding. Mount the box close to where it will be used most often and as near as possible to where the cable exits the house.

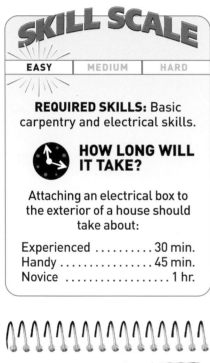

SKILL SCALE

EASY	MEDIUM	HARD

REQUIRED SKILLS: Basic carpentry and electrical skills.

HOW LONG WILL IT TAKE?

Attaching an electrical box to the exterior of a house should take about:

Experienced .... 30 min.
Handy .... 45 min.
Novice .... 1 hr.

STUFF YOU'LL NEED

✔ MATERIALS:
Screws or shields, conduit straps, electrical box, metal conduit, receptacle, nonstick plumber's tape, 4×4 post, posthole mix concrete, soil, gaskets, in-use cover plate

✔ TOOLS:
Screwdriver, posthole digger, shovel

ATTACHING TO AN EXTERIOR WALL

OUTDOOR BOXES ARE MADE FROM CAST ALUMINUM OR PVC PLASTIC. Both have gaskets and watertight covers to keep out the elements. If you are using PVC conduit, you can still use a PVC conduit connector to attach it to a metal box. PVC conduit attaches to PVC boxes with plastic pipe primer and solvent cement. If using a metal box, it's a good idea to wrap nonstick plumber's tape around the threads of the screw-in plugs. Outdoor boxes have flanges so you can fasten them to a structure with screws.

To protect against shock, the National Electrical Code requires either a GFCI breaker or GFCI receptacle in all outdoor outlets.

1 ATTACH THE ELECTRICAL BOX. Screw through the holes or through the flanges, if there are any, to attach the box. Seal unused openings with screw-in plugs, usually sold separately. To attach the box to a masonry wall, drill holes for self-tapping masonry screws and screw the box in place. For aluminum or vinyl siding, screw directly through the siding into the framing.

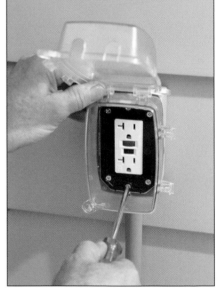

2 WIRE THE BOX. Install a GFCI receptacle and make the appropriate wire connections. Fix the gasket and waterproof cover plate to the receptacle with screws.

ELECTRICAL

MOUNTING AN ELECTRIC OUTLET ON A FREESTANDING POST

In some circumstances, you may need power in a place that's not convenient to a wall or structure in your yard. The solution is to run the cable to the spot where you need it, then sink a post in the ground at that point. The post serves as an anchoring point for your electrical box. Dig a posthole that's half as deep as the desired height of the post. Then run conduit from the trench up the post. Fasten the conduit and box to the post using straps and screws. Fill in around the post with concrete.

Check your local codes for any specifics concerning the support of freestanding electrical boxes.

1 **EXCAVATE FOR THE BOX.** Dig a trench at least 24 inches deep for the cable. With a posthole digger, dig a hole in the ground at the end of the trench. Make the hole half the exposed height of the post. Put the post in the hole.

THE BEST WAY TO SUPPORT A FREESTANDING ELECTRICAL BOX IS WITH A 4×4 POST. Conduit exits the box and is attached to the post with straps. The conduit runs down the post and into an 24-inch-deep trench. The cable will leave the conduit at that point and run along the bottom of the trench.

2 **ATTACH THE BOX.** Attach the receptacle box to the conduit first, then attach the box to the post with wood screws. Caulk the seam between the box and the post to prevent water from getting into the box. Attach the conduit to the post with straps.

3 **RUN CABLE.** Fish the cable for the box through the conduit with fish tape (see Step 2 , page 194). Mix up some ready-mix bagged concrete sold as posthole mix and fill the posthole with it. Fill the trench with the soil and sod you removed.

Installing a GFCI outlet

National Electrical Codes require you to protect outdoor outlets with a ground fault circuit interrupter (GFCI) and an in-use cover plate which allows the cover to be closed while a cord is plugged in. A GFCI shuts off the power if a short occurs and is essential for outdoor use, where dampness can make electrical shocks deadly.

SKILL SCALE

EASY	**MEDIUM**	HARD

REQUIRED SKILLS: Wiring and mechanical skills.

HOW LONG WILL IT TAKE?

Installing a GFCI outlet should take about:

Experienced .... 15 min.
Handy .... 15 min.
Novice .... 30 min.

STUFF YOU'LL NEED

✔ **MATERIALS:**
GFCI receptacle, gasket, cover plate

✔ **TOOLS:**
Screwdriver, needle-nose pliers, wire cutter or combination stripper

A+ WORK SMARTER

SURGE PROTECTION
If you live in an area prone to lightning, install a surge arrester at the main panel. It will protect the wiring in your home from huge surges in voltage caused when lightning hits a power line or strikes nearby. Individual protectors for the telephone, television, and other units are also available.

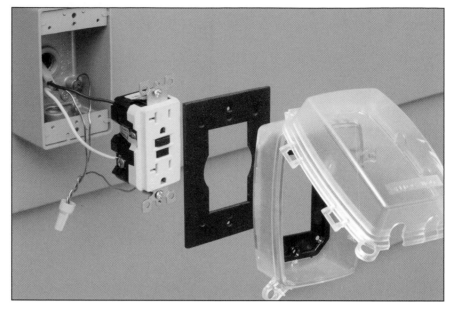

GFCIs LOOK LIKE OTHER OUTLETS EXCEPT FOR TWO SMALL BUTTONS. One simulates a ground fault, or a short in which power runs through something (or someone) and into the ground; the other is a reset button to restore power after the test. Push the test button once a month. If it cuts power to the outlet, it's working correctly. If it doesn't cut power, check the wiring and replace it, if necessary.

MAKING THE CONNECTIONS

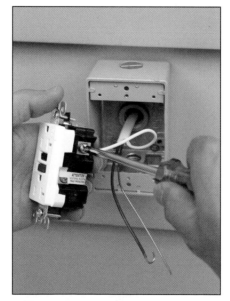

1 **HANG THE BOX.** Install the receptacle box on the wall or on a post. Use needle-nose pliers to make a loop in the end of the cable's white wire and wrap it clockwise around the silver terminal marked "line" on the GFCI. Then tighten the screw.

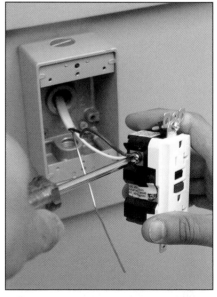

2 **CONNECT THE BLACK WIRE.** Connect the cable's black wire to the other line terminal on the GFCI outlet. Make a loop and place it clockwise around the screw. Tighten the screw.

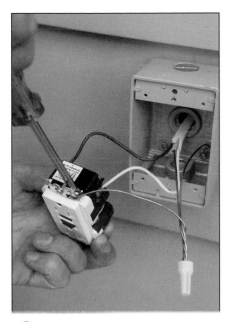

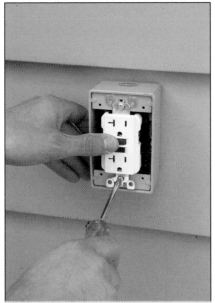

3 **CONNECT THE GROUNDING WIRES.** Connect a 6-inch bare or green wire to the grounding screw on the GFCI. Connect a similar wire to the grounding screw in the box. Twist the wires together with the bare wire from the cable and cover with a wire nut.

4 **INSTALL THE RECEPTACLE.** Fold the wires into the box, taking care not to disconnect them, and screw the receptacle into place at the top and the bottom of the box.

If you want to run power from a GFCI to another outlet or light, pay attention to the labels on the terminals. Some are labeled "line" terminals; others are labeled "load" terminals. Connect the incoming cable to the line terminals and the outgoing cable to the load terminals. Then connect the grounding wires to a pigtail attached to the grounding terminal.

5 **INSTALL THE IN-USE COVER PLATE.** Place the gasket over the receptacle and screw on the cover plate. Make the wire connections at the other end of the cable run, if necessary, and turn on the power.

6 **TEST THE CIRCUIT.** Plug a radio into the outlet. Press the test button. The reset button should pop out, and the radio should shut off. If not, check the connections to the box or replace the GFCI. Press the reset button to restore power.

An in-use cover plate keeps rain and moisture out of the receptacle box and is now required for new installations by The National Electrical Code. This applies to items that are plugged in for extended periods, such as outdoor holiday lights or a submersible pump.

ELECTRICAL

Installing switches

A single-pole switch has two terminals on one side and definite on and off positions. It controls one or more fixtures from a single location.

If you're replacing a switch, disconnect the wires that lead to it and reattach them to a new switch. If you're putting in a switch for a new fixture, look for an outlet or switch or tap into an existing circuit after first replacing the box with a larger one.

If the box has only one cable, it's an end-of-the run box, meaning that the power that leaves the box goes only to the light. If the box has two cables, it is in the middle of the run, meaning that the power comes into the box, then continues on to other receptacles, switches, or fixtures in addition to the light that the switch controls.

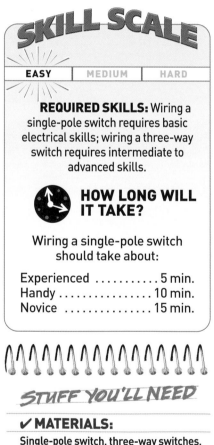
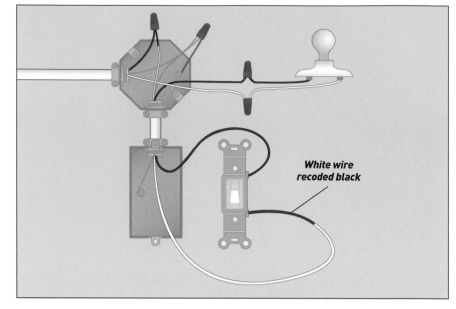

White wire recoded black

INSTALLING A SWITCH AT THE END OF THE RUN IS RATHER STRAIGHTFORWARD. The hot wire is routed through the switch, and the white neutral wire is connected directly to the light. Both switch wires carry electricity at one point or another and, therefore, must be connected to black wires. Because there's only one black wire, however, the white wire will have to serve as a hot wire. "Recode" the wire—wrap the ends with black tape—to remind you it carries power. The switch terminals are identical: Connect the black wire to either of them and the recoded white wire to the other. Screw the bare copper wire to the grounding screw in the box.

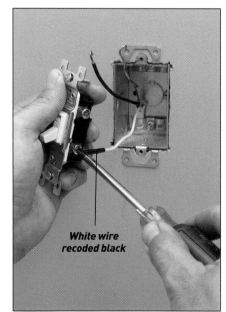

White wire recoded black

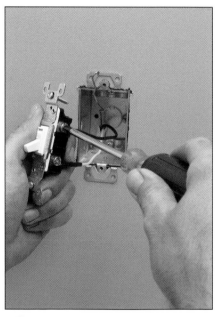

1 **TURN OFF THE POWER AT THE CIRCUIT BREAKER BOX THEN RECODE AND ATTACH THE WHITE WIRE.** Mark the end of the white wire with electrical tape or a black marker and use needle-nose pliers to loop it to fit around the terminal. Wrap the wire clockwise around one of the terminals and tighten the screw.

2 **ATTACH THE BLACK WIRE.** Loop the end of the black wire and screw it clockwise to the other terminal.

ELECTRICAL

3 **ATTACH THE GROUNDING WIRE.** Connect the grounding wire to the grounding terminal screw in the box.

4 **ATTACH THE SWITCH TO THE BOX.** Fold the wires into the box. Screw the switch mounting strap to the box and install the cover plate. If the switch is outside, make sure you use a box and cover approved for outdoor usage.

Middle-of-the-run switch

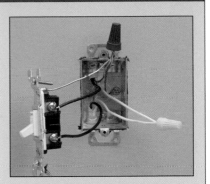

A single-pole switch in the middle of the run has two cables that enter the box: One cable leads back toward the service panel and the other takes power to another outlet. To add a switch, twist the white wires together and add a wire nut. Attach the two black wires to the two switch terminals. Connect the grounding wires to a jumper with a wire nut and connect the jumper to the grounding screw on the box.

WIRING A THREE-WAY SWITCH SEQUENCE

A three-way switch sequence allows you to control a light from two locations. Unlike other switches, three-way switches do not have set on and off positions.

The term three-way refers to the number of terminals on the switch: one common terminal, which is usually dark (black or copper), and two lighter-colored traveler terminals, which are used interchangeably. When wiring three way switches, use a cable with three wires and a ground. This cable has a red wire in addition to the usual black, white, and ground wires.

The general rule is that the power coming in from the source attaches to the common terminal of one switch. The wire carrying power to the light is attached to the common terminal of the other switch. The travelers of one switch are wired to the travelers of the other switch.

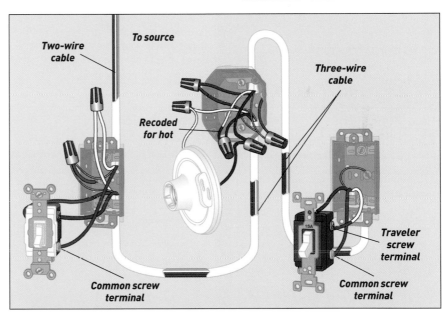

A THREE-WAY SWITCH SEQUENCE WITH A LIGHT BETWEEN TWO SWITCHES ALLOWS YOU TO TURN ON A LIGHT FROM EITHER OF TWO LOCATIONS—inside the house as well as from the garage, for example. Two-wire cable enters the switch box from the source. The white wire connects to the white wire of the light, and the black wire connects to the common terminal of the first switch. Three-wire cable runs between the switches, serving to connect the traveler terminals to each other. The black wire connects the common terminal of the second switch to the light. The second switch is a loop; the white wire is hot and must be recoded black. The grounding wires attach to the grounding screws.

Installing automatic control devices

Automatic control devices—timers, motion detectors, light sensors—serve double duty as convenience and security devices. A timer switch allows you to go on vacation confident the lights will come on at a certain time every night. A motion detector turns on a floodlight when an intruder enters the yard or when you get home and need to find your keys. A photoelectric eye automatically turns on the light when the sun sets and comes either with the light or as a screw-in attachment. A time-delay switch shuts off a light after a certain amount of time.

Purchase a specialty switch with a manual override so you can turn the light off if the kids want to play hide-and-seek, you want to look at the stars, or the neighbors ask you to turn off the light from time to time.

SKILL SCALE

EASY	MEDIUM	HARD

REQUIRED SKILLS: Basic to intermediate electrical skills.

HOW LONG WILL IT TAKE?

Installing an automatic control device should take about:

Experienced . . . . 15 min.
Handy . . . . 20 min.
Novice . . . . 30 min.

STUFF YOU'LL NEED

✔ MATERIALS:

Timer, time-delay or motion-sensor switch, wire nuts

✔ TOOLS:

Screwdriver, lineman's pliers, wire cutter or combination stripper, diagonal cutters

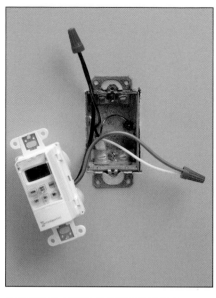

A TIMER IS AN ELECTRIC SWITCH that you can program to turn a light on and off at selected times. General instructions for installation follow; consult the manufacturer's directions for more details.

SAFETY ALERT

Always make sure the power is off at the service panel when installing automatic control devices.

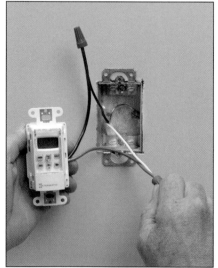

2 **CONNECT THE BLUE WIRE FROM THE TIMER TO THE WHITE CABLE WIRE** in the box. Secure with a wire nut. Attach the incoming grounding wire to the grounding screw in the box.

1 **REMOVE THE EXISTING SWITCH FROM ITS BOX.** Twist together the black wire from the timer and the black cable wire in the box and screw on a wire nut.

3 **FOLD THE WIRES INTO THE BOX AND MOUNT THE SWITCH** by screwing it to the box. Add a cover plate. Turn the power back on and program the switch as directed by the manufacturer.

WIRING A TIME-DELAY SWITCH

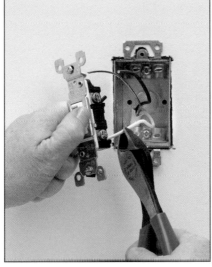

A TIME-DELAY SWITCH IS A MECHANICAL SWITCH that automatically shuts off a light after a designated amount of time. Begin installation by removing an existing switch from its box.

1 STRIP THE WIRES. Pull the switch away from the box and cut off as little as possible of the old wires. Strip off insulation to expose fresh wire.

2 ATTACH THE WIRES. Most switches have two push-in terminals. Push wires in the terminals. From the front, tighten the screws that hold the wires.

WIRING AUTOMATIC SENSOR SWITCHES

Motion detectors turn on the light when something moves within their range. Photoelectric sensors turn the light on at dusk and off at dawn. You can usually buy fixtures with one or the other sensor built in. Both are wired exactly the way a floodlight is. If you want to retrofit an existing light, however, buy a sensor separately. Photoelectric sensors screw into the light socket. A motion detector has to be wired.

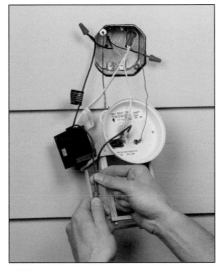

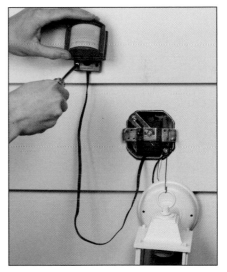

1 TO RETROFIT AN EXISTING LIGHT WITH A MOTION DETECTOR, turn off the power and disconnect the light. Wire the switch module as directed: Generally, a white module wire connects to the light's white wire; the incoming black wires connects to the module's black wire, and the light's black wire connects to a red wire on the switch module. Wrap electrical tape around the wire nuts and down the wire about 1½ inches.

2 ATTACH THE SENSOR. Plug the sensor into the module. Tuck the module into the junction box and screw the sensor to the wall somewhere near the light. Let the sensor cable loop down below the sensor to keep rain from dripping along the cable and into the sensor.

Installing outdoor light fixtures

Manufacturers offer several ways to light up your yard at night. Porch lights are one of the simplest. They provide security and shed enough light to help you unlock a door. Floodlights illuminate large areas in a yard, making it possible to use play areas even at night. A third alternative, lampposts brighten up a path and serve both aesthetic and security roles.

SAFETY ALERT

Always make sure the power is off at the main service panel before installing any light fixture.

SKILL SCALE

EASY	MEDIUM	HARD

REQUIRED SKILLS: Basic to intermediate electrical skills.

HOW LONG WILL IT TAKE?

Installing an outdoor light fixture should take about:

Experienced . . . . 15 min.
Handy . . . . 30 min.
Novice . . . . 45 min.

VARIABLES: Lamps mounted more than about 5 feet from the ground will take longer to install. Time does not include running cable.

STUFF YOU'LL NEED

✔ **MATERIALS:** Timer, time-delay or motion-sensor switch, wire nuts electrician's tape

✔ **TOOLS:**
Screwdriver, lineman's pliers, wire cutter or combination stripper, shovel, fish tape

WIRING AN END-OF-THE-RUN PORCH LIGHT

Metal fixture strap

Nipple

Cap nut

YOU HAVE THE OPTION OF MOUNTING A PORCH LIGHT ON THE CEILING OR ON THE WALL. Attach a metal fixture strap across the electrical box. Screw a nipple into the strap and into the porch light's base. A cap nut screws onto the nipple and holds the fixture to the wall or ceiling. Porch lights may differ in shape, size, and fixture installation, so follow the manufacturer's instructions. The wire connections, however, should be the same.

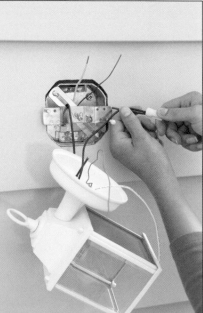

1 INSTALL THE HARDWARE. Screw a fixture strap to the box. This strap turns so you can adjust the position of the light.

2 ATTACH THE BLACK WIRE. Hang the fixture from the box with a hook made from a coat hanger. Twist the black fixture wire to the black cable wire and cover with a wire nut.

ELECTRICAL

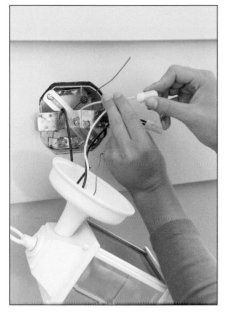

Middle-of-the-run porch light

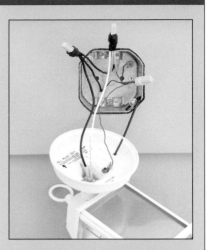

3 **ATTACH THE GROUND AND WHITE WIRES.** Twist the light's white wire and the white cable wire together and cover with a wire nut. Twist the light's ground wire the cable ground wire to a pig tail. Cover with a wire nut. Attach the pigtail to the box's grounding screw. Wrap electrical tape around each wire nut and about ½ inch of the wire coming out of them.

4 **INSTALL THE LIGHT.** Hold the base of the fixture over the electrical box, pushing all the wires inside. Screw the cap nuts onto the bolts in the hanger strap to attach the light fixture to the wall or ceiling.

A middle-of-the-run connection for a porch light is the same as an end-of-the-run connection except for three extra wires (black, white, and grounding). Twist all the black wires together and cover with a wire nut. Repeat for the white wires. Twist all the grounding wires together, add a jumper to them, and cover with a wire nut. Connect the jumper to the grounding screw in the box.

INSTALLING A LAMPPOST

A lamppost and light fixture are usually sold as a unit. The majority of the work is in digging a trench and running cable from the house to the spot where the lamp will be installed. The depth of the trench depends on whether you use conduit in the trench (see pages 192–195). In this case, UF wire is buried 24 inches deep.

Anchor the post in a footing made of quick-setting concrete poured in a fiber tube form. Keep the post vertical while the concrete sets using 2×4s staked to the ground and clamped to the post.

Lampposts may differ in fixture styles or in material used for the posts. However, the electrical connections are the same for all types of posts.

When working with electricity, always turn off the power by shutting off the appropriate breaker at the service panel.

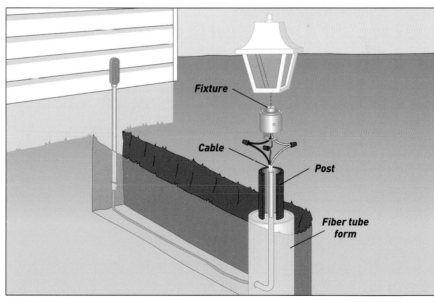

Fixture
Cable
Post
Fiber tube form

WHAT YOU DON'T SEE WHEN YOU LOOK AT A LAMPPOST IS THE WORK THAT WENT INTO IT. Here, waterproof UF (underground feed) cable is buried in a trench 24 inches deep and runs from the house to the location of the post. (If you run conduit, you can dig a shallower trench. See pages 192–195.) A concrete footing made with a fiber tube form provides support for the lamppost. The wire connections are a simple matter of joining three pairs of wires with wire nuts.

ELECTRICAL

Installing outdoor light fixtures

INSTALLING A LAMPPOST *(continued)*

1 **DIG THE TRENCH.** Dig a trench 24 inches deep and a hole deep enough for the lamppost and wide enough for a fiber tube form. Cut a form that reaches the bottom of the hole and cut a slot in the bottom for the conduit elbow. Fish cable from the trench through the conduit and lower the post into the form. Fill the form with quick-setting concrete per manufacturer's instructions. Brace with 2×4s staked in the ground and clamped to the post until the concrete is set.

2 **WIRE THE LIGHT.** Strip the cable wires and connect them to wires in the light. Twist and connect the black wire to the black wire, the white to the white, and the ground to the ground. Tuck the wires into the post.

3 **ATTACH THE LIGHT.** Screw the cap to the top of the post, then mount the light socket in the cap. The mounting method depends on the type of fixture. Check the instructions that come with the lamppost.

> **SAFETY ALERT**
>
> Halogen and mercury-vapor lights are extremely hot when they are on.

INSTALLING A HALOGEN FLOODLIGHT

Halogen floodlights are made of fused-quartz tubes filled with pressurized halogen gas. The tungsten filament inside gives off a very bright white light. When it comes time to replace the bulb, however, don't touch it with your fingers; the oil from your skin actually causes the bulb to burn out. Wear gloves or use a cloth.

Installation of a halogen fixture is straightforward—attach the light's black wire to the cable's black wire; the light's white wire to the cable's white wire, and ground wire to ground wire. You can also add a light-sensitive sensor that turns the light on at dusk and off at dawn. The fitting screws into a hole in the light fixture covered with a removable plug. Wire the light so that power goes through the sensor before it goes through the light.

When wiring, always turn the power off at the service panel.

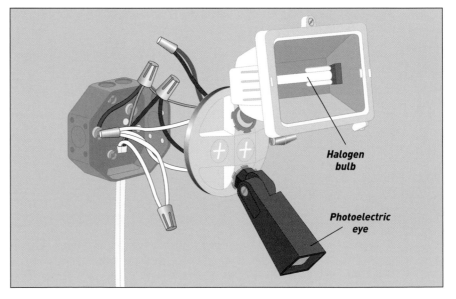

Halogen bulb

Photoelectric eye

HALOGEN FLOODLIGHTS COME IN VARIOUS SIZES AND OFTEN ARE SOLD IN PAIRS ON ONE BASE. Add a light sensitive fitting to automatically turn the light on at dusk and off at dawn.

ELECTRICAL

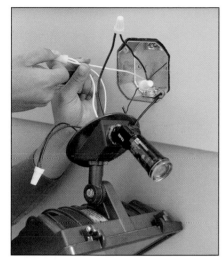

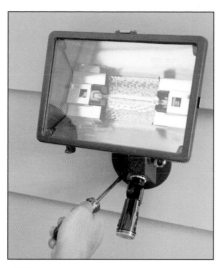

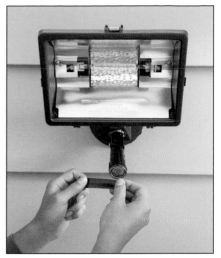

1 **ADD THE SENSOR AND WIRE THE LIGHT.** Remove the screw-in slug from the light, and replace it with a sensor. Twist the black cable wire around the black sensor wire. Twist the red sensor wire to the black light wire. Twist the white wires together. Attach the grounding wire from the light and the cable to a jumper and connect the jumper to the grounding screw in the box. Cover the connections with wire nuts. Wrap electrical tape around the caps, and about ½ inch of the wires.

2 **HANG THE LIGHT.** Assemble the fixture, if necessary. Push the wires to the back of the box and screw the base of the fixture to the wall.

3 **TEST THE CIRCUIT.** Turn on the power. Test the photoelectric eye by covering it with black tape. Once the eye is covered, the light should turn on. If it doesn't, check the wire connections for problems or return the light.

SAFETY ALERT

In any installation, the last thing you do is attach the wires to power.

INSTALLING A MERCURY-VAPOR LIGHT

Mercury-vapor lights belong to the family of high-intensity discharge lamps. They give off a distinctive bluish-green light. Mercury-vapor lighting is energy-efficient and often is used in street lamps. It's also popular for lighting large areas of a yard. Your local home improvement store sells a variety of models designed for homeowners. One disadvantage is that the light is intense. Make sure your light doesn't shine onto other people's property, or you may end up with an irate neighbor.

Always make sure you turn off the power at the source before installation. For added security turn off the power at the service panel by shutting off the appropriate circuit breaker.

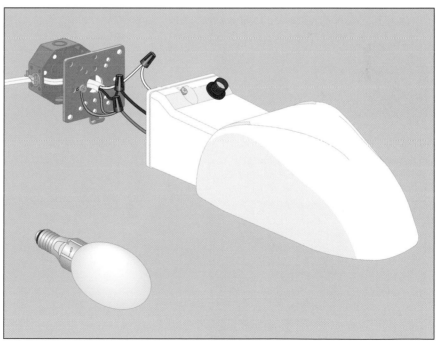

MERCURY-VAPOR LIGHTS TEND TO BE LARGE AND POWERFUL. Like an incandescent lightbulb, the bulb usually is screwed into a socket. Mercury-vapor lights come in a variety of fixture styles, each of which may have different installation instructions.

Installing low-voltage lighting

Low-voltage landscape lights—those that are 12-volt AC—literally are a snap to install. The lighting parts snap together, and the connectors snap into place. The cable looks like a lamp cord.

Landscape lights are available in a package that contains the transformer, the lights, and the connectors that you'll need. You also can buy the system piece by piece so you get exactly what you want. Talk with the sales staff to make sure you get the right transformer.

If necessary, splice low-voltage wires. Strip the wires, put in a silicone-filled cap (sold as a grease cap), and attach the new wire. Some caps are brand-specific, so make sure you buy a cap designed for your wire.

SKILL SCALE

EASY	MEDIUM	HARD

REQUIRED SKILLS: Basic electrical skills.

HOW LONG WILL IT TAKE?

Setting up a string of lights hooked up to a low-voltage system should take about:

Experienced . . . . 2 hrs.
Handy . . . . 3 hrs.
Novice . . . . 4 hrs.

STUFF YOU'LL NEED

✔ MATERIALS:
Wood screws or shields and screws, low-voltage lighting kit with transformer and cable

✔ TOOLS:
Drill and bits, screwdriver, shovel

MOST LOW-VOLTAGE LIGHTING SYSTEMS INCLUDE A TRANSFORMER THAT IS PLUGGED INTO A REGULAR OUTDOOR RECEPTACLE. The transformer steps the household current of 120 volts down to 12 volts. The size of the transformer varies; most are rated to handle a load of 100 to 300 watts. The higher the rating, the more cable and light fixtures you can connect to the system. A timer in the transformer turns the system on at dusk and off at dawn. One end of the cable connects to the transformer; you can attach lights to the cable anywhere you want.

1 WIRE THE TRANSFORMER. A transformer steps the voltage down from 120 volts to 12 volts. Attaching the cable for the lights is an easy task of screwing the wires in place. Details vary by manufacturer, so follow the directions that come with the transformer.

2 HANG THE TRANSFORMER. Mount the transformer on the wall next to a GFCI outlet. For most types of siding, you can make the attachment with a wood screw. Drive it into the plywood or the sheathing underneath the siding. For masonry, drill a hole for a lag shield, then screw into the shield.

3 **ASSEMBLE THE LIGHTS.** Light fixtures usually require assembly. You'll need to snap the sockets in place at the very least, and you may need to do some simple wiring. Follow the manufacturer's directions.

4 **PLACE THE LIGHTS.** Lay the light fixtures in the approximate spots they will be installed and run the cable across the ground from light to light.

HOMER'S HINDSIGHT

GET ENOUGH POWER
A friend has a long walk that leads to his garage. He wanted to light the path with low-voltage lighting and bought a kit, plus a few extra lights. Unfortunately, when he turned the system on, the lighting was extremely dim. The transformer couldn't supply enough power for a long cable with so many lights. Ask the salesperson if the transformer you're buying will do the job you want it to do.

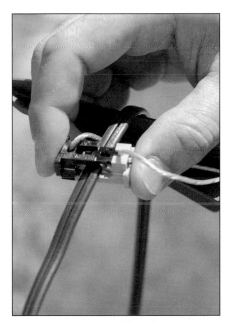

5 **CONNECT THE LIGHTS.** Attach the cable connectors. For this light, put half the connecter on each side of the cable and snap it together to connect the lights.

6 **DIG FOR THE CABLE.** Dig a 6-inch-deep trench alongside the cable and place the cable in the trench, but do not bury it yet.

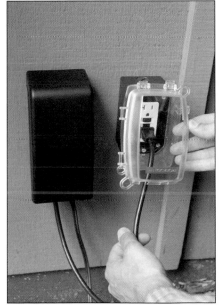

7 **SET THE TIMER.** Plug the transformer into the outdoor receptacle and set the timer. Cover the GFCI outlet with a plastic cover, usually sold separately. Test the lights; if they work correctly, bury the cable.

PLUMBING AND DRAINAGE

Outdoor water can be a blessing or a curse, depending on where you find it. If you're running water to a garden or a pond, it's a blessing. Water that's building up in the yard, however, can turn the yard into a muddy bog, erode foundations, wash away plants, and eventually work its way into the basement.

Like indoor plumbing, outdoor plumbing involves two systems: supply and drainage. Indoors the job is split between the two. What comes in must go out, and for every dripping faucet there can be a plugged drain.

Outdoors is a different story: For every person who runs a pipe out to the horse barn, countless others watch water build up in their yards. For those who plan to run pipes to the shed, the rules are simple: Use plastic pipes so they won't corrode, bury the pipes below the frost line so they don't freeze,

and slope the pipes toward the house so you can drain them if need be.

For drainage problems, few rules but numerous options exist. If water is working its way into your basement, start with the gutters. Make sure they're working, they're not leaking, and water is directed away from the foundation by a splash block at the least. Better yet route the water away from the foundation with drainpipes.

The problem may be geography: If you live at the bottom of a hill, water will run there when it rains. Solve problem geography with geography: Long, low berms direct water to a new path. Low, shallow depressions channel the water where it won't be a problem. Note, however, that directing water toward the neighbor's yard in order to dry out your own may create more problems than it solves.

CHAPTER 7

Plumbing and Drainage tool kit 212

Materials 213

Making supply-pipe connections 214

Tapping into supply pipes 218

Running supply pipes 220

Adding outdoor faucets 222

Gutters and downspouts 224

Installing outdoor drainage systems 226

REAL-WORLD SITUATIONS

MAKING CONNECTIONS

The process of joining pipes is easy, and a few guidelines help guarantee success.

If you work with PVC, the pipes are glued together, or more properly, they're solvent-welded together. The solvent, which you brush on both the pipe and the fitting you're attaching it to, melts the surface of the plastic. When you put the pipe in the fitting, the two melt together and once the solvent evaporates, they become a single solid surface. Here are a few tips to make sure the joint you make is a good one:

■ Cut the pipe with a cutter made for cutting PVC. Copper cutters won't work, and although handsaws will, they leave a ragged edge.

■ Cut and fit all the pipe before you glue any of the joints together. If you do, the pipe will be the right length and go to the right place. You'll also solve any problems you run into—such as a joist that's in the way—before you spend time making connections.

■ Prime. For a good joint, apply a PVC primer to the pipe before gluing it. The primer helps clean the pipe and softens the PVC before you apply the glue.

■ Turn the pipe. Brush on the solvent first, put the pieces together. Give the pipe ¼ turn to spread the solvent evenly over the entire surface.

You may use copper to get the water outdoors but once outside, always use plastic pipe. Copper and plastic are joined with special connectors, but copper pipes should be soldered to each other. (Plumbers call it sweat soldering, but it's safe to think of it as soldering.) Cut the pipe with a pipe cutter made for copper, and assemble the entire run before you solder anything. Some tips for a good joint:

■ Clean the pipe and fitting. Rub the pipe with emery cloth until the surface is shiny. Clean inside the fitting with a small wire brush made for the job.

■ Apply flux. Flux is an acidic paste that further cleans the joint, and if the joint isn't clean, the solder won't stick. Brush flux on both the fitting and the pipe before you put the two together.

■ Heat the joint with a torch and remove the heat before applying the solder. If the metal is hot enough to melt the solder, it will flow inside the fitting and seal the joint. If you melt the solder onto a cold pipe, the solder won't flow into the joint and may not even stick to the pipe.

PLUMBING AND DRAINAGE

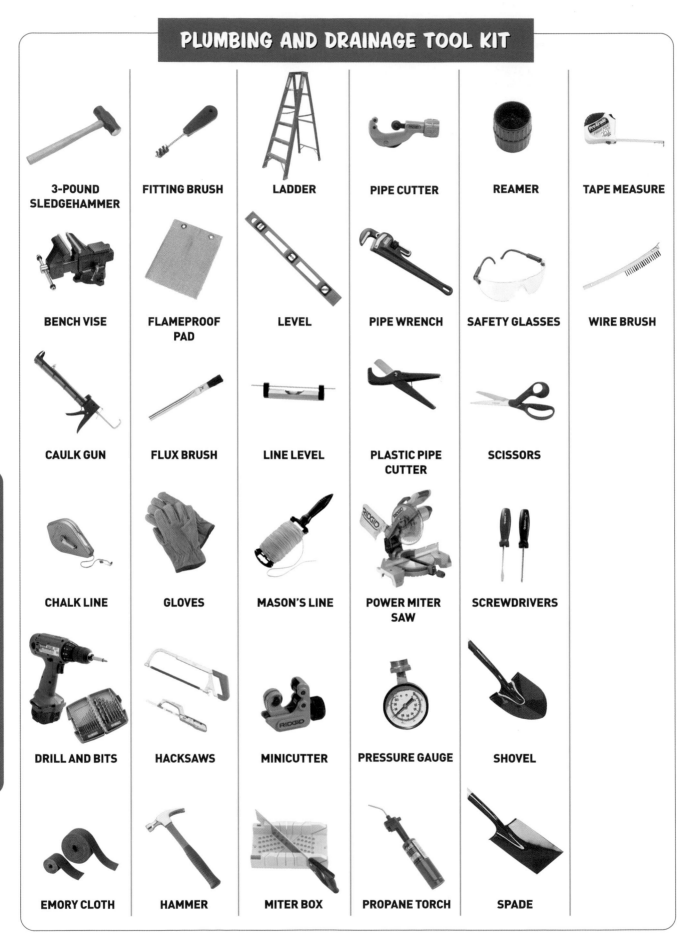

PLUMBING AND DRAINAGE TOOL KIT

3-POUND SLEDGEHAMMER

FITTING BRUSH

LADDER

PIPE CUTTER

REAMER

TAPE MEASURE

BENCH VISE

FLAMEPROOF PAD

LEVEL

PIPE WRENCH

SAFETY GLASSES

WIRE BRUSH

CAULK GUN

FLUX BRUSH

LINE LEVEL

PLASTIC PIPE CUTTER

SCISSORS

CHALK LINE

GLOVES

MASON'S LINE

POWER MITER SAW

SCREWDRIVERS

DRILL AND BITS

HACKSAWS

MINICUTTER

PRESSURE GAUGE

SHOVEL

EMORY CLOTH

HAMMER

MITER BOX

PROPANE TORCH

SPADE

PLUMBING AND DRAINAGE

Materials

The main types of plumbing pipes are **Ⓐ copper, Ⓑ galvanized steel, Ⓒ PVC, Ⓓ CPVC** and **Ⓔ PEX.** Attach them to joists or other supports with **Ⓕ pipe straps.** To connect two pieces of copper pipe, clean them with **Ⓖ emery cloth,** then join them by applying **Ⓗ soldering paste** or flux, heating the pieces with a torch, and applying **Ⓘ lead-free plumber's solder.** To join plastic pipes, apply **Ⓙ plastic pipe primer,** then glue with **Ⓚ solvent cement,** designed for the plastic you're using. Wrap **Ⓛ nonstick plumber's tape** around the threads of steel pipes when joining them. Prevent pipes from freezing by draining them through a **Ⓜ stop-and-drain valve.** Attach a **Ⓝ vacuum breaker** to **Ⓞ a faucet** to the outside of your house or a freestanding post. The breaker will prevent water from backing up into your water system. **Ⓟ A freezeproof faucet** drains automatically. **Ⓠ Sewer-and-drainage pipe** is laid hole-side-down in the ground to dispose of water underground. You also can use **Ⓡ perforated drainage pipe.**

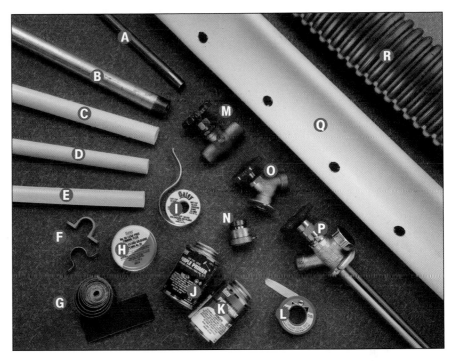

Each type of pipe has its own fittings. Connect **Ⓐ PEX** flexible plastic pipe with T fittings, crimp rings, and barbed splicers. (The connectors also come in plastic for residential applications.) Connect plastic pipes with **Ⓑ PVC** or **CPVC** fittings, choosing the same type of plastic for pipe and fitting. Connect copper pipe with **Ⓒ copper fittings,** solder, and flux. **Ⓓ Galvanized fittings** have threads that screw the pipes together. There also are **Ⓔ adapters** for reducing the size of a pipe or changing from one pipe material to another. Each fitting comes in different diameters to fit the different-size pipes. To go from ¾-inch pipe to ½-inch pipe, for example, use a **Ⓕ ¾×¾×½ T fitting,** which has two opposing ends with ¼-inch diameters and an exit source with a ½-inch diameter.

Types of pipes and tubes

TYPES	USES	JOINING METHOD
PVC (Polyvinyl chloride)	Cold water supply; outside irrigation systems; indoor drainage (SCH40PVC)	PVC primer and solvent cement
CPVC (Chlorinated polyvinyl chloride	Hot and cold water supply, indoors and out	CPVC primer and solvent cement
PEX (cross-linked polyethylene	Indoor and outdoor supply	Crimped or compression fittings on flexible pipe
Copper	Indoor supply	Soldering with lead-free solder and copper or brass fittings
Galvanized steel	Indoor supply	Threaded pipe to threaded steel fittings

Making supply-pipe connections

Fitting pipes together is to plumbing what driving nails is to carpentry—you can't do much without it. For outdoor plumbing tap into an indoor line and make connections to run pipe outside. Generally indoor pipe is ½ or ¾ inch in diameter and made of copper or plastic, although you'll sometimes find galvanized piping in older homes. Outdoor lines must always be plastic. Special adapters make connecting copper and plastic easy. Before you start tapping into the system, turn water off at the main shutoff valve and open all faucets to drain the system.

SKILL SCALE

EASY | **MEDIUM** | HARD

REQUIRED SKILLS: Using a pipe cutter and soldering copper with a torch or gluing plastic pipes together.

HOW LONG WILL IT TAKE?

Experienced .... 30 min.
Handy .... 45 min.
Novice .... 1hr.

STUFF YOU'LL NEED

✔ **MATERIALS:**
Copper pipe and fittings, galvanized metal pipe and fittings, CPVC/PVC pipe and fittings, PE pipe and fittings, lead-free solder, solvent cement, lead-free flux, thread-cutting oil, rag, nonstick plumber's tape, band clamps

✔ **TOOLS:**
Pipe cutter (copper, galvanized pipe, or PVC), fitting brush, propane torch, pipe threader, pipe wrenches, reamer, bench vise, flux brush, leather gloves, marker, flameproof pad, wire brush, screwdriver, emery cloth, safety glasses

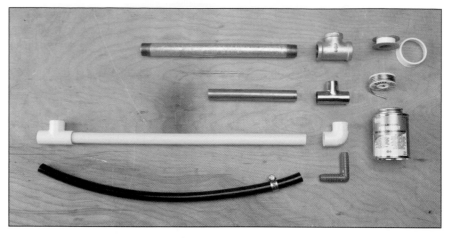

GALVANIZED METAL PIPE IS THREADED AND SCREWED TOGETHER. Connecting—or sweating—copper pipe involves heating the pipe before touching it with lead-free solder. Plastic pipe comes in three varieties: PVC, CPVC, and PE. Both PVC (polyvinyl chloride) and CPVC (chlorinated polyvinyl chloride) are used outdoors for supply lines. PVC is more practical, but you can use CPVC for hot-water lines. Connect plastic pipes with the solvent cement designed for the type of pipe; never substitute. PE (polyethylene) pipe is connected with barbed fittings and band clamps. You can purchase adapters to join two different types of pipe.

CONNECTING COPPER PIPE

1 **CUT THE PIPE.** Place a pipe cutter over the pipe and tighten the handle. Rotate the cutter around the pipe. As you do the cutting wheel scores a straight line. Tighten the wheel and cut again. Continue until you cut the pipe.

2 **REMOVE THE BURRS.** Pipe cutters have a triangular blade called a reamer. Twist it back and forth inside the end of the pipe to remove the burrs that cutting it created. Remove burrs from the ends of all pipes to be joined.

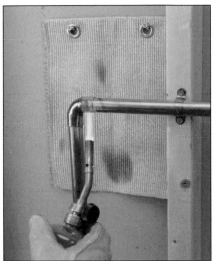

3 **CLEAN THE ENDS OF THE PIPES.**
Rub the ends with emery cloth until they are shiny. Clean the inside of the fitting with a fitting brush. Avoid files or steel wool; they are too rough. Don't touch the ends after cleaning them—the oil in a fingerprint can ruin the joint.

4 **APPLY FLUX.** With a small, stiff brush, apply lead-free soldering paste (called flux) to the last 1 inch of the pipes and the inside of the fitting. Wear gloves—flux is caustic. Insert one pipe into the fitting and twist it to spread the flux.

5 **APPLY HEAT.** Protect wood and wiring with a flameproof pad and keep a spray bottle filled with water nearby in case anything catches fire. Slide the second pipe into the fitting. Light a propane torch and adjust the flame until the blue part is 1 to 2 inches long. Hold the torch so the flame is vertical and heat the pipe and fitting until the flux begins to sizzle.

If drafts between floors make the flame flutter, stuff wet rags inside the wall.

6 **APPLY SOLDER.** Remove the torch and touch the joint with the end of a length of lead-free solder. It should melt evenly and completely around the joint. Use ½ to ¾ inch of solder for each joint. Although it may seem as if more is better, don't overdo it, or solder will flow into the pipe and reduce water flow.

7 **CLEAN THE JOINT.** Wipe off the excess solder with a clean, dry rag. If you don't, the pipe will oxidize and turn green. Be careful—the pipes are still hot at this point. Wait until the joints have cooled completely before turning on the water and testing for leaks.

BUYER'S GUIDE

ORDERING PIPE
Plumbing, heating, and refrigerating pipes have confused many customers. Make sure you buy plumbing pipes. The common size for most outdoor projects is ¾ inch, but you can use ½-inch pipe to install outdoor faucets. If you are replacing a pipe, you'll need to know both its outside and inside diameters so the new pipe will fit in the same fitting. You can do it with a tape measure or set of calipers, but the safest method is to take a sample to the store. Remember to include the distance the pipe extends into the fitting when calculating the length you need. If possible, take a piece of the old pipe with you to the store to make certain you buy the right kind and size.

CONNECTING THREADED PIPE

1 **CUT THE PIPE.** Clamp the pipe in a vise. Cut it with a rented iron pipe cutter that's equipped with a blade designed for metal. Tighten the handle after every two or three rotations. Cutting with a hacksaw is not advisable because the cut needs to be perfectly straight so the end threads properly.

2 **CLEAN OUT THE INSIDE OF THE PIPE.** Put the reamer attached to the pipe cutter inside the cut pipe end and twist it to scrape away any burrs that might restrict water flow.

3 **THREAD THE PIPE.** Rent a pipe threader that handles the diameter of the pipe. Fit the threader onto the pipe. Apply generous amounts of thread-cutting oil as you rotate the handle clockwise until one thread extends beyond the end of the threader. Remove the threader and clean the threads with a wire brush.

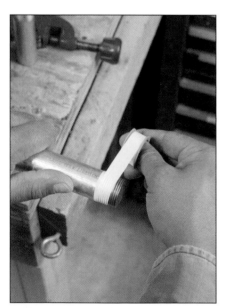

4 **APPLY NONSTICK PLUMBER'S TAPE.** Before you thread the pipe into a fitting, wrap nonstick plumber's tape 1½ turns clockwise around the male threads, pulling the tape tight. The tape seals the joint, preventing leaks and helping prevent rust.

5 **TWIST THE PIPE INTO THE FITTING.** Turn as far as possible by hand. Then clamp one pipe wrench on the pipe to hold it and another on the fitting, as shown. Place a short piece of pipe in the fitting so it doesn't collapse. Turn the wrench on the fitting clockwise and apply force only toward the open mouth of the jaws.

A+ WORK SMARTER

THE TURN OF THE SCREW
The problem with removing threaded pipe from a fitting is that it's next to impossible: As you turn the pipe to remove it from a fitting at one end, you're driving it into the fitting at the other end. Soon you've driven the pipe all the way into the fitting at the far end without freeing it at the other end. To solve this dilemma, cut the pipe first. Then clamp one wrench on the pipe and another on the fitting. Turn only the wrench attached to the fitting, applying force toward the open mouth of the jaws. Be sure to use the proper size of wrench for the job: a 12- to 14-inch wrench for ½- to 1-inch pipes or an 18-inch wrench for 1¼- to 1½-inch pipes.

PLUMBING AND DRAINAGE

CONNECTING PVC AND CPVC PIPE

1 **CUT THE PIPE.** Make a straight cut in the pipe with a pipe cutter made for plastic or cut it in a miter box. Use a reamer to remove burrs from the cut end. When you cut a pipe to length, add an extra ½ inch at each end for the pipe that slips inside the fitting.

PVC and CPVC take different primers and solvent cements; don't use one on the other.

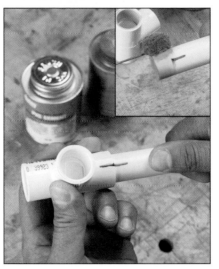

2 **PUT THE PIPE IN THE FITTING.** Test-fit the pipe in the fitting and mark the pieces so you can align them during installation. Test-fit the entire run of pipe. Apply primer to the end of the pipe and inside the fitting. Spread solvent cement on the end of the pipe, following the manufacturer's directions. Apply more lightly inside the fitting.

3 **PUT THE PIPE IN THE FITTING.** Slide the pipe completely into the fitting and give it a quarter-turn to help spread the solvent and remove bubbles. Adjust the fitting so the marks are aligned. Hold the joint for 10 seconds. Wipe off excess cement with a dry rag. Wait two hours before running water through the pipe to check for leaks.

Connecting PEX pipe

PEX (FLEXIBLE PLASTIC PIPE) (cross-linked polyethylene) is a flexible plastic pipe used for hot and cold supply lines. While it is gaining wider national acceptance, PEX is primarily used in the southern United States and in parts of southern California. In these areas it can also be used to run the main supply line from an outside water meter into a slab home. (Check local codes.)

The system uses two types of fittings: Plastic compression-type fittings. No tape or pipe compound is required. Brass ribbed fittings, which are permanently sealed to the pipe with a crimping tool and crimp ring (usually a professional installation).

PEX fittings are required by code to be accessible for inspection and repair and cannot be sealed in walls or ceilings. In order to make the fittings accessible, they are grouped in manifolds behind access panels.

1 **PUT THE FITTING IN THE PIPE.** PE, or polyethylene, pipe is a flexible black plastic pipe intended for outdoor use in rock-free soil; it is often used for irrigation systems. Cut PE pipe with a knife or fine-tooth saw. Slide a loose band clamp onto the pipe, then fit the pipe over the ribs on the fitting. First heat the end of the pipe with a hair dryer to expand it and make it easier to insert the fitting.

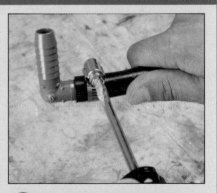

2 **TIGHTEN THE BAND CLAMP.** Move the band clamp so it is ¼ inch from the end of the pipe and beyond the ribs in the fitting. Tighten the screw on the clamp with a screwdriver.

PLUMBING AND DRAINAGE

Tapping into supply pipes

To get water outdoors, you need to work from indoors. Start by cutting through an existing pipe, adding a T fitting, and attaching the pipe that goes outdoors.

Before you cut, make sure you do two things:

■ Connect a water pressure gauge to the outdoor hose faucet. You'll need a minimum of 40 pounds of pressure to take the water any distance. Take an average of readings made at different times of the day.

■ When you're ready to cut into supply lines, turn off the house's main shutoff valve and open the faucets in your house to drain the pipes. Have a bucket handy, just in case.

STUFF YOU'LL NEED

✔ MATERIALS:

CPVC pipe, CPVC T fitting, PVC pipe, PVC T fitting, copper pipe, copper T fitting, adapters, lead-free plumber's solder, flux, solvent cement, plumber's tape

✔ TOOLS:

Minicutter, small hacksaw, emory cloth, plastic pipe cutter, pipe wrenches, propane torch, flux brush, flameproof pad, pressure gauge, emory cloth, fitting brush, safety glasses, work gloves

ATTACHING CPVC TO CPVC PLASTIC

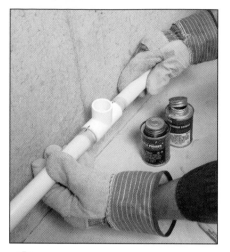

1 CUT THE EXISTING LINE. Turn off the water at the main shutoff valve. Cut through the cold-water supply pipe at the desired location with a plastic pipe cutter. Cut off an additional ½ inch for ½-inch pipe and ¾ inch for ¾-inch pipe. An alternative cutting tool uses a trigger pump action to cut the pipe

2 GLUE ON A T FITTING. Insert a T fitting and turn the stem in the direction of the new run. Mark the T and pipes with reference lines. Remove the T and apply pipe primer and cement to both cut pipe ends and the insides of the T. Apply a second coat of cement to pipe ends. Fit the T back onto the pipe, align the reference lines, and hold for 10 seconds. Glue the new run into the fitting.

ATTACHING COPPER TO COPPER

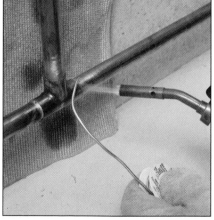

1 CUT THE PIPE. Cut out a piece from the cold-water pipe at the desired location with a pipe cutter—cut off an additional ½ inch for ½-inch pipe and ¾ inch for ¾-inch pipe. Use a close-quarters pipe cutter (a minicutter) like the one shown here if the space is cramped. Buff the cut ends with emery cloth and clean the fitting with a fitting brush.

2 SOLDER THE FITTING. Brush flux to the last inch of the cut pipe and the new pipe and to the inside of a T fitting. Put the fitting on the cut pipes and insert the new run of pipe in the opening. Solder the joints one at a time, starting with the lowest and working up. Heat the joints until the flux sizzles. Remove the torch and touch lead-free solder to each joint until it melts around each evenly.

ATTACHING PVC PLASTIC TO GALVANIZED STEEL

 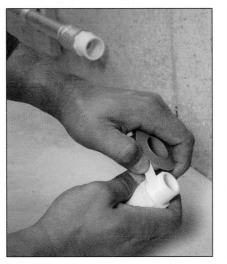 

1 CUT AND REMOVE THE PIPE. With a small hacksaw, cut through a section of the cold-water pipe. Clamp a pipe wrench to the fitting and another wrench next to it on the cut pipe. Turn the wrench that is clamped on the pipe counterclockwise.

2 SCREW ON TRANSITION FITTINGS. Wrap nonstick plumber's tape around the threads of two male ¾-inch transition PVC fittings. Screw them onto the fittings at each end, tightening them one turn beyond hand-tight.

3 GLUE ON PIPES AND A T FITTING. Cut pipe to run between the adapter and the T fitting; put it and the fitting in place without gluing. Measure the length of pipe needed to fit between the T and the second adapter. Cut and test it, then apply pipe primer and glue to attach the new pipe into the adapters and the T. Glue the pipe for the new run into the remaining hole in the T.

ATTACHING COPPER TO GALVANIZED STEEL

  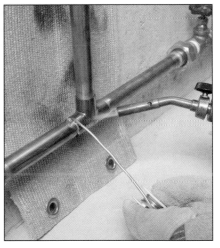

1 CUT AND REMOVE THE PIPE. Cut through the steel pipe with a small hacksaw. Twist each section out of its fitting using two pipe wrenches. Hold one on the fitting and the other on the pipe and twist the wrench that is on the pipe counterclockwise.

2 ATTACH ADAPTERS. Solder threaded brass fittings to two lengths of copper pipe that will run to a fitting for the new pipe. Connect one side of a dielectric fitting to the brass and another to the iron. A washer between the two pipes prevents corrosion that otherwise occurs between dissimilar metals. Wrap nonstick plumber's tape on the threads of the adapters, screw them in place, and tighten.

3 ATTACH THE NEW PIPE. Solder a T fitting between the two lengths of copper. Wipe away excess solder with a rag. Solder a new copper pipe into the T to extend a new run.

Running supply pipes

The next step in getting water outdoors for whatever application you want to install is to run supply pipes. Drill through the rim joist or concrete foundation to create an exit point for the pipe. Then tap into the supply line with a T fitting. If you live in an area with freezing temperatures in the winter, install a drainable valve—called a stop-and-drain valve—somewhere above the T but below the faucet. As winter approaches, open the drain on the valve to drain the faucet and the outside pipes. Once the valve is in, run pipe from it to the outdoors.

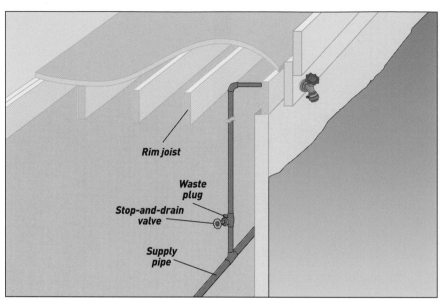

Rim joist

Waste plug

Stop-and-drain valve

Supply pipe

TO TRANSPORT WATER OUT OF THE HOUSE, cut into an existing supply line and insert a T fitting. The two openings opposite each other must be the same size as the existing pipe, but the third fitting can be any size. Use ½ inch for a faucet and ¾ inch for all other fixtures. When you're deciding where to run the pipe through the wall, look for a rim joist—it's easier than going through a masonry wall. You can use copper or plastic pipe for faucets that attach to the house. Any pipe buried in the ground, however, must be plastic, so consider using plastic for every pipe that comes after the T fitting.

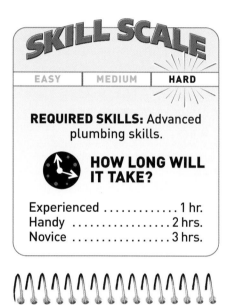

SKILL SCALE

EASY	MEDIUM	**HARD**

REQUIRED SKILLS: Advanced plumbing skills.

HOW LONG WILL IT TAKE?

Experienced . . . . 1 hr.
Handy . . . . 2 hrs.
Novice . . . . 3 hrs.

STUFF YOU'LL NEED

✔ **MATERIALS:**
Pipe, elbow fitting, stop-and-drain valve with a waste drain, pipe straps, flux, silicone caulk, lead-free solder

✔ **TOOLS:**
⅜-inch drill and bits, hammer, pipe cutter, tape measure, propane torch, flameproof pad, flame retardant work gloves, caulk gun, tape measure, safety glasses

In colder climates install a frost-free fitting.

EXTENDING THE SUPPLY LINE

1 **DRILL THROUGH THE RIM JOIST.** From inside the house, locate a spot on the joist just above the foundation where you want the pipe to exit. Drill a ¼-inch test hole at a slightly downward angle. Go outside and find where the bit went through the house. Drill a hole for the pipe at this point. Angle it upward and use a bit that's the same size as the pipe.

2 **ATTACH THE FITTING.** Solvent-weld, or solder, the fitting or faucet to the pipe while you can still slide it away from the house to work. Start by cutting a pipe a few inches longer that the thickness of the wall and attach a fitting to it. Slip the pipe, or nipple, through the hole.

3 **INSTALL A T FITTING INSIDE.** Tap into the supply pipe with a T fitting. Add a section of pipe and install a drainable valve, called a stop-and-drain valve. Water must flow through the valve in the direction stamped on the valve for it to work properly. The waste plug is the valve's drain. Turn off the valve, open an outdoor faucet, and unscrew the plug to drain pipes.

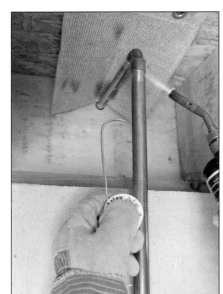

5 **CONNECT THE FITTINGS.** Cut pipe to the right length and sweat or solvent-weld it between the elbow and valve. Caulk around the outside of the hole you drilled to keep water from entering. On a faucet, caulk the flange; on a fitting, caulk around its perimeter.

4 **ATTACH AN ELBOW.** Install an elbow on the end of the nipple so it faces toward the stop-and-drain valve. For ½-inch pipe, measure from ½ inch inside the elbow to ½ inch inside the valve to determine the length of pipe needed. For ¾-inch pipe, measure ¾ inch inside each fitting.

SAFETY ALERT

Protect walls and ceilings with a flameproof pad and wear glasses and flame-retardant gloves when using a propane torch.

You may need to drill through a masonry wall to install pipe below grade. The pipe must fit inside a PVC sleeve to prevent abrasion, so drill the hole large enough for the sleeve. It's hard work; you may want to call a professional. If you are doing it yourself, rent a hammer drill with a ¾-inch carbide-tipped percussion bit. If you want to do it by hand, use a star bit with an extension that reaches through the house wall. Hit the bit repeatedly with a 3-pound sledgehammer to drill the hole.

Supporting pipe

To support pipe, run it along a joist and fasten it with pipe straps. Use a strap of the same size and material as the pipe. Slip the strap over the pipe and nail it to the joist.

If you are running pipe across joists, drill a hole slightly larger than the diameter of the pipe in the center of each joist. Don't drill closer than 2 inches from the edge, or you will weaken the joist.

PLUMBING AND DRAINAGE

Adding outdoor faucets

When choosing a location for an outdoor faucet, pick a spot that is close to the indoor cold-water pipe you plan to tap into. If possible locate it high enough on the wall to clear a bucket. If the faucet is freestanding, run the pipe through the foundation at the same level you'll run it through the yard—somewhere below the frost line. In colder climates install a frost-free faucet to prevent water from getting trapped in the pipe and freezing. Purchase a model with a vacuum breaker, which keeps the hose from sucking in water if the water pressure drops. If your faucet doesn't have one, you can screw one to the threads.

SKILL SCALE

EASY	**MEDIUM**	HARD

REQUIRED SKILLS: Basic plumbing skills.

HOW LONG WILL IT TAKE?

Experienced . . . . 30 min.
Handy . . . . 45 min.
Novice . . . . 1 hr.

VARIABLES: A freestanding faucet will take longer.

STUFF YOU'LL NEED

✔ MATERIALS:

Solder, flux, vacuum breaker, faucet or frost-free faucet, nonstick plumber's tape, scrap 2x4, silicone caulk, PVC pipe, PVC connectors, PVC elbow, solvent cement and primer, threaded PVC-to-metal adapter, sand, galvanized pipe, pipe clamps, steel rod

✔ TOOLS:

Caulk gun, propane torch, flux brush, ⅜-inch drill and bits, pipe wrench, 3-pound sledgehammer, screwdriver, shovel, safety glasses, work gloves

INSTALLING A WALL-MOUNTED FAUCET

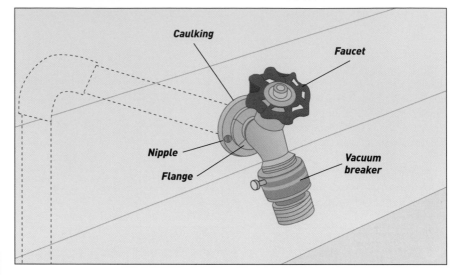

Caulking — Faucet — Nipple — Flange — Vacuum breaker

AN OUTDOOR FAUCET VALVE HANDLE TURNS WATER ON AND OFF. It is connected to a nipple that is attached to the supply pipe inside the house. The spout is usually male-threaded to accommodate garden hoses, although some models are female-threaded or unthreaded. Screw a vacuum breaker to the threads. The faucet has a flange that sits against the exterior wall of the house. Apply caulk to the flange before pressing it to the wall to ensure a weathertight seal.

BEFORE YOU RUN ANY OTHER PIPES, fit the flange over a nipple and solvent-weld, or sweat, the faucet onto it, leaving the valve open to protect the washers. Apply caulk. If you are using plastic pipe inside, use a plastic nipple and a plastic faucet. Insert the assembly in the wall and screw the flange to the wall.

A frost-free faucet

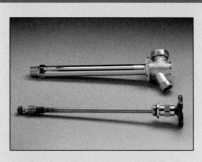

In climates where frozen pipes are a concern, install a frost-free faucet, which has a long body that extends through the exterior wall into the basement. A long stem runs through the body and into the house. When you turn the handle to turn off the water, a washer on the end of the stem stops the water inside the house, where it won't freeze. Install the faucet so it slopes downward toward the outside; excess water then can drain out. Some faucets have threaded fittings; others have to be sweated onto ½-inch copper pipe.

PLUMBING AND DRAINAGE

INSTALLING A FREESTANDING FAUCET

A freestanding faucet brings the source of water closer to the plants and flowers that need it most. Plan its location so the faucet doesn't get in the way of the traffic flow in your yard. It will take longer to install than a wall-mounted faucet. How long, of course, depends on how far from the house you want to install it—you'll have to dig a trench below the frost line for the pipe. Use PVC pipe underground (it won't corrode), but support the faucet riser on a separate piece of steel rod driven into the ground for stability.

Install a stop-and-drain valve indoors so you can drain away standing water in the the pipe before the first freeze.

You can use dirt or sand to support the pipe in the trench. Sand will fill voids beneath the pipe more effectively but the dirt is already there from digging the trench. It's your choice.

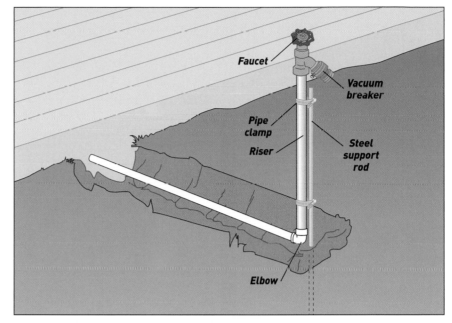

RUN PVC PIPE FROM THE HOUSE TO THE END OF THE TRENCH, where it's attached to a galvanized steel riser and the faucet. Support the riser with a steel pipe. Drive the support pipe 2 feet deeper than the trench bottom. The support should end about 2 inches below the faucet and be attached to the pipe with pipe clamps.

1 **DIG A TRENCH.** Make the trench about 12 inches deep and slope it uphill 1 inch for every 8 feet as it moves away from the house. Lay out lengths of PVC pipe from the house to the outlying faucet location and support them with scraps of 2×4. Solvent-weld the pipes together using couplings.

2 **SUPPORT THE PIPE WITH DIRT OR SAND.** Fill the trench below the pipe with dirt or sand, removing the 2×4 pieces as each section of pipe is supported. Attach a plastic elbow with one threaded end to the end of the PVC pipe.

Test the pipe for leaks before filling the trench.

3 **WRAP NONSTICK PLUMBER'S TAPE AROUND THE THREADS** of a galvanized pipe and screw the pipe into the elbow. Drive a piece of steel support rod 2 feet below the bottom of the trench next to the riser. Brace the riser to the support rod with pipe clamps. Screw on the faucet without damaging the fitting by placing a screwdriver in the spigot and turning clockwise until tight.

PLUMBING AND DRAINAGE

Gutters and downspouts

For gutters to carry water, make sure they slope toward the downspouts. For installation vinyl is easier to use than metal. It cuts easily with a hacksaw or power miter saw. You must allow for expansion and contraction, however, because vinyl expands with the heat and contracts with the cold.

In fact vinyl gutters are designed to allow for expansion. Each system is a little different, so follow the directions that come with your gutter carefully. At some point you'll need to skip a section of gutter, install the drop outlet, and then measure for and cut the missing piece of gutter, minus an allowance for expansion. You find the proper length by measuring from the last section of gutter installed over to a mark in the drop outlet that corresponds to the current temperature.

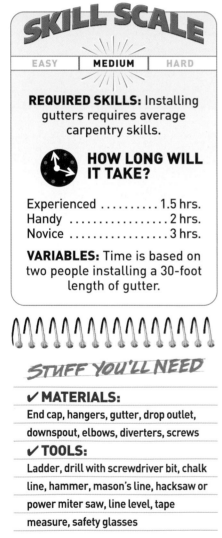

SKILL SCALE

EASY	MEDIUM	HARD

REQUIRED SKILLS: Installing gutters requires average carpentry skills.

HOW LONG WILL IT TAKE?

Experienced . . . . 1.5 hrs.
Handy . . . . 2 hrs.
Novice . . . . 3 hrs.

VARIABLES: Time is based on two people installing a 30-foot length of gutter.

STUFF YOU'LL NEED

✔ **MATERIALS:**
End cap, hangers, gutter, drop outlet, downspout, elbows, diverters, screws

✔ **TOOLS:**
Ladder, drill with screwdriver bit, chalk line, hammer, mason's line, hacksaw or power miter saw, line level, tape measure, safety glasses

1 **STRETCH A LEVEL LINE.** Drive a nail into the fascia at the end of the gutter that will be farthest from the downspout. Tie a mason's line to it and attach a line level. Stretch the line to what will be the other end of the gutter, level it, and mark the end of the line.

2 **LAY OUT A SLOPE.** Measure down from the mark ⅛ inch for every 10 feet of gutter and drive a nail. Stretch a chalk line between the two nails.

3 **SNAP THE CHALK LINE** to mark what will be the top of the gutter.

4 **PARTIALLY ASSEMBLE THE GUTTER.** Working on the ground, put an end cap in what will be the high end of the gutter. Slide the hanging hooks inside the gutter, spacing them 1 foot from each end and every 2 feet in between.

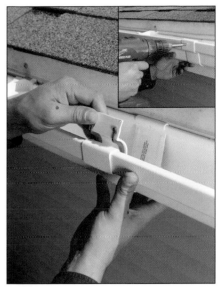

5 **HANG THE GUTTER.** Hold the middle of the gutter and put it up against the fascia. Align the top with the chalk line and screw the center hook in place.

Keep the gutter aligned with the chalk line and screw the rest of the hooks in place. Make sure the gutter will slide back and forth on the hooks; if it won't, find out which hook is either too high or too low and reposition it.

6 **HANG THE DROP OUTLET.** Hang the drop outlet next, before you install any more sections of gutter. Position the outlet so the downspout will run along the corner of the building. Screw the outlet in place, even though the gutter next to it hasn't been installed yet. There are some lines inside the gutter marked with various temperatures. Mark the fascia just above the one corresponding to the temperature at time of installation. Measure from the mark to the first section of gutter. Cut a piece of gutter to this length.

7 **HANG THE SECOND SECTION OF GUTTER.** Slide one end of the gutter you just cut into the drop outlet. Butt the other end against the first section of gutter, and put a two-piece connector across the seam. Start with the inner section, positioning it so it spans the seam. Then put the outer connector across the seam and snap it in place. Screw the connector to the gutter to keep it from moving.

8 **CONNECT GUTTER TO THE OTHER SIDE OF THE OUTLET.** Cut a piece of gutter to reach from the outlet to the end of the soffit. Put an end cap on it, slide the assembly into the drop outlet, and screw the hanger hook in place.

9 **PUT AN ELBOW ON THE DOWNSPOUT.** Hold an elbow against the wall 6 to 8 inches below the first. Measure the distance between the two, subtract the amount the manufacturer recommends for expansion, and cut a piece of downspout to this length.

10 **HANG THE DOWNSPOUT.** Measure from the elbow to the ground, subtract 6 inches, and cut a piece of downspout to this length. Hold it temporarily in place and mark the location of the downspout clips. Attach the clips and downspout. Put an elbow in the bottom and a diverter on the ground below to direct water away from the house.

For a tight seal make sure the gutter is clean when attaching connectors.

Installing outdoor drainage systems

A mushy yard is hard on plants and not particularly easy on the feet. One of the biggest culprits is the gutter, which takes water that falls on a few hundred square feet of roof and dumps it onto a few square inches of lawn. Corrugated pipe buried underground channels the water away from the house, the plants, and even the basement.

Make sure you use nonperforated pipe—perforated pipe is intended for use along the bottom of a basement wall.

SKILL SCALE

EASY	MEDIUM	HARD

REQUIRED SKILLS: Basic plumbing skills.

HOW LONG WILL IT TAKE?

Installing a 10-foot-long seepage trench with a dry well should take about:

Experienced . . . . 4 hrs.
Handy . . . . 6 hrs.
Novice . . . . 8 hrs.

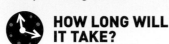

STUFF YOU'LL NEED

✔ MATERIALS:

4-inch nonperforated drainpipe, 2×4,1×2 stakes,90-degree drainage bend, downspout adapter, patio block

✔ TOOLS:

Shovel, level, line level, spade, hand saw, scissors, wheelbarrow, mason's line, tamper, 3-pound sledgehammer, safety glasses, work gloves

CONTROLLING DOWNSPOUT RUNOFF

CHANNEL WATER FROM THE DOWNSPOUT AWAY FROM THE HOUSE with nonperforated corrugated plastic pipe. Run the downspout into an adapter, which connects the downspout with the first length of pipe. Run the pipe to a 90-degree fitting and connect the fitting to more pipe that channels the water away from the house.

1 **DIG A TRENCH.** Start digging a trench at the downspout, sloping it downhill ⅛ to ¼ inch per foot. Run the trench either to a point where the bottom reaches the surface or to a dry well. To gauge the slope, put a 1-inch spacer between the end of a 4-foot level and a 2×4. The slope is correct when the bubble is centered. Line the trench with a corrugated plastic pipe 3 or 4 inches in diameter.

2 **ATTACH THE PIPE TO THE DOWNSPOUT.** Snap a 90-degree elbow to the end of the pipe that's nearest the downspout. Use a hand saw to cut enough pipe to reach from the elbow to the downspout. Snap one end to the elbow; snap the other to a downspout adapter. Slip the adapter over the downspout and fill in the trench.

CONSTRUCTING A DRY WELL

Despite its name, a dry well collects water. In this case the well takes water from a drain line when it isn't possible to drain it into a storm sewer or some other suitable spot. Dry wells are typically 2 to 4 feet wide and about 3 feet deep. Check local code for the appropriate size of well for your area; size usually is related to average rainfall. The well must be situated at least 10 feet from the house to keep water away from the foundation. Dig the drainage trench, then dig the dry well. Line the well with landscape fabric and fill it with gravel. Cover the well with a patio block to prevent it from filling up with water from above, rather than from the seepage trench. Then conceal the slab with earth and sod.

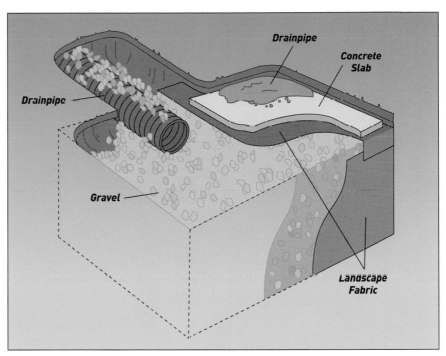

A DRY WELL IS A HOLE THAT SERVES AS AN OUTLET FOR A DRAINAGE TRENCH. Put the well at the low end of the trench at a minimum of 10 feet from the house. After digging the well, cover the inside of the hole with landscape fabric and fill it with gravel. The landscape fabric keeps the soil from mixing with the gravel. Cover the dry well with a patio block to keep rain from seeping into the well. Cover the slab with soil and sod.

1 DIG OUT THE TRENCH. After you dig the trench, dig the dry well at the low end of the trench. Check local code for the proper width and depth of the well.

2 SLOPE THE BOTTOM OF THE TRENCH. To work properly, the trench must drop $\frac{1}{8}$ to $\frac{1}{4}$ inch for every foot it travels on its way to the well. To gauge the slope, slip a $\frac{1}{2}$-inch spacer between a 4-foot level and a straight 2×4 that is at least 4 feet long. When the bubble in the level is centered, you have the right slope.

3 LAY DRAINAGE PIPE. Shovel in enough gravel to cover the bottom of the trench. Lay 4-inch-diameter drainpipe along the bottom of the trench and a few inches into the dry well. If you are using PVC, lay it with the perforated side down. Dry assemble the lengths of pipe with couplings.

Installing outdoor drainage systems

CONSTRUCTING A DRY WELL (continued)

4 **CUT A HOLE FOR THE DRAINPIPE.** Use scissors to cut a hole in the landscape fabric for the drainpipe.

5 **LINE THE DRY WELL.** Landscape fabric keeps soil from mixing with gravel. Line each side of the dry well with a piece of landscape fabric, leaving enough extra to fold over the hole later.

6 **FILL THE TRENCH.** Shovel enough gravel into the trench to cover the pipe and lay landscape fabric over the gravel. Backfill the trench with soil and cover the soil with sod.

7 **FILL THE WELL.** Fill the well with gravel. Leave enough room at the top for a patio block cover, a topping of 2 to 3 inches of soil, and a layer of sod. Fold the ends of the landscape fabric over the gravel.

8 **COVER WITH A PATIO BLOCK.** Place a concrete patio block on the gravel and landscape fabric to prevent water from the soil from filling the well. Leave enough room on top of the cover for 2 to 3 inches of soil and a layer of sod.

9 **REPLACE THE SOD.** Put a 2- to 3-inch layer of soil over the block and lay down the sod you removed earlier.

BUILDING A BERM TO DIVERT WATER

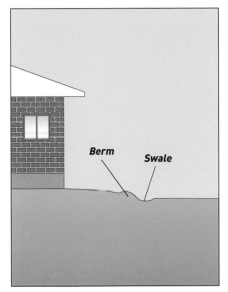

A BERM IS A SMALL EARTHEN BARRIER that redirects the flow of water. It's usually paired with a shallow ditch, called a swale, which helps drain away the water.

1 **REMOVE THE SOD.** Cut through the sod with an edger, removing a strip of sod as wide as a shovel. Pull up the sod and set it aside.

2 **BUILD UP THE SURFACE.** Use a wheelbarrow to dump loads of soil along the path of the berm. Smooth it out with a spade and a rake and create a small mound. Tamp. Cover the mound with the sod you removed and seed any bare patches.

BUILDING A SWALE TO CARRY WATER

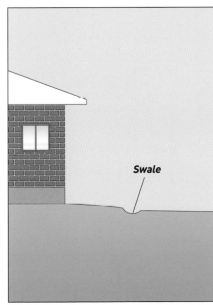

SWALES ARE SHALLOW TRENCHES that catch water and channel it away from the house and toward a more suitable spot, such as a storm sewer. The swale should run along the bottom of the slope to catch water and drain it away. Allow the swale to follow the natural slope of the land.

1 **LAY OUT THE SLOPE.** Remove the sod and drive a stake at each end of the swale. Stretch mason's line between the stakes and level it with a line level. On what will be the low end of the swale, lower the line ¼ inch for every foot that the swale is long.

2 **EXCAVATE TO CREATE THE SWALE.** Work your way along the line, digging so the bottom and the line are a constant distance apart. Throw the dirt to the downhill side as you go, then rake it to form a small berm. Tamp the berm and seed it. Cover the trench with the sod you removed.

CONCRETE

oncrete wears many hats in the construction trades. It's used to anchor fence posts, decks, piers, and basketball hoops. Concrete is used for sidewalks, driveways, the foundation for walls and sheds, and the base for patios—sometimes it is the patio.

Concrete is a mixture of cement, sand, and gravel. Masons refer to sand as a fine aggregate and gravel as a coarse aggregate, but no matter what you call them, concrete is a mixture, and that greatly affects the way you pour a pad.

When you first pull a board, or screed, across the top of the forms to level the concrete, the stones are spread evenly through the mixture, including along the surface. This look is fine for a foundation. To get

the smooth surface you're used to seeing on a patio or sidewalk, however, you'll need to do some more work. Enter the darby and bull float, two trowels used in the initial finishing phase of concrete. As you slide the trowels over the surface of the concrete, the stones on the surface of the cement sink, and the sand and cement rise, forming a thin layer of mortar.

Once the mortar surface forms, you'll need a different tool to create the finished surface. A broom creates a nonskid surface; a wood trowel creates a surface that, while flat, still has enough texture to help prevent slipping. If you use a metal trowel, you'll get a smooth, almost slippery surface—just the sort of thing you don't need outside.

CHAPTER 8

Concrete tool kit 232

Materials 233

Pouring a concrete pad 234

Mixing and pouring concrete 237

Anchoring posts for sports equipment ... 241

Making a molded concrete walk 243

Repairing concrete 246

REAL-WORLD SITUATIONS

CONCRETE EVIDENCE

Concrete may dry hard and stay hard, but it's not the rock-solid surface it appears to be.

Unlike wood, which has fibers running the length of the board, the structure of concrete runs every which way. Its random nature needs to be reinforced, or it's bound to crack.

Steel reinforcing mesh does the trick. Put mesh across the entire bed before you pour, supporting it on wire supports sometimes called chairs. (The old practice of supporting the mesh on brick or stone leaves too large a void in the concrete.)

Concrete will, of course, stick where you least want it to, namely to adjoining structures. All structures are moving—slowly perhaps, and not enough to see, but enough to cause concrete to crack. Expansion joints, which are thick, wide strips made of petroleum-impregnated felt or paper, help solve the problem. They're the black tarlike strips you see between a patio and the house. Because they are so oily, concrete won't stick to them, and the walk and the house can each move at their own rate without cracking the patio.

Once the mesh is in and the concrete poured, all large concrete surfaces need control joints. Control joints are the lines that run across the width of a sidewalk, and their purpose is to introduce a weak spot in the walk. If the ground under the walk settles for any reason, the resulting cracks are most likely to occur in the control joints. The result is not only neater, it's stronger than it would be if cracks ran all over the face of the concrete.

Think of a concrete pad as a system—parts of which are designed to make the pad stronger, others to make it weaker. Even the rounded edges you see on concrete are structural—rounded edges are less likely to chip than square ones. For the best results pay attention to the entire system while you work.

CONCRETE

CONCRETE TOOL KIT

3-POUND SLEDGEHAMMER

CAULK GUN

GARDEN HOSE

MASON'S LINE AND POWDERED CHALK

POWER TAMPER

TAPE MEASURE

BRICK AND COLD CHISELS

CHALK LINE

HAMMER

MATTOCK

RAKE

TROWELS

BROOM

CONTROL JOINTER

HANDSAW

MIXING TUB

SAFETY GLASSES

UTILITY KNIFE

BRUSH

FINISHING TROWEL (DARBY)

LEVELS

PAINT BRUSH

SHOVEL

WHEELBARROW

BUCKET

DUST MASK

MAGNESIUM AND WOOD FLOATS

PAINT ROLLER WITH EXTENSION

SPADE

WORK GLOVES

BULL FLOAT

EDGER

MASON'S HOE

POSTHOLE DIGGER

TAMPER

CONCRETE

Materials

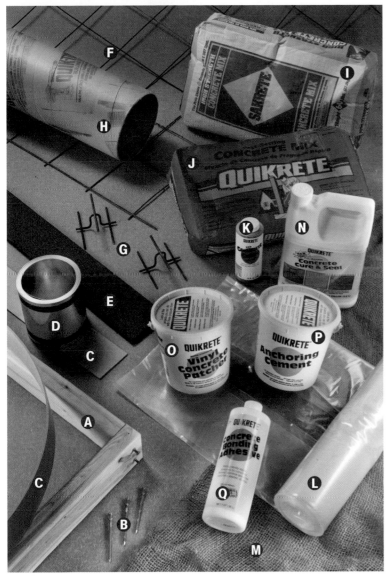

ⓐ Concrete made of three materials: **ⓑ Cement,** usually portland cement, **ⓒ sand,** and **ⓓ gravel. ⓔ Mortar,** which is used elsewhere in the book, contains **ⓕ lime** instead of gravel. Concrete works both as an underground foundation and as a slab poured on the surface. Mortar is used to bond materials together, such as bricks, stone, fence and mailbox posts. Both concrete and mortar can be hand-mixed from dry ingredients, but it is easier to buy them in **ⓖ pre-mixed bags.** Always mix concrete and mortar with clean, clear water—water that is clean and clear enough to drink.

Concrete pads start with forms made of **ⓐ lumber** and **ⓑ duplex nails**—the double heads are easy to remove. Form curves with **ⓒ tempered hardboard** or **ⓓ metal flashing.** Install **ⓔ expansion joints** along adjoining surfaces so new concrete moves independently. Add strength to slabs with **ⓕ 6×6-10/10 wire mesh**—6-inch squares of 10-gauge wire. Prop mesh and rebar on **ⓖ wire supports** (sometimes called chairs). If you're pouring piers, either as a foundation or to hold sports equipment posts in place, use **ⓗ fiber tube forms.** Use bags of **ⓘ pre-mixed concrete** for jobs needing up to 1 cubic yard. Additives in **ⓙ fast-set concrete** speed the curing process. Add color to concrete with **ⓚ a dye.** Cover fresh concrete with **ⓛ plastic sheeting** or **ⓜ burlap** to keep it from drying too quickly. Seal concrete with **ⓝ non-yellowing sealer.** Fill small cracks with **ⓞ vinyl patching compound. ⓟ Anchoring cement** expands as it dries to create an extremely secure bond with regular concrete. **ⓠ A bonding agent** helps repairs adhere to damaged surfaces.

Assembling forms for a concrete pad

STUFF YOU'LL NEED

✔ MATERIALS:

¾-inch gravel, 2×s, ½-inch plywood, 10d (3-inch) duplex nails, ½-inch expansion joint, 6×6-10/10 wire mesh, chairs, construction adhesive, form-release agent or vegetable oil, tie wire, concrete

✔ TOOLS:

Mattock, spade, power tamper, shovel, wheelbarrow, rake, line or water level, tape measure, chalk line, hammer, 3-pound sledgehammer, handsaw, caulk gun, paintbrush, safety glasses, dust mask, work gloves

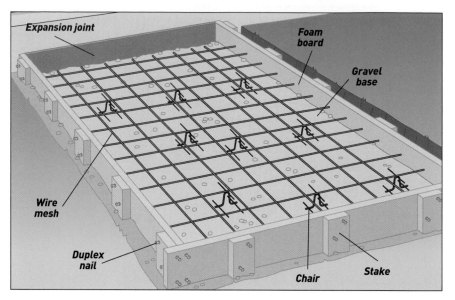

A CONCRETE PAD IS A SYSTEM OF STONE, METAL, AND CONCRETE. The top 4 inches is a concrete slab. A wire mesh running through the middle of the pad supported by rebar supports called chairs, ties it together to help prevent cracks. Beneath the concrete is a gravel bed, which improves drainage and is easier to level than soil. An expansion joint between the pad and house allows the two to move separately when the ground shifts. Forms hold concrete in place as you pour and act as guides when you drag a board across the forms to level the surface. The forms usually are removed after the concrete cures.

In most areas a concrete slab begins with 4 inches of compacted stone, which provides drainage below the concrete and helps prevent flooding and perhaps cracking as the ground shifts. Areas with excellent drainage don't need a stone base, so check with your local building office to see what's required locally.

To keep the slab from cracking, the pros put mesh in the middle of the pour to help tie the slab together. Next they put a strip of tar-impregnated felt, called an expansion joint, between the new pad and any existing structures. If an adjacent structure, such as the house foundation, stays stationary while your new pad shifts, the expansion joint allows them to move independently, thereby preventing cracks in the slab or foundation.

Control joints act as magnets for cracks. The joints are lines that are weaker than the rest of the slab. Cracks are more likely to form along the control joints, where they are hidden, than in the middle of the pad.

1 **LAY OUT AND EXCAVATE THE PAD.** Lay out the pad with batterboards and string. Remove the sod and dig out 8 inches of soil across an area that is 1 foot larger than the pad in each direction. Compact the surface that remains with a power tamper.

CONCRETE

2 **ADD GRAVEL AND COMPACT AGAIN.** In areas that require gravel beds (most do; check local code), spread gravel on the surface in 2-inch layers, compacting the layers and adding gravel until you get a bed 4 inches thick.

3 **LAY OUT THE OUTSIDE EDGE OF THE FORMS.** Install a second set of layout lines, putting them on stakes. Position the stakes outside the first set of lines, offset from the first set by the thickness of the forms you'll use. Level them with a line level or water level.

4 **DRIVE STAKES ALONG THE NEW LAYOUT LINES.** Drive stakes along the layout lines, putting them at the corners of the pad and every 2 feet in between. Drive the stakes so they're plumb and firmly bedded in the ground. Don't worry about their height; you'll trim them to height later. Remove the first set of layout lines; you don't need them anymore.

5 **MARK THE STAKES.** The pad must slope away from the house at a rate of 1/8 to 1/4 inch per foot—check local code for the proper amount. Measure down from the batterboards and mark the corner stakes at the finished height of the pad. Hold a chalk line tight at the marks you made and snap the chalk line to mark the rest of the stakes.

6 **NAIL THE FIRST FORM IN PLACE.** Align the form with the mark on the stakes and nail it in place with two duplex nails. Brace the form board with a 3-pound sledgehammer while you pound in the nails. Nail the rest of the stakes to the form board the same way.

7 **CUT OFF THE STAKES.** Cut the stakes flush with or slightly below the top of the forms. You will use the tops as a guide to level the concrete surface, and any stake rising above the surface will keep you from getting a smooth result.

Assembling forms for a concrete pad (continued)

8 **INSTALL THE REMAINING BOARDS.** Cut the boards long enough to span each of the remaining sides. Position them one at a time so their tops are level with the marks you made on the stakes earlier. Nail them to the stakes with duplex nails.

9 **SPLICE BOARDS TOGETHER, IF NECESSARY.** On sides too long for a single board, butt two boards together. Cut a strip of ½-inch plywood and nail it across the joint. Drive a 2×4 stake at each end of the plywood strip and nail it to the forms with duplex nails.

10 **INSTALL THE EXPANSION JOINT.** With construction adhesive, attach a ½×4-inch expansion joint to the foundation of the house and any other existing concrete that meets the pad. The joint will prevent the pad and foundation from bonding and cracking if they shift or settle at different rates.

11 **COAT THE FORMS WITH RELEASE AGENT.** Coat the form boards with a commercial form-release agent or vegetable oil to prevent the concrete from sticking to the form boards.

12 **PLACE THE MESH.** Reinforce the concrete with 6×6-10/10 wire mesh (6-inch squares, made of 10-gauge metal). Put the mesh on wire supports, called chairs, and sold separately, so it sits roughly in the middle of the slab's thickness. Keep the mesh a few inches away from the edges of the forms to prevent rust. Overlap sections by 4 inches and tie them together with wire. Wire the mesh to the chairs.

CONCRETE

Mixing and pouring concrete

Concrete is sold three ways—bagged mix, concrete mixed from the raw ingredients, or concrete ordered from a ready-mix company. The easiest method for small jobs—under 1 cubic yard—is to buy premixed bags. All you have to do is add water. Mixing the concrete from ingredients—portland cement, sand, gravel, and water—is more labor-intensive, but it saves money because you're not paying for the convenience of an all-in-one package. If you're dealing with more than a cubic yard, you're better off ordering the concrete from a ready-mix company. Remember, even if you need only part of a yard, you'll have to round up to the next full yard. If you need 2.4 cubic yards, for example, you'll have to order 3 cubic yards.

Cubic yards of concrete needed

AREA (SQ. FT.)	3" SLAB	4" SLAB	5" SLAB	6" SLAB
10	.10	.14	.17	.20
25	.25	.34	.42	.51
50	.51	.68	.85	1.02
100	1.02	1.36	1.70	2.04
200	2.04	2.72	3.40	4.07
300	3.06	4.07	5.09	6.11
400	4.07	5.43	6.79	8.15

THE CHART ABOVE TELLS YOU HOW MUCH CONCRETE YOU'LL NEED FOR SOME TYPICAL JOBS. If the chart doesn't apply to your job, some simple math will tell you what you need. Multiply the length of the proposed slab by its width (both in feet) to find the area in square feet. Multiply this amount by the desired depth or thickness of the concrete in feet. Divide this figure by 27 (the number of cubic feet in a cubic yard) to find the volume in cubic yards. Add 10 percent for subgrade variations and waste.

BUYER'S GUIDE

CHOOSING CONCRETE

A variety of specialized concretes are available: vinyl concrete, fast-setting concrete, fiber-reinforced concrete, sand-mix concrete, and anchoring concrete. Vinyl concrete, also called patching mix, is used generally for repairs. To make your own vinyl concrete, add a bonding agent to the mix of dry ingredients. Fast-setting concrete (or quick-setting) is made with Type III portland cement and dries faster than regular concrete. This allows you to get back to work on your site more quickly. However, Type III cement is expensive and difficult to find. Use a ready-mix with a quick-set additive instead. Fiber-reinforced concrete is expensive and normally not used in do-it-yourself applications. Sand-mix concrete has no gravel, only sand and portland cement. It is useful as a grout but shrinks more than regular concrete because it has no gravel. Anchoring concrete contains an epoxy cement that allows it to adhere to regular concrete. Also, it is 2½ times stronger than regular concrete.

Concrete recipe

MATERIAL	PARTS
Portland cement	1
Sand	2½
Gravel	2½
Water	½

WORK SMARTER

FAST IN, FAST OUT

If you decide to order your concrete ready-mixed, make sure you're prepared to unload the concrete as quickly and efficiently as possible. The longer the truck is at your site, the more money you'll pay. This is the time to call in a few friends to give you a hand. To keep costs down, prepare the site as thoroughly as possible. Lay a pathway of 1×8 planks from where the truck will park to the site. Make sure all forms are in place and secured. And don't overfill the wheelbarrow: Concrete is heavy, and a top-heavy load is more likely to tip.

Mixing and pouring concrete

MIXING CONCRETE

FOR SMALL BATCHES OF CONCRETE, fill a wheelbarrow no more than three-quarters full with pre-mixed concrete or dry ingredients. Pile the ingredients into a mound and make a small crater in the center. Pour water into the crater a little at a time. Mix well with a mason's hoe or shovel, then test the consistency. The concrete should cling to the side of the tool.

IF YOU NEED LARGER AMOUNTS OF CONCRETE, rent a concrete mixer. Fill the mixer no more than half full with premixed concrete from bags or add each dry ingredient separately. Turn on the mixer and mix the dry ingredients, then add the required amount of water from a bucket. Let the mixer rotate for about five minutes, then test the consistency.

TO TELL IF THE CONSISTENCY IS RIGHT, slice through the mixed concrete with a spade. If ready, the edges of the slices should hold straight, not crumble, and be the consistency of oatmeal. If the edges crumble, the concrete is too dry and you need to add some water. If the edges fall over, it is too wet and you need to add more dry ingredients.

POURING CONCRETE

EVEN AIR DISTRIBUTION
Air-entrainment agents may sound like unnecessary extras, but they make your concrete much stronger, especially in climates with frequent freezing and thawing. Air entrainment creates evenly distributed air bubbles in the concrete, which strengthen the mix and increase its workability. Air-entrainment agents for dry, premixed concrete—usually sold in liquid form—are available at home centers. For ready-mix concrete, consult your supplier. Whatever method you choose, talk to a pro. The necessary amounts may vary from brand to brand and affect the quantities of sand and water needed.

1 POUR THE CONCRETE IN THE FORMS. If you're using a wheelbarrow, build a temporary ramp over the forms so the wheelbarrow won't displace them. Dump the loads of concrete against each other on the side farthest away from the ramp. Have a helper with a shovel spread the concrete into corners and against the forms and expansion joints.

2 REMOVE TRAPPED AIR. Lay a wide board across the forms so you can reach the interior of the pour. If the concrete causes the wire mesh to sink, pull it up with a rake so it's in the middle of the slab. Work a shovel or rake up and down to remove air pockets, especially alongside the forms.

3 **FLATTEN THE SURFACE.** With a helper, pull a screed (a long, straight 2×4) across the form to level the concrete. Tilt the screed forward and slide it from side to side as you push it forward. Stop to shovel off excess concrete in front of the screed or to fill in low spots. Make a second pass with the screed tilted the other way.

4 **FLOAT THE CONCRETE.** Work a bull float back and forth with the blade flat against the surface to smooth and compact the concrete. Work the concrete until water forms on the surface.

FOR SMALLER PADS FLOAT THE CONCRETE WITH A LARGE FLOAT CALLED A DARBY. The technique is the same even though the tool is different. Slide the darby across the concrete, smoothing and compacting it, until water forms on the surface.

FINISHING CONCRETE

Designer Tip

GETTING THE RIGHT SURFACE
Function often dictates how a pad should be finished. For a smoother finish, use a magnesium float instead of a wooden one. Avoid finishing concrete with a steel trowel because it will create a finish so smooth that it becomes slick and dangerous when wet. A skid-free broomed finish is an especially good idea around pools.

1 **ROUND THE EDGES.** When you've finished floating, separate the concrete from the forms by running the tip of a pointing trowel between the two. Then slide the cutting edge of an edger along the forms to round over the pad edge to make it less likely to chip. Tilt up the leading edge of the tool to avoid marring the concrete.

2 **CUT CONTROL JOINTS.** Cut shallow grooves, called control joints, in the wet cement pad. The joints are the pad's weakest spots, so if the ground shifts, the resulting cracks will most likely form along these lines. You need a joint every 8 feet, so make marks every 8 feet along the forms. Place a control jointer at the mark and guide it against a board that spans the pad.

Mixing and pouring concrete

FINISHING CONCRETE *(continued)*

3 **FLOAT THE SURFACE.** After you've cut the control joints and once any water sheen leaves the surface, run a wood or magnesium float over the surface for a final smoothing. Raise the leading edge of the float slightly as you work to avoid making lines on the surface of the concrete.

4 **BRUSH THE SURFACE.** For improved traction, pull a stiff-bristled broom toward you over the concrete. Draw the broom in either straight or wavy lines. If you don't like the pattern or if it is too coarse, trowel, wait, and broom again. The longer the concrete dries, the finer the broomed surface. Make another pass along the perimeter with an edger.

5 **LET THE CONCRETE CURE.** Lay plastic sheeting over the finished surface. The moisture trapped inside eliminates the need for watering during the curing stage. Let the concrete cure at least 48 hours, then remove the form boards. For more information, see "Curing Concrete," below.

Curing concrete

Concrete is not like glue, which hardens as the water in it dries out. A chemical reaction, or curing, requires water, which causes concrete to dry. Let a slab dry out as it cures, and it's liable to crack. One way to keep it wet is with a sprinkler. Turn it on whenever the concrete appears dry.

You can also cover the slab with plastic sheeting to trap evaporating moisture. If the final appearance of the slab is critical, staple the plastic to a frame of 1×2s. Otherwise you'll end up with a mottled look where the plastic touched the concrete.

A final option is to cover the slab with clean burlap and keep the burlap wet with a hose or sprinkler for the duration of the curing. Adjust the flow of water so it doesn't puddle on the burlap. Turn the sprinkler on for a few minutes every few hours, as needed, to keep the burlap damp.

CONCRETE

Anchoring posts for sports equipment

Some sports equipment—basketball nets, for example—work best with posts that are firmly anchored in concrete.

Dig a hole half as deep as the exposed height of the post. Set the post in the hole and plumb and brace it before adding concrete. You can pour concrete directly into the hole or set the post in a fiber tube form. A form results in consistent strength throughout the base, and you are guaranteed not to waste concrete because of a hole that is too wide.

SKILL SCALE

EASY	MEDIUM	HARD

REQUIRED SKILLS:
Basic masonry skills.

HOW LONG WILL IT TAKE?

Experienced . . . . 3 hrs.
Handy . . . . 4 hrs.
Novice . . . . 5 hrs.

STUFF YOU'LL NEED

✔ **MATERIALS:**
6-inch-diameter fiber tube form, duct tape, 2×2 stakes, 1×4 braces, gravel, concrete

✔ **TOOLS:**
Posthole digger, 3-pound sledgehammer, shovel, hammer, trowel, level, utility knife, tamper, mason's hoe, wheelbarrow, safety glasses, work gloves

SAFETY ALERT

Locate all underground utilities before excavating.

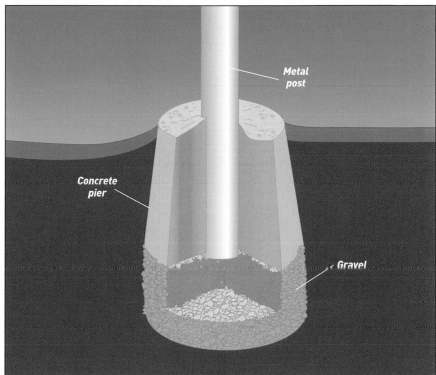

Metal post

Concrete pier

Gravel

THE SIZE OF THE HOLE DEPENDS ON WHETHER THE POST YOU'RE SETTING IS FOR A TENNIS NET, VOLLEYBALL NET, OR BASKETBALL HOOP; follow the manufacturer's instructions. The easiest way to anchor the post is to pour concrete directly into the hole. Put a little gravel in the hole before pouring the concrete to provide better drainage.

1 DIG A HOLE FOR THE POST. Select a site for your post. Using a posthole digger, dig a hole half the exposed height of the post. Add 4 inches of gravel at the bottom of the hole for drainage.

2 PUT THE POST IN THE HOLE. Drive 2×2 stakes into the ground and nail 1×4 braces to them. Plumb the post and tape the braces to the post with duct tape.

Anchoring posts for sports equipment (continued)

3 **MIX THE CONCRETE.** Pour bagged concrete mix into a wheelbarrow and add half the recommended amount of water. Mix with a mortar hoe, adding water a little at a time until the desired consistency is achieved.

4 **PUT CONCRETE IN THE HOLE.** Shovel 6 to 8 inches of concrete into the hole, then tamp it with a 2×4 to remove air bubbles. Continue, adding 6- to 8-inch layers and tamping until the hole is filled.

5 **TAMP AGAIN AND CROWN THE TOP.** Once the hole is filled, give it a final tamping. Add a bit more concrete, then crown the top so water will drain away from the post. Let the concrete cure for 48 hours.

ANCHORING POSTS WITH A FIBER TUBE FORM

1 **PUT THE FORM IN THE HOLE.** Place a 6-inch-diameter fiber tube form in the hole. Support the form about 6 inches above the bottom of the hole by nailing two 2×4s to it, as shown above. Shim under the 2×4s to level the form.

2 **PUT THE POST INTO THE FORM.** Drive stakes into the ground and nail braces to them. Plumb the post and tape it to the braces with duct tape. Fill the form in 6- to 8-inch layers. When you finish pouring a layer, work a scrap 2×4 up and down in the concrete to remove trapped air. When the form is full, crown the top so water drains away from the post.

3 **REMOVE THE 2×4S AND CUT OFF THE EXPOSED SECTION OF THE FORM.** Let the concrete cure for at least two days, then backfill around the form with soil. Use a utility to cut off the part of the form that sticks out of the ground.

Making a molded concrete walk

Even when the installation is relatively easy, working with concrete involves heavy lifting. Don't strain yourself, work methodically, and take breaks when you can so you'll be able to enjoy using the project into which you've put so much effort.

Forget everything you've ever heard about pouring a walk. Forget digging out 8 inches of soil; forget hauling in tons of stones; forget compacting the stone or building and squaring forms.

Concrete molds, made by the companies that sell bagged concrete, simplify the job immensely. The mold is usually a 2×2-foot plastic square with interior dividers that create a stone or brick pattern in wet concrete. You put the form on the ground, fill it up with concrete, and trowel the surface flat. Next you remove the mold, put it next to the concrete you've poured, and pour again. If the walk curves, angle the form to get the shape you want.

An 80-pound bag of concrete fills the mold, simplifying mixing and measuring. You can pour and mix more concrete one square at a time with no worries about a large batch of concrete drying while you work. Pour and move the mold as many times as it takes to lay the walk, or stop whenever you like. If you're using a mold with a stone pattern, you can use the concrete right as it comes out of the bag. If you're using a brick pattern, such as the one shown here, mix dye with the concrete to give it a brick color.

The job requires some digging. You'll need to remove the sod so that the walk has a firm base. But once you've removed the sod, leveling the walk is much simpler than it is with traditional forms. In fact you have a choice: You can let the mold follow the contour of the ground, the same way a footpath would, or you can level the mold before pouring, giving you the level surface of a city sidewalk. The choice is yours. Leveling instructions are included here to give you an idea of what's involved.

1 **LAY OUT THE WALK** with stakes and mason's line. (Mason's line won't sag and stretch like string does.) Lay out any curves as described on page 18. Spray paint or sprinkle powdered chalk along the lines to mark the walk on the ground.

2 **REMOVE THE SOD.** Cut along the edge of the walk with an edger or spade. Hold the handle of the spade low to the ground and kick it to remove a strip of grass. Repeat until you've removed all the sod.

CONCRETE

Making a molded concrete walk (continued)

3 **REMOVE ABOUT 1 INCH OF SOIL.**
Dig a trench about 1 inch deep, checking from time to time with a 2-foot level to make sure the surface is relatively level. The surface need not be flat because the concrete will conform to any irregularities. It must, however, be firm: Shovel out any soil you knock loose, or the concrete may crack.

4 **MIX THE CONCRETE.** If you're using a brick pattern, such as the one shown here, dye the concrete red before putting it in the mold. You'll need one 80-pound bag of fiber-reinforced concrete per 2×2-foot section of walk and about 10 ounces of liquid color per 80-pound bag. If using a mixer pour in color and water before you pour in the concrete.

IF MIXING BY HAND, MIX THE COLOR AND WATER TOGETHER, then add it to the concrete mix. If you're using a mold that imitates stone, mix the concrete following the directions on the bag but leave out the dye.

5 **PUT THE MOLD IN PLACE.** Put the mold on the ground and check it for level. Prop it on small stones, as needed, to level it.

6 **FILL THE MOLD TO THE SURFACE.** Shovel concrete into the mold, filling it to the top. Smooth the top with a mason's trowel.

CONCRETE

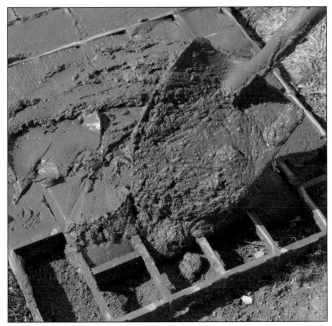

7 **REMOVE THE MOLD.** Lift the mold from the wet concrete. The edges of the concrete will be somewhat rough. Trowel lightly to remove imperfections.

8 **REPOSITION THE MOLD.** Turn the mold a quarter-turn and put it next to the concrete you just poured. Check for level and shim with small stones, as before. Mix and pour concrete, and trowel it smooth. Work your way down the walk, section by section.

9 **POSITION THE MOLD TO MAKE A CURVE.** Start a curve by putting the mold at an angle so it overlaps a straight section of walk. The angle should position the edge of the mold along the curve you've laid out, and the overlap should be just enough to accommodate the angle.

10 **FILL THE MOLD.** Shovel concrete into the mold. Trowel until smooth all the concrete within the mold, including any concrete from the previous section. Move the mold as often as needed to create the curve, keeping the angle and overlap constant from square to square.

11 **SEAL THE CONCRETE.** When the concrete is fully cured (approximately 72 hours), brush on a concrete sealant to protect it from oil, grease, and salt. Fill the gaps around the edges of the walk with soil.

Repairing concrete

Although it's extremely tough, even concrete needs a helping hand to keep it attractive and strong over many years. Common repairs can include cleaning stubborn stains, replacing expansion joints, or fixing cracks. If the concrete needs many little repairs, you may be better off resurfacing or replacing an entire section of a slab. Because concrete and cleaning solutions can be caustic, wear a dust mask when mixing them and safety glasses and rubber or heavy work gloves when handling them.

SKILL SCALE

| EASY | MEDIUM | HARD |

REQUIRED SKILLS: Basic to intermediate masonry skills.

HOW LONG WILL IT TAKE?

Experienced . . . . 30 min.
Handy . . . . 1 hr.
Novice . . . . 1.5 hrs.

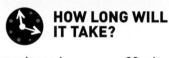

STUFF YOU'LL NEED

✔ MATERIALS:
Muriatic acid, sealer, expansion joint, bonding agent, vinyl concrete, patching compound, 2× lumber, duplex nails, wire mesh, concrete, burlap or plastic

✔ TOOLS:
Fiber or wire brush, paint roller with extension handle, bucket, cold chisel, 3-pound and 6-pound sledgehammers, metal trowel, caulk gun, tamper, pointing trowel, garden hose, paintbrush, hammer, wheelbarrow, mason's hoe, control jointer, edger, broom, bull float, darby, wood or magnesium float, safety glasses, work gloves

CLEANING AND SEALING CONCRETE

1 **TO GET RID OF CONCRETE STAINS,** add one part muriatic acid to nine parts water in a bucket. Apply the solution evenly with a stiff push broom. Wear rubber gloves and eye protection because the acid is caustic. Rinse the slab with water when done.

2 **IF THE CONCRETE IS NOT PAINTED,** apply an acrylic or non-yellowing silicone sealer with a short-nap paint roller to protect the surface from future damage. Let it dry 48 hours.

REPLACING EXPANSION JOINTS

1 **EXPANSION JOINTS ALLOW SECTIONS OF THE SLAB TO SHIFT INDEPENDENTLY,** thereby avoiding cracks in the concrete. If the strip of expansion joint material has rotted, chisel it out with a 3-pound sledgehammer and cold chisel. Remove all debris.

2 **BUY A NEW STRIP OF EXPANSION JOINT MATERIAL** and cut it to size. Slide the new strip into the joint so the top is ½ inch below the concrete surface. Caulk the joint with a rubber silicone sealant or apply a polyurethane sealant to preserve the new expansion joint.

REPAIRING CRACKS

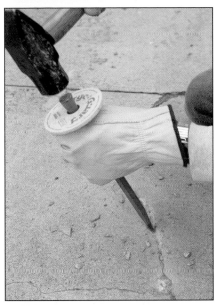

1 **NEW CONCRETE DOES NOT STICK WELL TO OLD.** To anchor a patch make the crack wider at the bottom than at the top. Place a cold chisel in the crack, angle it slightly outward, and rap it with a 3-pound sledgehammer.

2 **CLEAN OUT DEBRIS THOROUGHLY WITH A STIFF FIBER OR WIRE BRUSH.** Crumbs and pebbles weaken a concrete patch.

3 **FILL THE CRACK WITH A PATCHING MIX**—also known as vinyl concrete—made from vinyl, portland cement, and sand. It covers cracks up to ½ inch wide. Dampen the area around the crack, then trowel on the mix. Smooth the surface with either a trowel or a small float.

REPAIRING POP-OUTS

1 **POP-OUTS ARE SMALL CONICAL-SHAPE CHUNKS OF CONCRETE** that have popped out and left a hole behind. Using a cold chisel and a 3-pound sledgehammer, undercut the hole by making the pop-out wider at the bottom than at the top. Clean the hole with a stiff fiber or wire brush.

2 **WET THE SURFACE AND APPLY A CONCRETE BONDING AGENT** inside the hole with a paintbrush. Wait about 10 to 15 minutes or until it gets sticky.

3 **PACK A SMALL AMOUNT OF ANCHORING CEMENT INTO THE HOLE** and smooth the surface with a putty knife or trowel. Anchoring cement expands as it hardens. It is primarily used for anchoring bolts in holes drilled in concrete, but it also works well here. Keep the area moist until the patch cures.

Repairing concrete

RESURFACING CONCRETE

1 **SOMETIMES A CONCRETE SLAB IS BEYOND A FEW EASY REPAIRS** and must be resurfaced. In a bucket carefully add one part muriatic acid to five parts water. Wet the concrete, then apply the solution with a fiber brush. The acid will etch the old surface so the fresh concrete will adhere to it.

2 **WAIT UNTIL THE SOLUTION STOPS BUBBLING**—about 15 minutes—then rinse the solution, as well as any debris, from the concrete surface with a jet of water from a garden hose. Flush thoroughly with water; any leftover acid may weaken the bond.

3 **DIG A TRENCH 2½ INCHES DEEP AND 6 INCHES WIDE AROUND THE ORIGINAL SLAB.** Lay 2×4 form boards in the trench against the slab and stake them so the forms are 1 inch above the level of the old concrete surface.

4 **CONCRETE WON'T STICK TO CONCRETE IN THIS CASE,** so apply a concrete bonding agent to the area with a paint roller. Then mix 2½ parts sand, 1 part portland cement, and ½ part water. Spread the sand mix inside the forms. Screed the surface by placing a straight 2×4 across the forms and drawing it across.

5 **FINISH THE SURFACE LIKE ANY OTHER CONCRETE SLAB.** Smooth with a bull float or darby, making sure to flatten high spots and fill depressions. Then match the previous texture with a metal trowel, wood float, magnesium float, or broom. Cure for two to three days.

Correcting a slope

To correct the slope of a slab, resurface it. Set the forms in a trench against the existing slab so the tops are ½ inch above its highest point. The size of the 2× lumber used for forms depends on how many inches they rise above the surface of the slab at the lowest point. Use boards at least 2 inches wider than this height. For a ¼-inch slope, attach a 1-inch-thick spacer to a 4-foot 2×4 and lay it on the form. Set a 4-foot level on the 2×4. Adjust the form until the bubble is centered on the level. Once you've gotten the proper slope, stake the form boards securely in place. Etch and rinse the concrete, roll on the bonding agent, and place the new sand mix in the forms. Then screed and finish it.

REPAIRING CONCRETE STEPS

1 **SCRUB THE BROKEN AREA CLEAN WITH A STIFF, WET BRUSH.** Apply concrete bonding agent to the exposed concrete with a paintbrush. This helps the patching compound adhere to the old concrete.

2 **WAIT UNTIL THE BONDING AGENT GETS STICKY,** then apply patching compound to the damaged area with a mason's trowel. Apply enough compound to replace the missing concrete. If you are using a vinyl concrete-patching mix, no bonding agent is required.

3 **TAPE TOGETHER A WOOD FORM TO FIT AROUND THE CORNER.** Place pavers against the form so it doesn't move while the compound is hardening. If the area to be patched is large, you may want to create this form before Step 2.

Patching compounds are also available that do not require forms to hold the material until it sets. Check with your local home improvement center to see if the product is available in your area.

REPLACING CONCRETE

1 **BREAK UP THE DAMAGED SECTION OF CONCRETE** with a 6-pound sledgehammer. If the area is more than a few square feet, you may want to rent a jackhammer. Break the concrete into small pieces that are easy to handle, and remove them or brush them away.

2 **BUILD A FORM FOR THE NEW CONCRETE OUT OF 2× LUMBER.** Slope or level as necessary. Nail 2×4 stakes to the forms with duplex nails. In freezing climates or in areas with poor soil, a base of gravel is needed. If the existing gravel is mixed with soil, dig it out and replace with a new 4-inch layer.

3 **ALONG ANY ADJOINING STRUCTURES, SUCH AS A FOUNDATION OR DRIVEWAY, ATTACH AN EXPANSION JOINT** with nails or construction adhesive. The joint allows the concrete to move independently. Tamp the gravel.

Repairing concrete

REPLACING CONCRETE (continued)

4 **LAY WIRE MESH WITHIN THE FORM,** resting it on bricks. Add water to premixed concrete in a wheelbarrow and mix until it is firm and workable. Fill the damaged area with the concrete.

5 **REST A STRAIGHT 2×4 ON OPPOSITE FORM BOARDS** or on the existing concrete if you are replacing a single section. You may need a helper on the other end if the area is large. Level and smooth the concrete by drawing the screed across the fresh surface in a zigzag motion. Then make a second pass to finish screeding the concrete.

6 **CUT EDGES AND CONTROL JOINTS** into the new concrete. Run a pointing trowel between the form and the concrete, then pass an edger along the forms a few times to make smooth edges. Lay a straight 2×8 across the forms as a guide to cut control joints with a jointer.

7 **SMOOTH OUT HIGH AND LOW SPOTS** by passing a darby quickly over the surface in broad sweeps. Be careful not to disturb the control joints. When the surface appears to be dry and stepping on the concrete leaves less than a ¼-inch depression, smooth the surface with a wood or magnesium float.

8 **FOR A BROOMED SURFACE,** finish the surface with a metal trowel. Then pull a broom across the surface, perpendicular to the traffic flow. Rinse the broom as soon as you're done. Touch up the edges and control joints, if necessary.

9 **COVER THE REPAIRED AREA WITH A SHEET OF PLASTIC** and allow the concrete to cure for at least two to three days. If using burlap instead of plastic, mist it often to keep it wet.

CONCRETE

Glossary

3-4-5 triangle: A triangle with two sides that measure 3 feet and 4 feet and a third diagonal side (hypotenuse) that measures 5 feet. The angle formed by the 3- and 4- foot sides is always 90 degrees. Used by builders to lay out square corners in indoor and outdoor structures. Will work with any multiple or fraction of 3, 4, and 5.

3-pound sledgehammer: A sledgehammer 12-18 inch handle and a 3-pound head. Useful for driving stakes.

Anchor: A metal slug placed in concrete to hold a hex-head bolt The inside of the slug is threaded for the bolt; the outside of the slug has teeth that grip the masonry as the bolt causes the slug to expand.

Ashlar: Building stone that has been milled so that it is reasonably flat, smooth, and has 90-degree corners.

Batterboards: Two stakes with a crosspiece nailed between them used to lay out a building project. The batterboards are connected by a stretch-resistant string, called mason's line, which marks the edge of whatever you're building.

Benderboard: A thin piece of wood that will flex to follow a curve. Used as edging along the curved edge of a walk or patio.

Berm: A long, low mound built to divert water away from a walk, patio, or the house.

Bonding agent: A liquid painted onto masonry to help concrete or mortar stick to it.

Bull float: A large trowel mounted on a broom-like handle, used to smooth wet concrete.

Chair: A wire structure used to support reinforcing mesh keeping the mesh elevated while concrete is poured.

Cold chisel: A metal handled chisel designed for chipping away at masonry.

Common nails: Nails with a large flat head, used where strength matters more than appearance.

Concrete broom: A broom, similar to a push broom, made especially for pushing across wet concrete to create a slip-resistant surface.

Concrete pavers: Brick-like blocks made for use in building patios and walks. Made of concrete instead of clay, they come in a variety of colors and shapes, and are designed to simplify laying masonry surfaces.

Conduit: Tubing designed to protect wiring from damage. It can be made of either PVC or metal. Plastic must be used underground.

Construction adhesive: A thick, sticky glue that comes in a caulk-like tube. Used in some applications as a fastener instead of nails.

Curing compound: A liquid sprayed or painted over wet concrete to control the rate at which it hardens and helps keep the concrete from cracking.

Darby: A long, narrow trowel used to create a smooth surface on concrete. Often used together with a bull float, a long-handled smoothing trowel that reaches sections of concrete you can't reach by hand.

Dry saw: A portable saw with a diamond rimmed blade used to cut through masonry.

Dry well: An underground drainage area, filled with stone and covered with soil and grass. Used where drainage is otherwise poor or where a drain for gutters, foundation or patio has nowhere else to run.

Duplex nails: Used in nailing together wood forms for concrete. The nails have two heads on the shank, one head about ¼ inch above the other. The first head controls how deep you can drive the nail. The second remains exposed and makes it easy to remove the nail.

Expansion joint: An ½-inch divider put along the edge of a concrete pad to keep it from sticking to an existing concrete structure. Usually made of an asphalt impregnated material.

Fiber tube forms: Cylindrical tubes put in the ground as forms for pouring a concrete footing for a post.

Footing: An underground structure that supports a post, wall, or foundation. A footing must be below the frost line so that freezing and thawing won't cause it to move.

Form: A fiber tube, or a wood or metal structure used to contain wet concrete when its poured. The forms are placed around the edges of the pour. The top of the form is often used as a guide along which you pull a straight-edge to create a flat surface.

Framing square: An L-shaped square used by carpenters to lay out roofs and walls. Also called a rafter square, it is useful when laying out outdoor structures.

GFCI: Ground Fault Continuity Interrupter. A device which cuts power to an outlet if electricity passes directly from the outlet into the ground—as might happen outdoors, or in a kitchen or bath. A GFCI is either built into the outlet or into the circuit breaker.

Hex-head bolts: Bolts which have a six-sided head and which are tightened with a wrench or ratchet set. Fastening requires washers and a nut.

Lag screws: A lag screw, like a hex head bolt, has a head with six sides. It has a pointed tip however, so that it can be driven into wood like a screw. Before driving a lag screw, drill holes slightly smaller than the diameter of the lag screw. Lag screws should be sued with a washer but do not require and will not work with a nut.

Landscape blocks: Precast concrete blocks designed for building landscape walls. They often have a lip on the back to make aligning them easier.

Landscape fabric: A coarse-weave plastic fabric put on the ground to discourage weeks or to keep dirt from filtering down into the gravel drainage bed below.

Landscape spikes: Large galvanized spikes that look like common nails; used to nail landscape timbers together or to anchor timbers or edging into the ground.

Line level: A very short level that hooks onto a layout line so that you can see if the line is level.

Mason's blocks: L-shaped wooden blocks used to attach a guide line along the length of a masonry wall. The tension of the line holds the blocks in place. Once the line is leveled it serves as a guide to keep the courses of a brick, stone, or block wall at the proper height.

Mason's hoe: A hoe for mixing mortar or concrete. A hole or holes in the middle of the hoe make it easier to pull through the mixture and help mix the ingredients together.

Mason's line: A string designed for layout work that is made of synthetics and which won't sag.

Mason's trowel: A triangular trowel with slightly curved edges, used to apply mortar when building walls or when building walks and patios laid in a mortar bed.

Masonry nails: Hardened nails with four flat sides, designed to be driven into concrete.

Mortar: A mixture of portland cement, lime, sand, and water, used to bind bricks, cement block, and tile to another surface.

Plugging chisel: A narrow mason's chisel used to remove mortar from between bricks when repointing.

Pointing trowel: A trowel with a narrow point and a wide back used for applying mortar when repointing.

Portland cement: A cement mixture in which the dry ingredients are mixed, baked and then pulverized before being mixed with water. Mixing water

with portland cement results in a chemical reaction that makes for a high-strength cement.

Power auger: A gasoline engine which drives a bit that looks like a large drill bit. Used when digging holes for footings and fence posts.

Power tamper: A gasoline-powered compacting tool used to compress gravel and sand beds in patios and walkways.

Pre-mixed concrete: Premixed concrete is a dry mixture sold in bags. It is mixed with water on the job site. (Ready-mix concrete has already been mixed with water and is delivered by truck.)

Pressure-treated lumber: A softwood building lumber that has been treated under pressure with chemicals that discourage rot and decay.

Rafter ties: Metal fasteners that tie a rafter or joist to the framing that supports them.

Ready-mix concrete: Ready-mix concrete is mixed with water at the factory, and is delivered while still wet by truck. (Premixed concrete is a dry mixture sold in bags and mixed with water on the job site.)

Rebar: A metal bar that is put in concrete to reinforce it and prevent cracking.

Reinforcing mesh: A metal mesh put in concrete pads to prevent cracking. It is usually referred to both by the size of the square and the gauge of the wire. For a concrete pad, use 6x6 10/10 mesh. It has six-inch squares made of 10-gauge wires.

Repointing: Removing crumbling mortar from between bricks, stones, or concrete blocks and replacing it with new mortar.

Rise: The vertical distance between two steps in a stairway. Also used to mean the total height of the stairs.

Riser: The vertical board installed between two steps.

Run: The width of a step from front to back, excluding any overhang. Also used to mean the horizontal length of a stairway.

Screed: A straight edge pulled along the top of a concrete form used to flatten the concrete when it is still wet.

Seepage trench: A gravel-lined trench that surrounds a perforated drainage pipe. Water seeps out of the pipe and drains into the ground. The trench is usually covered with soil, and grass or other plants.

Seismic/hurricane anchors: Metal fasteners that tie a rafter or joist to the framing that supports them. Also called rafter ties.

Self-drilling concrete anchors: A heavy-duty screw that can be driven into slightly smaller hole that has been predrilled concrete.

Shade fabric: A waterproof woven material designed to let some, but not all, sun pass through it.

Swale: A shallow trench dug to divert water away from a structure. Often used in combination with a berm.

Tamper: A tool used to compact the ground. There are both hand and power versions.

Tread: The part of the stair that you walk on.

Water level: A level made of a long water-filled tube, which operates on the principal that water always seeks its own level. When held against two points, the top of the water column in each end will be at the same level. Electronic versions are designed to beep when one end of the tube reaches the same level as the other.

Wet saw: A saw used to cut tile, brick, stone and concrete, with a blade cooled by water.

Wythe: Brick and stone walls are made of two bricks or stones placed in rows back to back. Each row is called a wythe.

Index

A

Air-entrainment agents, 238
Amperage, drawn by motors, 180
Arbors, 152–155
    arch-top, 172–175
    building, 163–171
    materials, 153, 155
    posts for, 152, 163–166, 172, 175
    real-world situation, 153
    reed/bamboo covering, 170
    shade fabric, 171
    tool kit, 154
Augers, 19, 20
Automatic control devices,
    installing, 202–203

B

Bamboo, arbor covering, 170
Batter gauge, 81, 93, 95, 96
Berms, 229
Block
    concrete block wall, 97–103, 107
    landscape block wall, 62, 77–79
Brick walls
    common-bond, 90–92
    mortar estimates, 67
    repairing, 104–106
    running-bond, 87–89
    stucco application, 102
Building codes, 4, 10, 75, 82, 84

C

Cable. See also Wire
    materials, 179
    mounting tips, 195
    running through conduit, 194–195
    running through joists, 195
    sizes, 179
    stripping, 181
    voltage drop, 179
Cap rail, 33, 36, 44–45
Caulk, 134, 143, 194, 197
Cedar, 11
Cement, 65–67, 100, 233
Chain link
    fence, 16, 50–52, 60
    gate, 53–54
    privacy slats for, 52
    repairing, 60–61
Circuit tester, 184, 187
Circuits
    extending, 183–189
    GFCI, adding, 190–191
    load, 183
    mapping, 183
Cleaning
    concrete, 246
    fences, 56

Concave jointer, 89, 92, 94, 96, 100, 105, 106
Concrete, 230–250
    air entrainment, 238
    amount needed, estimating, 85, 119, 237
    for arbor posts, 162–165, 175
    block wall, 97–100
    cleaning, 246
    control joints, 120, 231, 234, 239, 250
    cracks, repairing, 247
    curing, 86, 240, 250
    drilling, 221
    expansion joints, 231, 233, 234, 236, 246, 249
    for fence posts, 19, 43, 58, 59, 61
    finishing, 119–120, 239–240
    floats and floating, 120, 230, 232, 239–240
    form-release agent, 83, 236
    forms, for pad, 234–236
    forms, for shed slab, 118–119
    forms, tube, 116, 165, 206, 242
    materials, 231
    mixing, 85, 238, 242, 244
    molded walk, 243–245
    pouring, 85–86, 119, 238–239, 243
    ready-mix, delivery of, 85, 237
    real-world situations, 231
    recipe, 237
    reinforcement, 118–119, 231, 233, 234, 236, 250
    repairing, 246–250
    replacing, 249–250
    resurfacing, 248
    safety, 84, 119
    sealing, 245, 246
    shed footings, 117
    shed ramp pad, 151
    shed slab foundation, 117–120
    slope, correcting, 248
    for sports equipment posts, 241–242
    steps, 249
    tools, 230, 232
    varieties of, 237
    vibrator, 86
Concrete block wall
    building, 97–100
    repairing, 107
    stuccoing, 101–103
Conduit
    cutting, 194
    installing PVC, 192–194
    metal, 193
    running cable through, 193, 194–195
Construction adhesive, 65, 79, 128, 236
Control joints, 120, 231, 234, 239, 250
Copper pipe, 211, 213, 214–215, 218–219
Corners, laying out square, 18, 68, 69, 112–113, 121, 138, 161, 164
CPVC (chlorinated polyvinyl chloride) pipe, 213, 217, 218
Curing, concrete, 86, 240, 250

D

Deed restrictions, 10
Design, 6–11
Dogs, fence for, 55
Doors, shed
    metal, 149
    vinyl, 141, 143
    wood, 133
Downspouts
    controlling runoff, 226
    installing, 224–225
Drainage
    berm, 229
    downspout runoff, 226
    dry well, 227–228
    materials, 213
    retaining wall, 70–71, 73, 79
    for sheds, 113
    swale, 229
    tool kit, 212
Dry well, 227–228

E

Efflorescence, 104
Electrical, 176–209
    amperage drawn by motors, 180
    automatic control devices, 202–203
    connecting wires, 182
    electrical box, mounting, 196–197
    extending circuits, 183–189
    GFCI circuit, adding, 190–191
    GFCI outlet, installing, 198–199
    light fixtures, 204–207
    low-voltage lighting, 176, 208–209
    materials, 179–180
    real-world situation, 177
    running cable and conduit, 192–195
    safety, 181, 186, 188, 189, 190, 196, 202, 204, 206, 207
    service panel, joining into, 190–191
    stripping wire/cable, 181
    surge arrester, 198
    switches, installing, 200–201
    tool kit, 178

transformer, 208
voltage drop, 179
Electrical box
capacity, 184
external clamp, 185
junction box, 189
mounting on exterior wall, 196
mounting on post, 197
tapping into, 188–189
Expansion joints, 231, 233, 234, 236, 246, 249

F

Faucets, 222–223
Felt, roofing, 131
Fences, 12–61
alternate-board, 30–32
basket-weave, 35–36
board-and-batten, 33
cap rail, 33, 36, 44–45
chain link, 50–54, 56, 60–61
cleaning, 56
curved, 18, 25
gates, 37–40, 47, 53–54, 61
height restrictions, 28
hillside, 26–27
for horses, 43
kickboards, 31
laying out, 17–18
louver, 34–35
materials, 15–16
metal, 61
mortised posts and rails, 42–43
panels, installing prefab, 22–23
pet, 55
pickets, 28–29
post-and-rail, 41–43
posts, 19–21
real-world situations, 13
repairing, 56–61
screws, installation with, 31
sections, building, 28–29
solid-board, 33
tool kit, 14
tree incorporation into, 32
vinyl, 46–49
wire, 44–45
wood rails, 24–25
Finishing, concrete, 120, 239–240
Fish tape, 194
Fittings
conduit, 192
pipe, 213, 219, 221
Floats/floating, concrete, 120, 230, 232, 239–240
Floodlight, 206–207
Floors, shed
metal, 144

vinyl, 137
wood, 123
Flux, 211, 215
Footings
fence post, 20–21, 58–59, 61
regional requirements, 84
shed, 115–116
sizing, 20
wall, 82–86
Forms
for concrete pad, 234–236
for concrete shed foundation, 118–119
release agent, 83, 236
tube, 116, 165, 206, 242
for wall footing, 83–84
Foundations, shed
concrete slab, 109, 117–120
materials, 111
metal shed, 144
precast concrete pier, 115–116
skid, 114
vinyl shed, 137
Friends, working with, 127
Frost depth, 82

G

Gates
building, 37–38
chain link, 53–54
double, 40
fixing, 61
hanging, 39–40
hardware, 16, 38–40, 49, 54
heavy, 38
laying out, 17–18
stops, 61
tool kit, 14
vinyl fence, 47
GFCI (ground fault circuit interrupter)
circuit, adding, 190–191
outlet, 177, 196, 198–199, 208–209
Grade, wood, 11
Gutters, 224–225

H

Halogen floodlight, 206–207
Hangers
galvanized, 155, 169
wooden fence, 22

I

Inspector, building, 4

J

J-bolt, 120
Joists
pipe support and, 221

running cable through, 195
shed floor, 121–122
Junction box, tapping into, 189

K

Kickboards, 31

L

Lamppost, 205–206
Landscape fabric, 65, 71, 77
Lattice
arbor, 170, 175
fence, 29
trellis, 155, 156–158
Ledger
shed ramp, 150
trellis, 159, 160
Lighting. See also Electrical
end-of-the-run porch light, 204–205
halogen floodlight, 206–207
lamppost, 205–206
low-voltage, 176, 208–209
materials, 180
mercury-vapor, 207
middle-of-the-run porch light, 205
sensor switches, 203
tapping into a light fixture, 188
Low-voltage lighting, 176, 208–209

M

Masonry
attaching trellis to, 160
drilling through, 221
Mason's blocks, 87, 89
Mercury-vapor light, 207
Metal
fence posts, 45
fencing, 61
shed, 144–149
Mortar, 233
amount needed, estimating, 67
brick patio, 67
brick walls, 63, 88–92, 104–106
concrete block wall, 97–100
lime-free, 67
making your own, 66
mixing, 66
repairing joints, 104
retempering, 67
stone walls, 93–96
types, 67
Mortised post-and-rail fence, 42–43
Motion detector, 203
Muriatic acid, 104

O

Outlets
  checking for power, 184, 185, 187
  connecting wire to, 182
  end-of-the-run, joining into, 183–186
  GFCI, 177, 196, 198–199, 208–209
  installation, 184
  middle-of-the-run, joining into, 186–187
  types, 180
  waterproof cover for, 199

P

Painting, shed, 134
Patio, brick, 67
Pet fence, 55
PEX (flexible plastic pipe), 213, 217
Photoelectric sensor, 203
Pickets, 28–29
Piers
  setting posts on, 165–166
  shed foundation, 115–116
Pipe
  cutting, 214, 216–219
  drainage, 71, 73, 79, 115, 226–229
  fittings, 213, 219, 221
  joining, guidelines for, 211
  materials, 213
  ordering, 215
  running supply, 220–221
  supply connections, 214–217
  supporting, 221
  tapping into supply, 218–219
  threading, 216
Plastic pipe, 211, 213, 217
Plumbing, 210–229
  drainage, 226–229
  faucets, 222–223
  gutters and downspouts, 224–225
  joining pipe, 211
  materials, 213
  ordering pipe, 215
  real-world situations, 211
  running supply pipe, 220–221
  supply line connections, 214–217
  supporting pipe, 221
  tapping into supply pipe, 218–219
  tool kit, 212
Porch lights, 204–207
Posts
  arbor, 152, 163–166, 172, 175
  chamfered, 76
  decorative tops, 21
  digging holes for, 17, 42, 46, 50, 75, 161–162, 164, 241
  fence, installing, 19–21
  gate, 37
  hanging rails between, 25
  lamppost, 205–206
  leaning, 58
  metal, 45, 50–52
  metal anchor spikes for, 162
  mortised, 42–43
  mounting electrical box on, 197
  on piers, 165–166
  plumbing and bracing, 20, 43, 58, 59, 61, 76
  post-and-rail fence, 41–43
  repairing, 58–59
  retaining wall, post-and-board, 75–76
  sister post, 58
  for sports equipment, anchoring, 241–242
  trellis, 160–162
  trimming, 21, 166
  vinyl, 46–49
Pressure washing, 56
Pressure-treated lumber, 11, 65, 114, 153, 167
Privacy slats, fence, 52
PVC (polyvinyl chloride)
  conduit, 192–194
  pipe, 211, 213, 217–219, 223

R

Rafters, arbor, 168
Rails, fence, 24–25, 57
Ramp, shed, 150–151
Real-world situations
  arbors and trellises, 153
  concrete, 231
  design, 7
  electrical installation, 177
  fences, 13
  landscape walls, 63
  plumbing, 211
  shed, 109
Rebar, 65, 73, 84, 118–119
Receptacle analyzer, 185
Redwood, 11
Reed, arbor covering, 170
Reinforcement, steel mesh, 118, 231, 233, 234, 236, 250
Release agent, 83, 236
Resurfacing, concrete, 248
Retaining wall
  drainage, 70–71, 73, 79
  landscape block, 77–79
  post-and-board, 75–76
  timber, 72–75
Roof
  arbor, 170–171
  metal shed, 148–149
  vinyl shed, 142–143
  wood shed, 130–132
Roofing cement, 132
Router jig, for arch-top arbor, 172–174

S

Safety
  concrete work, 84, 119
  electrical, 181, 186, 188, 189, 190, 196, 202, 204, 206, 207
  general guidelines, 5
  mortar, 67
  utility lines, 10, 19, 113
Service panel, 190–191
Shade fabric, 171
Sheds, 108–151
  drainpipe, laying, 113
  foundation, concrete slab, 117–120
  foundation, precast concrete pier, 115–116
  foundation, skid, 114
  hardware, 133–134
  kits, 108, 109, 111
  laying out, 112–113
  location, 137
  materials, 111
  metal, 144–149
  painting, 134
  ramp, 150–151
  real-world situation, 109
  roofing, 131–132
  subfloor, 121–122
  tool kit, 110
  trim, 133–134
  vinyl, 137–143
  window, 135–136
  wood, 123–130
Shingles, 131–132
Siding, attaching a trellis to, 158
Site map, 8–9
Slope, checking, 113
Sod, removal of, 243
Solder, 215, 218
Sports equipment, anchoring posts for, 241–242
Steel pipe, 213, 216, 219
Steps, repairing concrete, 249
Stone wall
  dry-set, 80–81
  footing for, 82–86
  mortared, 93–96
Story pole, 87, 89, 92, 97
Stringers, 150–151
Stucco
  applying to block wall, 101–102
  applying to brick wall, 102
  making, 101
  repairing, 107

texturing, 103
tinted, 103
Subfloor, shed, 121–122
Surge arrester, 198
Swales, 229
Switches
    automatic sensor, 203
    end-of-the-run, 200–201
    middle-of-the-run, 201
    three-way, 201
    time-delay, 203
    timer, 202
    types, 180

T
T stakes, 45
Tamper, 74–75, 79
Tension bar, 50–54, 60
Threaded pipe, 213, 214, 216
Timber walls, 72–75
Time-delay switch, 203
Timer switch, 202
Tool kit
    concrete, 232
    electrical, 178
    fences and gates, 14
    landscaping walls, 64
    plumbing, 212
    shed, 110
    trellises and arbors, 154
    walls, 64
Transformer, 208
Trees, incorporating into fence, 32
Trellis, 152–162
    building a panel, 156–158
    hanging, 159–162

on hinges, 160
materials, 153, 155
posts for, 160–162
real-world situation, 153
tool kit, 154

U
Utility lines, 10, 19, 113

V
Vapor barrier, 118
Vinyl
    cleaning, 56
    cutting, 49
    fence, 15, 46–49, 56
    gutters, 224–225
    lubricating for sliding, 139
    shed, 137–143
    trellis lattice, 155, 156–158
Vinyl concrete, 237
Voltage drop, 179

W
Walk, molded concrete, 243–245
Walls, 62–107
    batter gauge, 81, 93, 95, 96
    block walls, 62, 65, 77–79
    brick, common-bond, 90–92
    brick, running-bond, 87–89
    concrete block, 97–100
    corners, 78
    curves, 77
    drainage for retaining wall, 70–71,
      73, 79
    dry-set, 63, 80–81
    footing for a stone or brick wall,

82–86
    laying out, 68–69
    maintaining, 104–107
    materials, 65
    metal shed, 146–147
    mortared, 63, 66–67
    mounting electrical box on, 196
    post-and-board, 75–76
    real-world situation, 63
    stone, 80–81, 93–96, 106
    stuccoing a block wall, 101–103
    timber, 72–75
    tool kit, 64
    vinyl shed, 140
    wood shed, 124–127, 129
Window, shed, 135–136
Wire. See also Cable
    connecting, 182
    extending circuits, 183–189
    gauge, 179
    jumper, 182, 185–189
    stripping, 181
    voltage drop, 179
Wire fence, 44–45
Wood
    fence, 15, 17–43
    grade, 11
    pressure-treated lumber, 11, 65,
      114, 153, 167
    retaining wall, 72–76
    shed, 123–130

Z
Zoning ordinances, 10